D0014765

WITHDRAWN
UTSA LIBRARIES

RENEWALS 458-4574

DATE DUE

JUN 27

DEC 14

NOV 27

PRINTED IN U.S.A.

GAYLORD

The Challenge of Fundamentalism

Comparative Studies in Religion and Society
Mark Juergensmeyer, editor

The Challenge
of Fundamentalism

Political Islam and the
New World Disorder

—⚬— —⚬— —⚬—

Bassam Tibi

UNIVERSITY OF CALIFORNIA PRESS
Berkeley · Los Angeles · London

University of California Press
Berkeley and Los Angeles, California

University of California Press, Ltd.
London, England

© 1998 by
The Regents of the University of California

Library of Congress Cataloging-in-Publication Data

Tibi, Bassam.
    The challenge of fundamentalism : political Islam
and the new world disorder / Bassam Tibi
        p.   cm. — (Comparative studies in religion and
    society ; 9)
    Includes bibliographical references (p.) and index.
    ISBN 0-520-08868-9 (alk. paper)
    1. Islam and politics.   2. Islamic fundamental-
ism.   3. Islam—20th century.   I. Title. II. Series.
BP173.7.T56   1998
320.5'5'0917671—dc21   97-17138
                                                   CIP

Printed in the United States of America
9 8 7 6 5 4 3 2 1

The paper used in this publication meets the minimum
requirements of American National Standard for In-
formation Sciences—Permanence of Paper for Printed
Library Materials, ANSI Z39.48-1984.

**Library
University of Texas
at San Antonio**

Contents

Preface

This book focuses on the question of order in current world politics. What we shall be examining in that context is Islamic fundamentalism, not the trumpeted "Islamic Threat." For me as a Muslim, Islam itself, being a tolerant religion, is not and cannot be a threat, and it is a disservice to world peace to speak of Islam, one of the world's major religions, in terms of "threat" and "confrontation." My religion is an open-minded faith, neither an intolerant political ideology nor a concept of world order, as Islamic fundamentalists—and some in the West—so fiercely contend. The Qur'an unmistakably commands: "[There is] no compulsion in religion" (Qur'an: Surat *al Baqarah,* 2/256). But Islamic fundamentalism, or political Islam, is a horse of another color: this brand of fundamentalism poses a grave challenge to world politics, security, and stability.

This, then, is a book about one variety of the world's panoply of religious fundamentalisms, not a study of Islam as a religion. In the course of examining the fundamentalist challenge, the book seeks to make two points clear. First, religious fundamentalism—as a political phenomenon not restricted to the World of Islam—is an aggressive politicization of religion undertaken in the pursuit of nonreligious ends. Second, fundamentalism, Islamic or otherwise, is only superficially a form of terrorism or extremism; I do not—and others should not—use the terms *usuliyya* / fundamentalism and *tatarruf* / extremism interchangeably. In delineating the views of Islamic fundamentalists on order, both domestic and international, I hope to demonstrate the ominous political challenge inherent in their brand of fundamentalism.

The fate of Nasr Hamid Abu-Zaid, an Egyptian university professor and Muslim scholar, illustrates my thesis well. In recent years Abu-Zaid has become the topic of front-page coverage in the international press. In thus rising to prominence, he had done nothing more than to express the view, in print, that linguistic research can be extended to theological matters by submitting Islamic scripture to this kind of inquiry. In his *Naqd al-khitab al-dini/A Critique of Religious Discourse* (Cairo: Maktabat Madbuli, new edition 1995), he sets forth his conviction that Muslims need to learn how "to differentiate between religion itself and human understanding of religion. . . . My argument was, if we want to live in the twenty-first or twentieth century, we have to know how to pursue scientific knowledge" (*International Herald Tribune*, July 23, 1993, front page). For this seemingly innocuous statement the Cairo professor must pay dearly: he has been declared a *murtad*/apostate by Islamic fundamentalists who, in this case, were not terrorists. Among them, in fact, were distinguished lawyers who went to court to divorce Abu-Zaid from his wife Younes against the will of both, on grounds that he had been shown to be a heretic. The Cairo judges endorsed the plea of the fundamentalist lawyers, for according to the *shari'a*/Islamic law, a Muslim woman cannot be married to an "apostate."

Two years later, in June 1995, a Cairo court approved the lawsuit and ruled that the married couple must separate, and consequently be divorced (*Süddeutsche Zeitung*, June 19, 1995, p. 9). Abu-Zaid then fled with his wife to Leiden, Netherlands, and went to the appeals court to contest the ruling. The Egyptian Supreme Court, however, upheld the *murtad* sentence and thus the ruling of divorce imposed on the couple. The evidence for apostasy was found in Abu-Zaid's writings (see *Frankfurter Allgemeine Zeitung*, August 10, 1996, p. 4), and the legal basis for the ruling was the new *hisbah* law passed by the Egyptian parliament on January 29, 1996 (see my examination of the Abu-Zaid case and the new *hisbah* law in the German daily *Frankfurter Allgemeine Zeitung*, July 3, 1996, p. 34). The *hisbah* law sanctions the punishment of Muslims deviant from the *shari'a* even when those who denounce them, and bring suit, are not directly involved in the legal dispute. This precedent in Egypt, a secular state, as well as the rise of Turkish fundamentalists to power in secular Turkey (where Erbakan was Prime Minister from July 1996 to June 1997), constitutes an institutional intrusion of the state by fundamentalists. Even though the *"nizam Islami /* Islamic order" is their avowed goal, these fundamentalists are creating disarray, not order.

It is not so much the outrageously unjust fate of Abu-Zaid and his wife that matters for our purposes here, but rather the implications it has for the virulent spread of fundamentalism. In a major interview in the German weekly *Der Spiegel,* Abu-Zaid rightly stated that the strength of the Islamic fundamentalists lies not in their pursuit of

> terrorism and bloodshed. They can bring this country nearer to [the] abyss through their infiltration of the legal system and the state. These attempts are much more dangerous than the slayings and use of explosives. In fact, the Egyptian government has been able to contain fundamentalist terrorism. . . . I advise the president [of Egypt] to push forward the intellectual battle [against the fundamentalists]. . . . Their power in the schools and universities is already disastrous. (*Der Spiegel,* issue 27, 1995, pp. 122f.)

The Abu-Zaid story illustrates the two pivotal issues I shall deal with: on the one hand, that Islamic fundamentalism is not Islam per se and, on the other, that in the long run the Islamic fundamentalists are far more dangerous as ideologues of power than as extremists who kill, cut throats (as they have in Algeria), and throw bombs. Fundamentalism is a *Weltanschauung,* or worldview, that seeks to establish its own order, and thus to separate the peoples of Islamic civilization from the rest of humanity while claiming for their worldview a universal standing. The decoupling thus envisaged and the concurrently espoused universalist claims are only seemingly in contradiction, for they are in fact seen by the fundamentalists as two successive steps in the same process.

Islamic fundamentalists challenge and undermine the secular order of the body politic and aim to replace it by a divine order, the so-called *hakimiyyat Allah.* The order they envisage is not simply a domestic one, but the foundation for the new world order they expect to mount in place of the existing one. Seen in this light, Islamic fundamentalism becomes a grave challenge to current standards of world politics. To be sure, the movement lacks the capabilities and resources necessary for achieving that goal, but I am not prepared, as some are, to dismiss this challenge as "just rhetoric." Certainly, Islamic fundamentalists will not be able to impose their "order" on the world, but they *can* create *disorder,* on a vast scale. They are already doing so, on domestic grounds, in Algeria, Afghanistan, Egypt, Saudi Arabia, and elsewhere. Turkey has a fundamentalist prime minister but remains a secular state; the traditionalists currently in the ascendancy in Afghanistan, ethnic Pashtuns, envisage a divine order, though it is difficult to identify them as fundamentalists in the terms I use herein. But in Iran and Sudan the fundamentalists are *already* in power: both countries are supporting a variety of underground fundamentalist movements by funding them, training their irregular warriors, and providing the logistics necessary for fomenting disorder. This is a challenge that must be taken seriously, and events in the years since I began writing this book have served to confirm my grave concern for what awaits.

But at the same time we must never lose sight of the distinction between Islam and Islamic fundamentalism; any promotion of hostility to Islam itself in the guise of a clash of civilizations would unwittingly play into the hands of the fundamentalists in their efforts to antagonize the West.

This book, then, is not a litany of sensational events and outrageous tactics, but rather an in-depth analysis of the global phenomenon of the politicization of religion, a phenomenon that is not restricted to Islamic civilization. My analysis seeks not only to explain the phenomenon, as it is manifested in the Islamic case, but also to inquire into the deeper recesses of its background and appeal.

Our world is rapidly becoming a "global village," and global issues must be addressed within the framework of global solutions. I seek not only to enlighten my readers about the burgeoning global phenomenon of religious fundamentalism but also to present an alternative. In my view, that alternative is a compact based on secular democracy and human rights. These twin goals should be made the substance of an international cross-cultural morality, one that might bring people of different civilizations and cultures to live together in peace instead of perpetually clashing with one another. The book concludes with an assessment of this alternative.

My work on "*al-Islam al-siyasi* / political Islam" and the crisis of Islamic civilization in modern times began in the late 1970s. Earlier, my research had been on Arab nationalism, as a secular ideology, and on the Arab military, the leaders of which were in that era alleged to be modernizing elites. My first two books, published in German in 1971 and 1973, were on these secular subjects. *Arab Nationalism: Between Islam and the Nation-State* has been available to readers of English since 1981 (second edition 1990, revised and enlarged third edition 1996, London and New York: Macmillan and St. Martin's Press). But as has become painfully clear, both secular Arab nationalism and the equally secular Arab military elites have failed: the secular nationalists have been unable to develop the existing nominal nation-states into genuine nation-states based on democratic institutions; and the so-called modernizing military elites have turned out to be rank dictators. These elites imported the "most advanced governmental technology" (Gabriel Ben-Dor) and combined it with modern versions of the domestic tradition of arbitrary rule.

My book *The Crisis of Modern Islam*, published in German in 1981 and in English in 1988 (Salt Lake City: Utah University Press), was an effort to offer some answers to the pending questions. I continued this research in *Islam and the Cultural Accommodation of Social Change* (Boulder, Colo.: Westview Press, 1990), in which I inquired into the failure of attempts to introduce modernity into the Islamic civilization. This failure followed the humiliating Arab military defeat in the June War of 1967, which I dealt with in *Conflict and War in the Middle East* (London: Macmillan, 1993), and has been the very breeding ground for fundamentalist ideology and its project of a new world order.

Having departed a political culture that subordinates the individual to the group—I was born in Damascus and lived in that culture through my formative years—and having become fascinated in Europe by the culture of *individual* human rights, I have always been a lone toiler in the intellectual vineyards, enjoying my work despite my seeming isolation. Recently, however, the Fundamentalism Project of the American Academy of Arts and Sciences, of which I was a member in the years 1989–92, showed me that work in research teams can be very stimulating. I am most grateful to the directors of this project, Martin Marty and Scott Appleby, and to the coordinator of my team, Everett Mendelsohn of Harvard, for offering me intellectual guidance while I pursued my work on political Islam and fundamentalism. I had the honor to co-author Volume 2 in the project on *Fundamentalisms and Society* (1993).

I began work on the present book during my affiliation as a visiting research associate (1988–93) at Harvard University. The first draft of chapters 1 to 8 was written directly in English during my term as a visiting professor for peace and conflict studies at the University of California, Berkeley, in spring term 1994. Profiting from an intellectual association with Douglas Arava, my sponsoring editor at the University of California Press, and my most able developmental editor Bill Carver, I continued to revise and rewrite successive drafts of the book after leaving Berkeley and returning to my home university in Göttingen, where the book as it stands was completed in the years 1994–96. The many assistances of Marilyn Schwartz, managing editor at Berkeley, are also greatfully acknowledged.

The final two chapters of this book, 9 and 10, are based on a decade of research and on further intercultural communication efforts pursued both in the West and in the World of Islam. The ideas discussed in Chapter 9 were presented to the scholarly community of Asian Studies at the Université Catholique du Louvain, Belgium, in May 1994, after my return from Berkeley to Europe. Here my gratitude goes to Professor Michèle Schmiegelow for many inspirations. A year later I was given an opportunity to discuss my ideas at length at Bilkent University of Ankara, Turkey, where I acted as visiting professor. I owe much to my Turkish host, Professor Ali Karaosmanoglu, for his many insights. Chapter 10, which deals with the topic of human rights, pursues ideas discussed in different intercultural forums like *Pen International,* and in cross-cultural dialogues focused on the Mediterranean as a bridge or boundary between Europe and the World of Islam. In that concluding chapter I explain why human rights matter for the study of fundamentalism. In regard to Islam and human rights, the open discussions in Jakarta, Indonesia, with intellectuals of ICMI (Association of Muslim Intellectuals of Indonesia) have been most inspiring. I believe Southeast Asian Muslims offer us some hope for easing the desperate situation of Islamic civilization and the disintegrating order of the world at the turn of the new century.

My associates in Göttingen deserve great gratitude for supporting me in the completion of this final version. My staff assistant Anke Ringe unfailingly committed my many drafts to the computer; and my research assistants, Katja Bruder, Jost Esser, and Daniela Heuer, were most helpful in many ways, from proofreading the several drafts to rethinking my arguments and checking my notes. In particular, Katja Bruder offered a genuine intellectual challenge during the rewriting of the final version. Without the assistance of all four associates I would not have been able to complete this work. I am also grateful to the developmental and copy editors enlisted by the University of California Press in Berkeley. Special gratitude goes in particular to Bill Carver for superbly straightening out my language imperfections. My beloved wife Ulla gave me much emotional support during my absence from home in Harvard and Berkeley as well as in many parts of the World of Islam and during the long working weeks following every return to Göttingen.

I do not want to conclude this preface without emphasizing that I take my stand against fundamentalism on Islamic grounds, or, as my reformist coreligionist Muhammad Said al-Ashmawi puts it in reverse in French, "*l'islamisme contre l'Islam* / Islamism against Islam." To me religious belief in Islam is, as Sufi Muslims put it, "love of God," not a political ideology. In my heart, therefore, I am a Sufi, but in my mind I subscribe to *'aql*/reason, and in this I follow the Islamic rationalism of Ibn Rushd/ Averroës. Moreover, I read Islamic scripture, as any other, in the light of history, a practice I learned from the work of the great Islamic philosopher of history Ibn Khaldun. The Islamic source most pertinent to the intellectual framework of this book is the ideal of *al-madina al-fadila*/the perfect state, as outlined in the great thought of the Islamic political philosopher al-Farabi. Al-Farabi's "perfect state" has a rational, that is, secular order and is best administered by a reason-oriented philosopher. This is my alternative to the fundamentalists' concept of a divine order, the order on which they base their challenge and their efforts at remaking the world. A combination of these Islamic sources, the Sufi love of Ibn 'Arabi, the reason-based orientation of Ibn Rushd, the historicizing thought of Ibn Khaldun, and al-Farabi's secular concept of order, seem to me the best combination of cornerstones for an Islamic enlightenment. I maintain that this is the true Islam, in contrast to the political Islam of Islamic fundamentalists. As the "open society" has its enemies, to use the phrase of Sir Karl Popper, so too does an "open Islam" have its enemies: the fundamentalists. They are a challenge not only to world order but also to us liberal Muslims.

July 1997
Center for International Affairs
Georgia Augusta University of Göttingen
Bassam Tibi

—∽—

ONE

The Context

*Globalization, Fragmentation,
and Disorder*

No prudent observer of world politics would deny that with the breakdown of communism and the end of bipolarity the West has lost the political factor that secured its unity for a period of four decades from 1945 on. The Western responses to the war in the Balkans have made obvious the disunity of the West since the fall of communism. During the Cold War, peace researchers and pacifists dismissed attacks on communism as an instrument adopted by the West to play down its own problems. Such views might not have had great impact in North America, but they surely did in Western Europe. Not only left-wing writers but also liberals rejected anti-communism as unethical and denounced critics of communism, whether in Europe or the United States, as "Cold War warriors." The then-prevalent silence about the expansive nature of communism was extended even to human rights violations in the Soviet Union and Eastern Europe. This silence was practiced not because peace researchers encouraged these violations, but simply so that international conflict might be minimized in the name of peace. Do we see here an ominous similarity between the West's approach to communism then and its approach to fundamentalism today?

It is most disturbing to observe the very people who denounced criticism of the totalitarian character of communism resorting to the same tactic when required to think critically about religious fundamentalism as a new factor in global politics. In this case the new fashion of "political correctness" is being employed. On ethical grounds I share the concerns of some liberals regarding the use of fundamentalism for the demonization of other civilizations. But as a devout Muslim I am greatly concerned about equating Islam with fundamentalism, not only by people who are hostile to Islam but also by those who believe Islam must be defended against a misperceived "Islamic Threat." In short, I disavow the view that it is politically incorrect to speak and write in blunt terms about fundamentalism, as this book shall demonstrate.

In what follows, I shall argue that Islamic fundamentalism is simply one variety of a new global phenomenon in world politics. At issue in each case is a political ideology, not the religion so cynically linked with that ideology. In my view, fundamentalism is an ideology symptomatic of the "clash of civilizations." It is not the cause of the current crisis of our world, but both an expression of it and a response to it. Fundamentalism, however, is not a solution. By inciting conflict and deepening the ongoing cultural fragmentation of the world, it leads to disorder. Many of the scholars who agree with me in stating that fundamentalist agitation leads to turmoil in the Islamic world stop short of conceding that this trend touches on world politics as well. I shall begin by establishing the argument that Islamic fundamentalism is not simply an intra-Islamic affair, but rather one of the pillars of an emerging new world disorder.

ISLAMIC FUNDAMENTALISM, THE WEST, AND WORLD ORDER

Long before the end of the Cold War, scholars had recognized the politicization of religion as a new global phenomenon. They proposed to describe and analyze the new tide as a *religious fundamentalism*.[1] The term, of course, soon became highly charged, owing to its sensationalized application to the revolution of the Ayatollahs in Iran in 1979 and the ensuing climate of religious fanaticism and extremism there. A decade later, after the fall of the Berlin Wall, some observers, mostly on the left, argued that with the breakdown of communism the West had lost its arch-enemy. Ever since, of course, the West has been accused of being on the lookout for a substitute ogre, and Islamic fundamentalism seemed to have the right qualifications. The underlying argument is that the West needs to identify a new enemy so as to ensure the continuity of its political and military unity and hegemony. It is unfortunate that in this cynical climate the former NATO Secretary-General Willy Claes issued a statement that seemed to support this suspicion. Claes in fact proposed to view Islamic fundamentalism as the next major threat to Western civilization, and indeed the rhetoric of Islamic fundamentalists strongly supports NATO's taking such a position. But does rhetoric alone, unsupported by wherewithal, suffice for establishing trends in world politics?

Islamic fundamentalists do indeed attack the West, believing fervently that the world is already witnessing its decline and that they will therefore be in a position soon to proclaim a new order to supplant the discredited Western world order. Their view of a new order is based, so they say, on the political tenets of Islam, certainly as interpreted by them. One need not be an expert on Islamic movements to know how weak and divided these movements are, in relative terms, and to infer from their weakness their inability to bring about the new world order they proclaim with such electrifying rhetoric. To be sure, fundamentalists can engineer frightening levels of terrorism and otherwise throw the streets into turmoil, but it is difficult to imagine the diverse and rivalrous Islamic fundamentalist movements coming together long enough to create a new order, even had they the requisite economic, political, and military wherewithal. The argument of this book is that these movements can nonetheless create disorder within their own countries sufficient in the long run to lead to a combined regional and global disorder, addressed here as the new world disorder. My approach here is intended to be neither sensational nor accusatory. Rather, it describes an international trend. The analysis presented maintains that we are even now witnessing a simultaneity of structural globalization and national and international cultural fragmentation. The net effects of these simultaneous processes underlie the rise of religious fundamentalisms worldwide.

The new world disorder is, however, much more than turmoil; its broader ramifications are already made credible by the crisis of the nation-state in most countries of Asia and Africa. Again, fundamentalism is much more than extremism or terrorism; it is rather a powerful challenge to the existing order of the international system of secular nation-states. Given that this institution is Western in origin, the revolt against it is also a "revolt against the West."[2]

What has Islam to do with this revolt, and why is a link being drawn between Islam and fundamentalism? In fact, Islam is both a world religion and a major civilization, embracing one-fifth of the people on the planet. In our age of the "clash of civilizations"[3] world peace means accommodation between civilizations on grounds of mutual equality, respect, and recognition.[4]

To question the ongoing hegemony of the West is, from this point of view, not to claim a substitute for its hegemony, be it Islamic or whatever, but rather to argue for intercivilizational equality and justice, in preference to anyone's hegemony. A closer look, however, shows clearly that this is not the outlook of the Islamic fundamentalists, who envisage a new world order, in the twenty-first century, to be led by Islamic civilization. Again, it is crucial that a distinction be drawn between Islam as a religion and civilization and Islam as a political ideology, the latter characterized in this book and elsewhere as fundamentalism. These are two completely different issues. To offer enlightenment about Islamic fundamentalism is one thing, and to warn of a demonization of Islam and a reactionary anti-Islamism is quite another!

In the course of dismissing the perception of an "Islamic Threat,"[5] an effort that I share, some scholars nonetheless seem to confuse the two aspects of Islam. Islam as a religion is definitely not a threat, but Islamic fundamentalism is. It is a threat, however, only in the sense of creating disorder on a grand scale, not—as is often contended—in the sense of replacing communism as a "new global enemy for the Western alliance." Moreover, it is important to make clear at the outset that "Islamic fundamentalism is very different in different places, and a basis for common cause is difficult to achieve,"[6] as Horsman and Marshall rightly observe in their book *After the Nation-State*. Interesting in this regard are the issues addressed by the Islamic ruler King Hassan II of Morocco, in an interview prior to a visit to Washington. It is more enlightening to listen to Muslim leaders talking about fundamentalism than to consult Western views on this phenomenon.

The Moroccan king is well aware of the fundamentalist challenge, but unlike those left-wing Westerners who accuse the West of having invented this imaginary challenge in an effort to replace communism, he knows fundamentalism firsthand, as a fact of political life in the World of Islam. In discreetly alluding to the statement by former NATO Secretary-General Willy Claes, referred to above, the king argued that "NATO is a defense organization for the North Atlantic region. I do not think NATO was created to fight fundamentalism, but to fight Soviet guns and missiles. . . . Anyway, if fundamentalism has to be engaged in battle, it would not be done with tanks. Fundamentalists don't have armored divisions, they have no Scud missiles, and not an atomic weapon."[7] Although concerned about the demonization of Islam in the West, King Hassan did not refrain from—implicitly—rebuking those who see fundamentalism as a cultural revival of Islam in the ongoing search for identity. He sees fundamentalism as a challenge, but a political challenge, not a military one. The king knows, too, that fundamentalism is not a religious renaissance: "[On] the day I see a fundamentalist who preaches religion for the love of God then I'll say, fine, let's listen. But so far I haven't heard that. . . . [Fundamentalism] is a behavioral question, a psychology which cannot be fought with armadas, but [only] with other ideas" (ibid.).

In facing the challenge of fundamentalism, we need first to understand it and then to seek out instruments for dealing with it. This book seeks to provide the requisite understanding. Being both a Muslim and a student of Islam, and having worked also in non-Islamic countries, I am aware of the global character of the phenomenon at issue.[8] In India I was able to observe the Hindu-Muslim conflict over the character of the Indian secular state. Hindu fundamentalism, in fact, is another variety of the challenge to secular order, and Hindu fundamentalists have a vision of India as a Hindustan, that is, an exclusively Hindu state. But their fundamentalism does not seek more than a political territorialization of Hinduism within the boundaries of India.[9] Unlike territorial Hindu fundamentalism, Islamic fundamentalism is an absolutist universalism, a vision of a worldwide order based on Islam. It is for this reason—and not because of an "enmity to Islam"—that the debate on fundamentalism and world politics must be centered around Islam and the West. Traditionally, the two have had a hostile image of one another,[10] but the context of globalization and fundamentalism is—despite all analogies—an altogether different one.

FUNDAMENTALISM: A RESPONSE TO THE PROBLEMS OF GLOBALIZATION AND FRAGMENTATION

My point of departure here is the argument that globalization is rampant in economy, politics, communication, transportation, and technology, but not in culture or civilization. Note that I do not use the terms "culture" and "civilization" interchangeably. In keeping with the cultural anthropology of Clifford Geertz,[11] I view culture as a local production of meaning, that is, as the lineaments of life in a local setting. In Islam there exists a great variety of cultures. In a single Islamic country like Indonesia, there are three hundred different cultures, not to speak of the manifold versions of Indo-Islam, Arab Islam, and African Islam elsewhere. These cultures, however, all share a worldview that can best be described as an Islamic *Weltanschauung*.

This worldview is the basis of the holistic Islamic civilization of the past, a civilization that continues to prevail in Islam today in the midst of a world of modern nation-states. In other words, we are dealing with a great variety of local cultures more or less embedded in a single great civilization. This is so also in other civilizations. The West, for example, is uniquely Western on the one hand, but culturally multifaceted on the other.

Globalization has affected most realms of life, chiefly the economy (that is, the world economy) and politics (that is, the international system of states), but—as contended—it has not notably affected culture or civilization. There exists, then, a world *system*, but not a correspondingly holistic world *civilization*. The "technological unification of the world" has led to the emergence of global structures underlying the "shrinking of the globe," but it "does not in itself create a unity of outlook and has not in fact done so,"[12] as the late Hedley Bull, a leading scholar of international relations, rightly put it. The result is a more globalized but equally more fragmented world. Globalization is structural; fragmentation is cultural. Cultural fragmentation manifests the deficiencies of structural globalization.

In relating the argument of globalization and fragmentation to the postulated disorder to come—a disorder promoted, as I argue, by fundamentalism as a divisive political force—I shall focus on the nation-state. The "revolt against the West" begins as a revolt against the domestic nation-state.

THE SECULAR NATION-STATE: PRIME TARGET OF FUNDAMENTALISM

The nation-state was initially a European institution, formulated in the early nineteenth century, on which the once exclusively European system of states was based. "From the state system that was once the peculiarity of Europe there has developed a system of nation-states covering the globe in a network of national communities . . . [and] tribal societies have been either destroyed or absorbed into larger social entities,"[13] as Anthony Giddens puts it in the best study on the nation-state. In describing major changes in the world order in modern times he points to two processes that have "been responsible for producing these extraordinary changes, the global consolidation of industrial capitalism and the global ascendancy of the nation-state."[14]

The globalization thus addressed is a structural process. The universal outlooks determined by it derive from specific norms and values underpinning a secular worldview. These norms and values are Western in origin and have *not* become universal. In the past century, progress in the globalization of structures has not been matched by comparable progress in the universalization of norms and values. True, the ascendancy and spread of Western education have contributed to the emergence of Westernized elites in non-Western civilizations, but it has failed to gain roots there.[15] Even these elites are decoupling themselves from Western norms and values, in an effort to de-Westernize, first, themselves and, then, in the case at hand, the World of Islam. Cultural revival ends in political strategies that turn upon a return to allegedly authentic, local, cultural roots. For this reason it is not at all peculiar to see among the leaders of Islamic fundamentalism some who are holders of Western doctorates, for example the Algerian Abbasi Madani (doctorate from the University of London) and the Sudanese Hassan al-Turabi (doctorate from the Sorbonne, in Paris).

Islamic civilization has its own views, coupled with a claim to their universality, but unlike Western civilization it has never been able to trigger globalization processes of its own design. During the period of Cold War bipolarity, the concerns of Islamic civilization were subordinated to the global conflict, but in the post-Cold War international system, the Western and Islamic civilizations are once again competing. In terms of its image of itself, political Islam constitutes both a claim and a mandate to mobilize Islamic civilization against the West and, in the bargain, to contest the Western institution of the nation-state. And the significance of the nation-state does not lie "so much in the acknowledgment of any particular state boundaries, but [in the] recognition of the authenticity of the nation-state as the legitimate arbiter of its own internal affairs," as Giddens puts it.[16]

Did the globalization of the system of nation-states contribute to establishing a comparable legitimacy pattern in the governments and affairs of non-Western countries? Unlike the European nation-states, those of the World of Islam, in particular those in the Middle East, grew neither from political processes of mobilization and integration nor from economic processes of growth; these newly formed nation-state superstructures were, rather, an imposition laid on after the West's dissolution of Islamic order.[17] From this discouraging background follows the weak legitimacy of the contemporary institution. Islamic fundamentalists view these states as *hulul mustawrada*/imported solutions. The "primacy of the nation-state as the universal political form of the current era"[18] is not a construct acceptable to

Islamic fundamentalists, and their revolt against the nation-state leads to a process of de-legitimization.

To be sure, the legitimacy crisis[19] of the nation-state in the World of Islam has not been brought on by religious fundamentalism. It is, rather, the other way around: the crisis of legitimacy derives from the failure of the nation-state to strike roots in an alien civilization, and fundamentalism, seeing its opportunity, is the political articulation of the crisis. (In fact, these developments are not restricted to Muslim countries; nation-states in the so-called Third World have been described in general as "quasi-states,"[20] and in my work I refer to them simply as "nominal nation-states"; see note 17.) Following the distinguished Egyptian ambassador Tahsin Bashir I have described the contemporary Arab states of the Middle East and North Africa, with the exception of Egypt and Morocco, as "tribes with national flags."[21] In this broad heartland of the World of Islam the nation-states have failed to meet the twin challenges of promoting economic growth and erecting institutions for political participation. They have failed, in short, to combine economic prosperity with democracy. (Two states of Southeast Asia—Malaysia and Indonesia—are by all odds the only Islamic exceptions in that regard.) Islamic fundamentalists point to this failure as grounds for justifying their de-legitimization of the nation-state in the World of Islam.[22] As their alternative to the order of the nation-state they preach the *nizam Islami* / the Islamic order[23] (see chapters 5 and 6).

One of the major processes addressed in this book is that Islamic (and other) fundamentalists, in their vision of "remaking the world," reclaim not only the sciences, the family, and education (see note 8), but also the concept of order.[24] Even while they are dismissing the nation-state as an expression of a Western understanding of order that is alien to Islam, and in its place seeking their own authentic order, they are unleashing disorder, and the effects of this process may be global.

Why are these processes gathering strength and significance in our time? Why did they fail to in earlier periods? Is the end of the Cold War truly relevant?

AFTER THE COLD WAR: FURTHER FRAGMENTATION

The observer of world political developments cannot be unaware of the repercussions of the end of the Cold War, in particular the demise of the bipolar structure of the international system. As Horsman and Marshall

argue, in their study *After the Nation-State*, "the effects of the recent geopolitical changes have been extreme. . . . [F]undamentalism in countries with
large Islamic populations will . . . serve to slow any progress toward even
rudimentary forms of liberal democracy. . . . [P]artitions, border skir
mishes, and secessionist movements are now far more likely to prolifer-
ate."[25] In the epoch of the Cold War, regional and domestic conflicts—like
those in the Middle East and South Asia—were subordinated to the global
system of bipolarity and worldwide superpower competition.[26] The two superpowers effectively contained the escalation of existing conflicts (the
Iran-Iraq War was an exception) and kept the antagonists at bay. But as the
interminable, barbaric, and costly war in the Balkans has demonstrated,
the world has changed radically. Such a hot war could not have taken place
in the years of the Cold War. It is true that during the years of the East-
West conflict many wars took place (think also of the Arab-Israeli[27] and
Indian-Pakistani wars[28]), but with the exception of the Iran-Iraq War of
1980–1988, none of them was as protracted as the war in the Balkans
has been.

In supporting their belief that there can *be* no peace between the West
and the World of Islam, the Balkan War has served well the purposes of
the Islamic fundamentalists. In their view the Balkan War, as the Gulf
War before it, was evidence of a Christian crusade against Islam.[29] The
West itself is at once powerless and disunited in responding to these
changes. As Horsman and Marshall argue, in their pondering on the
age *After the Nation-State*, "[t]here is as yet no adequate international
political security structure to manage these changes in any systematic
way. NATO is of little use in its current state; the organization is structured to respond to threats from the East, not to internecine strife in the
Balkans."[30] Nor is NATO structured to respond to the political actions of
fundamentalist movements, I would add, in recalling the interview with
the Moroccan king cited above. References to an emerging "world power
Islam"[31] are misleading and useless—they serve only to revive interest
in the outdated strategies of NATO. There is a great need to think about
the new frontiers of security and to develop new patterns for meeting
recent challenges.

Most important for international security are the political events related
to the de-legitimization of the nation-state in the World of Islam. In the
Middle East, in particular, these states "have poor human rights records, little experience of peaceful transition between regimes, and few of the liberal

institutions of civil society. Many are authoritarian regimes led by ruling, dynastic families . . . or praetorian regimes backed by force."[32] The Middle East is the most unstable as well as the geopolitically most important region in the World of Islam, and exacerbating the instability of the region has been the powerful instrument of resurgent Islamic fundamentalism. Fundamentalists may not be able to achieve better records than the regimes they are beginning to replace, but in de-legitimizing them they are creating disorder and contributing to a further intensification of the ongoing global fragmentation. Obviously, "this fragmentation makes the task of making political systems work harder, not easier."[33]

Any analysis of the simultaneity of structural globalization and cultural fragmentation leads to the question, why should this process matter to the international system as a whole and to the West in particular? How can the unrelieved turmoil and the de-legitimization of the nominal nation-state that we see in the World of Islam lead to global disorder?

THE "ISLAMIC RESURGENCE": TWO VIEWS

The contested contention that "Islam" is emerging as a "new world power" in the post-Cold War period is a view that can be found both in the West (see note 31) and among the Islamic fundamentalists themselves as they strive for an "Islamic world order." Fred Halliday, one of the most knowledgeable experts on Middle Eastern politics, dismisses this claim as "demagogy on both sides" and argues that "the contemporary challenge of 'Islam' is . . . not about inter-state relations at all, but about how these Islamic societies and states will organize themselves, and what the implications of such organization for their relations with the outside world will be. The dynamic is an internal, often destructively involutionary one."[34] This observation, though correct as far as it goes, overlooks the fact that international relations in the post-Cold War period are becoming increasingly less state-centered and more or less elevated to relations among civilizations—despite the formal persistence of the state as the putative primary actor in international politics. It also overlooks the fact that the dismissal of the nation-state, beginning with its de-legitimization in the World of Islam, is not exclusively an intra-Islamic affair. This "internal dynamic" will have great effects on the outside world, and here, precisely, lies the challenge. Political theorists like David Beetham, who involve Islam in the general study of the legitimization of power, acknowledge that the prospect of an Islamic state, as opposed to the array of secular nation-states in the region, is a clear challenge to the exclusively secular basis of legitimacy in the Western tradition.[35] Given that the system of globalized secular nation-states is the political framework of interaction on which the international order is based, any challenge to this pattern can be expected to have repercussions on world order itself.

The argument I am dismissing here is that international politics in our era continues to be basically state politics. Halliday, for one, infers that even if Islamic fundamentalists were to seize power they would pose no challenge, given that the Islamic states are weak: "They are incapable of mounting a concerted challenge, let alone redrawing boundaries. . . . Europe [is] in this sense, . . . immune—the flow of migrant workers and the incidence of terrorism by Middle East groups being very different from the military and piratical attacks of previous centuries."[36] Halliday's effort to enlighten the Western audience about the "demagogy of the Islamic threat" is an admirable one, and I share that honest motive wholeheartedly. One cannot overlook the anti-Islamism that is emerging in the West, which derives in part from the revival of archaic fears of Islam, as reflected in Halliday's reference to the "piratical attacks" represented by early Islamic incursions into Europe and later forays from North Africa's Berber Coast. Still, this need to enlighten the Western audience ought not unburden the analyst from the necessity of addressing *real* threats. There *is* a challenge, and it cannot be reduced to the growing "tendency of ethnic and communal movements involving Muslim interaction with non-Muslims to take an Islamist form."[37]

The effects of this tendency are not limited to making those "living on the boundaries of the Islamic world . . . face many difficulties in the years ahead," as Halliday argues. The results will be both domestic and regional, seldom simply state-centered conflicts that can be resolved through the "promotion of democracy and political tolerance," as Halliday himself rightly emphasizes. Clearly, the resolution of these conflicts not only is not on the priorities list of Islamic fundamentalists, but in fact is among their targets for destruction.

Ali Benhaj, one of the major leaders of the Algerian Front Islamique du Salut / Islamic Salvation Front (FIS), unequivocally dismisses democracy as "*kufr* / unbelief."[38] Another leading Islamic fundamentalist, Hassan al-Turabi (doctorate in law from the Sorbonne), who serves as ideologue-in-chief of the Islamic fundamentalists in the Sudan, has spoken of individual human rights with contempt in identifying them as "an import from the West" for which Muslims "have no need."[39]

POLITICAL ISLAM AS A VARIETY OF FUNDAMENTALISM

In this book I conceptualize political Islam as "fundamentalism," but it is fair to ask whether this is a reasonable characterization. Halliday believes the term is "misleading" (see note 34), and he is not alone in this. But unlike Halliday, other authors—despite sharing his dismissal of the term—do not overlook the global significance of the phenomenon. The use of religion in igniting conflict in international affairs is a very serious novelty in contemporary world politics. Mark Juergensmeyer, in referring to the confronting of the secular state by religious factions, speaks of a "New Cold War." The longing for "an indigenous form of religious politics free from the taint of Western culture has been expressed by . . . persons of a variety of faiths throughout the globe."[40] This longing is not new, but the role it is establishing in international politics *is*, and Juergensmeyer recognizes that only the end of the Cold War could have opened the way for this "New Cold War." In his view, "[t]he new world order that is replacing the bipolar powers of the old Cold War is characterized not only by the rise of new economic forces, a crumbling of old empires, and discrediting of communism, but also by the resurgence of parochial identities based on ethnic and religious allegiances."[41] The "New World Order" conceived by the West (consider Francis Fukuyama and former President George Bush) as a promising new era is a horse of another color, and its rhetoric need not be taken seriously; it is promulgated simply as an opposition to the realities of a new world disorder resulting from the "confronting [of] the secular state," as Juergensmeyer rightly observes. He prefers not to conceptualize the new challenge as fundamentalism but, rather, subscribes to the concept of "religious nationalism," for three reasons: first, "the term [fundamentalism] is less descriptive than it is accusatory"; second, "fundamentalism is an imprecise category for making comparisons across cultures"; and third, fundamentalism describes attitudes "motivated solely by religious beliefs rather than broad concerns about the nature of society and the world."[42]

In the Fundamentalism Project of the American Academy of Arts and Sciences, of which I was a member,[43] cross-regional and interdisciplinary research has contributed to repudiating all three of Juergensmeyer's reservations against the use of the concept of fundamentalism. To be sure, it is important that we free the concept of its loose and sensational use in the media, which contributed to the term's becoming so highly charged. But in the first place, it is precisely the politicization of religion that fundamentalism addresses. It is in this sense that I subscribe to a strict distinction between *Islam as a religious belief,* to which I myself adhere, and *Islamic fundamentalism as a political ideology* based on an equally selective and arbitrary politicization of religion. In the Fundamentalism Project we came ultimately to the conclusion that fundamentalism is a global phenomenon, one that can be found in all of the world's major religions.[44] When the world-politics perspective is restricted to Islamic-Western relations, it may well be that for some people the talk about fundamentalism takes on an accusatory character. This more narrow dispute, however, is neither the frame of reference of this book nor its concern. Prejudice in international politics is an important area of study, but it is not what we shall pursue here.

In the Fundamentalism Project, again, area-studies experts engaged in a comparative study of fundamentalisms in *all* major world religions. In so doing, they have shown that the concept of fundamentalism—as I have interpreted it here—is the right framework for "making comparisons across cultures." And, finally, fundamentalism does not address religious beliefs, but rather a sociopolitical worldview (see note 43), that is, a broad concern about the nature of state, society, and world politics, however that concern might be articulated in religious symbols.

As Martin Marty and Scott Appleby, the directors of the Fundamentalism Project, put it, the research of the project has demonstrated that "[t]hose people and groups now known as fundamentalists emerge from different regions of the world, cite different holy books, or have different interpretations of the same holy book, or follow no holy book at all but a venerable tradition instead."[45] These "fundamentalists see themselves as actors in an eschatological drama unfolding in the mind of God and directing the course of human history" (ibid., p. 819).

Despite their pragmatic use of religion, the context is clearly more political than religious, and it embraces politics both domestic and global. Fundamentalists "reaffirm the old doctrines; they subtly lift them from their original context, embellish and institutionalize them, and employ them as *ideological weapons against a hostile world.* . . . [In] remaking the world, fundamentalists demonstrate *a closer affinity to modernism than to traditionalism*" (ibid., pp. 826f). And, finally, fundamentalism is *not* an expression of a religious revival, but rather a pronouncement of a new order, for "fundamentalists seek to replace existing structures with a comprehensive system emanating from religious principles and embracing law, polity, society, economy, and culture. . . . [F]undamentalism contains within it a totalitarian impulse" (ibid., p. 824).

Fundamentalists, again, are modernists, not traditionalists, because they evaluate tradition in the light of modernity, and selectively retrieve salient elements of both in order to put forward a concept of political order, be this domestic, as in the case of Hindustan (Hindu India), or global, as is the case in *nizam Islami*/ the Islamic order, which is—in rhetoric—expected to encompass the entire globe (see chapters 5 and 6). *Dar al-Islam*/ the territoriality of Islam is identical with *dar al-salam*/ the world in peace, but only under the banner of Islam.[46] In short, fundamentalists gain a boost from the failed policies of the secular regimes and proceed to question the secular nation-state as such. The divine order they envisage as an alternative model in reality leads to disorder, though this, of course, is not their intention.

The emerging domestic disorder (in Algeria, for example) is truly a "challenge to Muslim peoples themselves," as Halliday rightly argues. But how could this challenge be restricted to the peoples of a civilization numbering 1.3 billion people living as a majority in 52 states and as minorities in many others? How can such momentous changes (in terms of disorder and turmoil) in the World of Islam have no repercussions in the outside world? Halliday, nonetheless, believes that the challenge of "Islamism" (his term for fundamentalism) is "not to the non-Islamic world."

Fundamentalists politicize religion and fragment loyalties. "The process is apt to be violent. In sum, managing international order in an age of fragmented loyalties will not be easy."[47] The age we are already witnessing, following the regional decline of the nation-state, seems to be the onset of a new world disorder unleashing what has been described as the "coming anarchy."[48]

Given the distortion, in the Western media, of the distinction between Islam and Islamic fundamentalism, it is important not only to distinguish clearly between the two but also to make clear that the phenomenon is not restricted to the Islamic world. As a global phenomenon it can also be encountered in other civilizations. The changes prompted by the end of the Cold War suggest that a decisively new epoch in world politics has begun, during which new phenomena are being introduced while old ones are taking on new shapes and assuming greater importance. Among these phenomena is the politicization of major world religions. Although the nature of that politicization varies from one civilization to another, owing to existing concrete conditions, this new phenomenon is generally being characterized as an expression of religious fundamentalism.

My work on fundamentalism in several areas of the Islamic world (the Middle East, North and West Africa, Central Asia, and, most recently, Southeast Asia) has led me to conclude that the rise of competing political religions, each imbued with its own ethnic identity, is one of the significant characteristics of our age and will remain with us well into the next century. The decline of communism in the East and the crisis of meaning plaguing the West have together paved the way for non-Western civilizations—above all Islam—to pose their competing challenges to Western modernity and Western hegemony.

THE CLASH OF TWO UNIVERSALISMS: A "CLASH OF CIVILIZATIONS"?

I argue that Islam has become the West's leading challenger for one simple reason: in contrast to those of Hinduism, for example, Islamic perspectives are not restricted to national or regional boundaries. In this respect, Islam resembles Western civilization, in the sense that it is universal in both its claims and its outlook. It is thus easy to understand why Islam and the West clash, more consistently than do other competing civilizations. Unlike Western civilization, however, Islam, though universal, has not been able to spread the *da'wa* / Islamic mission throughout the modern world. The globalization process unfolding in the course of European expansion proved Western civilization to be more competitive, and severely challenged Islam. Contemporary Muslims feel that the West has deprived Islam of its core function, that is, to lead humanity. Those who are familiar with the pronouncements of Muslim fundamentalists and have read the writings of Sayyid Qutb and Abu al-A'la al-Mawdudi know that this political movement does not arise simply from a nostalgia for past glory, or to foment a political revolt against Western hegemony. In fact, the concept of world order posed by these fundamentalists *competes* with Western universalism. I agree with Halliday that Islamic fundamentalists lack the capabilities needed for a broad implementation of their concepts, but their vision is not simply rhetoric, and they are already able to launch considerable disorder.

To make the issue more concrete, let me relate it to major political events. Many Muslims and even the CIA analyst Anthony Arnold[49] share the view that Islam, owing to the repercussions of the Afghanistan war, has given its share to the breakdown of communism. These Muslims then ask, why not defeat the West, too? They asked this question during the Gulf War, and they continue to ask it, though that war led to an Islamic defeat. Saddam Hussein, in labeling the war a *jihad*/holy war, thus claiming to battle the West in the name of Islam, received the support of most of the fundamentalist movements in the Muslim world. Few in the West are aware that most Muslims outside the West view the Gulf War as a clash between their own civilization and that of the West. The fact that books and articles expounding this view are still being published by Muslims years after the Gulf War supports the observation that most Muslims continue to believe that the war was a "crusade of the West" against their civilization. As I have indicated, the war in Bosnia, too, is perceived by Muslims as a continuation of the same ongoing "crusade." To be sure, in both cases the perception runs counter to the hard facts of reality. Still, the perception alone is sufficient to incite the call for *jihad*, which is seen as the Islamic *response* to a powerful external threat, not an Islamic *initiative*.

This reading of the classical history of Islamic *jihad* and the Christian crusades into contemporary politics is designed to address the question, who will lead the world after the crumbling of the communist bloc? The question establishes a clear link between the breakdown of communism, the end of the Cold War, and the new boost given the *jihad* doctrine by Islamic fundamentalism after the Gulf War,[50] despite the militarily shattering defeat it imposed. It would appear, in fact, that the West won the Gulf War militarily but lost it politically. Scholars of international relations preoccupied with international politics as inter-state relations can understand neither this phenomenon nor the "clash of civilizations" it brings to the fore. Indeed, the recent debate over the "clash of civilizations" provoked by the Harvard scholar Samuel P. Huntington indicates—despite its deplorable shortcomings—a welcome change in perspective among many in the international relations community. "Culture" and "civilization" are issues that had earlier been mostly ignored by scholars of international studies preoccupied with the "state."

In this context I have suggested that we might view fundamentalism as an ideology contributing to what I have called the "War of Civilizations." By "war" I do not address military issues, but rather a competition between worldviews seen as different frames of reference for dealing with politics. Certainly it is not the *term* that matters; French scholars, for instance, use their distinct term *"intégrisme"* in referring to the same process with the same meaning I allude to here. What matters is that in some of these cases a politicization of worldviews has linked religion to a variety of nationalisms. Serbian Orthodox fundamentalism, for example, which has politicized Eastern Orthodox Christianity,[51] pursues in fact a nationalist strategy, albeit in a religious disguise. Thus the conflicts involved in these cases are seemingly domestic, with the avowed political goal of establishing a "Greater Serbia" in the Balkans, or a "Hindustan" as a Hindu state in India. Despite the fact that one can find similar mixes of religion and politics in other local cultures and civilizations, it does not seem to me appropriate to call this phenomenon in general "religious nationalism." In my view, "fundamentalism" is the more appropriate term for addressing the politicized worldviews of competing civilizations.

In the case of Islam, in fact, it is not "the nation"—in the sense of contemporary national boundaries—that is at stake. The revival of the Islamic notion of *umma* in the meaning of "universal Islamic community" differs significantly from the secular notion of *umma* in the meaning of "nation." Indeed, in the course of resisting the Western world order the Islamic revivalists direct their views and actions *against* the institution of the nation-state and the domestic Muslim elites who rule it. That is, Islamic fundamentalists accuse their rulers of fulfilling Western strategies aimed at dividing the universal *umma* into an array of secular nations along the Western model of the nation-state (see note 22). Again, "fundamentalism" seems to me the most appropriate term to depict this ideological stance, because it suggests, on the level of civilization, the politicization of religion that is involved. To be sure, the fundamentalist challenge is multifaceted; its ideology is not monolithic. For this reason, all five volumes of the already mentioned Fundamentalism Project address the issue in plural, that is, in terms of "fundamentalisms."

The reason why this book includes no area studies is that my focus is not on the day-to-day events related to political Islam. The mass media and popular writings consistently expose us to these sensations, and it is not my desire to summarize news coverage in some manner or other. Rather, I am interested in Islamic fundamentalism as a pivotal issue in world politics. In creating disorder it might conceivably change the character of the international system in the coming decade. As I shall show in Chapter 3, the Gulf War, once a most exciting event for television audiences, was in the Islamic perception the arena for competition between the formula of the "New

(Western) World Order" and an envisaged Islamic world order. With President Bush losing the 1992 election, his rather simplistic vision of a "New World Order" vanished. Still with us, however, is the Islamic formula of a *nizam Islami*/Islamic system that aims to give the political world a new shape. The vision of an Islamic world order is a long-term goal that relies *not* on state policies but on public choices made by politically active members of the Muslim community. The *umma*, not the existing Islamic states, lies at the heart of these choices. Nor does this analysis contradict the fundamentalists themselves, who aim to establish the "Islamic state" after having overthrown the various existing state structures. Conspicuously, then, it will not be the Saudi-dominated community of Islamic states—as rallied in the Organization of the Islamic Conference (OIC)[52]—that will pose this kind of challenge.

If we recognize the challenge emerging from the politicized notion of the *umma* itself, then we also understand that the "clash of civilizations" moves beyond geographic and state-centered boundaries. The ever-increasing migration from parts of the Islamic world to the West, Europe and America alike, contributes to the complexities of this clash. In his book *Islam and War*, John Kelsay puts it like this: "The traditions we call 'Western' and 'Islamic' can no longer strictly be identified with particular geographic regions. . . . The rapidity of Muslim migration, . . . suggests that we may soon be forced to speak not simply of Islam *and*, but of Islam *in* the West."[53]

Drawing upon reference to multiculturalism and an instrumental use of Western-liberal tolerance, Islamic fundamentalists operating in Western Europe and the United States are in fact claiming, in the name of *communitarianism*, ghetto rights for Islamic minorities.[54] This claim is a great disservice to Islam—as a religion—and to its democratic incorporation into Western democracies, the latter not a concern of fundamentalists. The argument that Islamic fundamentalism is a political ideology rather than a purely religious phenomenon finds support in the fact that fundamentalists are not particularly engaged in theological debates. I agree with the French writer Jean François Revel, who sees Islamic fundamentalism as the most serious challenge to secular democracy precisely because its proponents professedly aim to replace secularity with a divine order.[55] The notion of *hakimiyyat Allah*/Allah's rule, to which most of the Islamic fundamentalists subscribe, is nothing less than a vision of totalitarian rule[56]—exercised, shamefully enough, in the name of God. Students of Islam know well that this notion is recent, and that one fails to find it either in the Qur'an or in the *hadith* tradition of the Prophet, the only two authoritative sources of Islam recognized by all Muslims. Again, Islam as a faith is very different from Islamism as a contemporary *political ideology* of fundamentalism. My experience in Germany of being deliberately misunderstood on this point compels me to reiterate that I direct my criticism *not* toward Islam as a faith I as a Muslim adhere to, but toward fundamentalism as an ideology. The point that only few Westerners understand is this: Islamic fundamentalists acting in Western exile present themselves as the true spokesmen of Islam. For discrediting or deflecting any criticism of their totalitarian views, they deliberately accuse their rivals of anti-Islamism.

I subscribe to genuine, more political than interdenominational, Islamic-Christian-Jewish dialogue as the route to peace in the new century and new millennium. The Jewish-Palestinian political dialogue in the pursuit of peace is a case in point; this dialogue is rejected by both Islamic and Jewish fundamentalists. I reject therefore all efforts to politicize religions so as to employ them as tools in the "clash of civilizations."

I subscribe also to an international morality, based on democracy and human rights, as an alternative to be shared by all religions, and I therefore dismiss equally the persistence of Western hegemony and aspirations for an Islamic domination. I shall return to these alternatives in the final chapters (9 and 10) of this book.

If humanity fails to find common ground in the precepts of international morality, then our world will become an arena for the new world disorder. It is distressing to observe, the more so in an age of crisis, the ever-growing appeal of religious fundamentalisms, in all civilizations. Some international-security experts, like the knowledgeable Albert Wohlstetter of the University of Chicago, predict that Bosnia presents, in miniature, a scenario for international conflicts throughout the world. Well, the war in Bosnia appears to be over, but Wohlstetter's scenario remains a frightening prospect for the turn of the century. Although the signs of a new world disorder are already apparent, humanity might still prove able to avert it as a scenario for the twenty-first century. The critique of religious fundamentalism is a contribution toward this end.

—∞—

TWO

The Study of Islamic Fundamentalism and the Scope of the Inquiry

Again, I identify religious fundamentalism not as a spiritual faith, but as a political ideology based on the politicizing of religion for sociopolitical and economic goals in the pursuit of establishing a divine order. By definition, then, this ideology is exclusive, in the sense that it attacks opposing options, primarily those secular outlooks that resist the linking of religion to politics. Fundamentalisms are thus absolutist, by their nature, and as we move into the next century, they seem to be placing their imprint on world politics.

RELIGION, FUNDAMENTALISM, AND CIVILIZATIONS

For fundamentalists, religion is the expression of a divine order, as schematically opposed to our secular order. In this perspective, God's rule replaces humanity's rule. This distinction makes perfectly clear the fact that fundamentalism is not simply a revival of premodern religious worldviews. It is, rather, a practical policy preference. Fundamentalists do not debate in intellectual clubs, nor do they engage in theological controversies. Religious fundamentalists are ideologues and political activists, primarily concerned with political power. Nor is religious fundamentalism confined to Islam. Rather—as any thoughtful review of political events around the world will demonstrate—it is a global phenomenon. The use of religion to further political ends can be observed in all major world religions, including Hinduism, Buddhism, Confucianism, Christianity, and Judaism.[1]

Anthropological theory views culture[2] as an expression of a social production of meaning, with a specific, local frame of reference. Some religions embrace a number of cultures but are confined to a single geographical region, as is the case with Hindu civilization in South Asia, which has neither a mission to all of humanity nor a universal outlook. Except for Judaism, however, the monotheistic religions consider themselves to be universal, and their truth to be absolute for all of humanity.[3] If politicized, these religions develop ideologies of political universalism that may also entail a concept of world order. Toward that end, these religions aim to unite the local cultures of their heartland, thus forming a wider *civilization* and building a greater capacity to shape the world beyond according to their own neo-absolutist vision. Islamism, as a political ideology, but not Islam as a religion, presents an excellent example.

In the modern world, which like worlds of the past is characterized by cultural diversity, regions or worldviews seek civilizational awareness by gathering related local cultures together politically. In this context, religious fundamentalisms move to center stage as expressions of political ideologies. In establishing in each case a *Weltanschauung*, that is, a particular conception of the world based on religion, they provide the grounds for drawing fault lines between competing civilizations. In this capacity, religious fundamentalism becomes an ideology for inciting conflict, not a strategy for fostering peace between local cultures and regional civilizations.

These fault lines notwithstanding, humanity must attempt to build bridges, not battlements, between civilizations. We must look beyond the nation-state to understand how civilizations function and interact, and we need to identify what really determines people's sense of identity and the commitments that grow out of this framework. In chapters 5 and 6, particularly in Chapter 6, I will show, for most people in non-Western civilizations, how meaningless the modern state has been for defining their identity. Most non-Western people find the framework for their identity in their local communities, that is, in their ethnicities. This identification takes place on a local or regional level, with secondary reference to the subsuming civilization.[4] An exposure to another civilization generally fosters the perception of it as alien. In the country I come from, Syria, and the dozens of countries I have lived and worked in throughout Asia and Africa in the past two decades, I have come across only a few people who identified themselves— as citizens—with the existing state. Regularly, people turn to other identity references. For them, the existing states are both superficial and imposed.

Underlying this perception is the fact that the new nation-states are simply nominal formations lacking the substance of the modern state—as exemplified, for example, in Europe—and commanding no great loyalty. They provide no real identification as a basis for substantive citizenship.[5]

Under these circumstances, and on a local level, people perceive themselves as members of communal groups, sectarian and ethnic alike. In the larger context they see themselves as Arabs and Muslims, but not, however, as citizens of any state—unless they are formally asked for their passports. Religious fundamentalists working in such an environment employ a dual strategy: they draw on their particular civilizational framework to distinguish themselves collectively from those in the world beyond, while in their concrete communities they mobilize kinship and ethnic commitments. The best example of this strategy is Afghanistan, with its *mujahidin*, past and present. The *mujahidin* are the warriors who fought against the Soviet troops following the invasion of Afghanistan. There were seven major Afghan *mujahidin* groups united as a fundamentalist force against the Russian enemy. But after the withdrawal of the Soviet troops they have split into ethnic factions fighting one another in an endless war that will be with us for years to come. As the case of Afghanistan demonstrates, ethnic loyalties tend to undermine holistic fundamentalist views. Ethnic divides close only when a uniting external threat appears on the horizon. During the Soviet invasion the Afghan *mujahidin* waged their holy war as fiercely as if they had been the united warriors of Allah, but today, sadly, they are ethnic militants slaughtering one another.[6] On a global level the civilizational framework allows Islamic fundamentalisms to call on the entire Islamic *umma* of 1.3 billion Muslims when a major external threat is perceived. As the Afghan case shows, however, the strength of that power base is undermined by sectarian and ethnic strife on the local and domestic levels. It is for this reason that the fundamentalist movements so often fail to establish the divine order they call for; their actions yield more disorder than order. They can unify their forces only under the effects of a perceived or real external threat, and they are therefore not above inventing one.

Religious fundamentalisms couple a premodern sensibility with an instrumental exploitation of modernity (for example, the employment of modern arms and technologies), and it is for this reason that I consider the politicization of religion as the greatest challenge to cultural modernity and the gravest threat to world stability. In our age, world peace can be established only as a peace between civilizations, and because we are dealing with a global phenomenon, we must learn more about the workings of religious fundamentalisms if we are to face the challenge posed.

It is obvious that the political revival of religious civilizations reflects a revival of parochialism in an age dominated by the global standards of modern science and technology. Many scholars with a sound knowledge of world civilizations, like Leslie Lipson, believe that the "future does not belong to the Khomeinis," because science and technology create a globalization of civilization that cannot be reversed.[7] This belief, which resonates with the Enlightenment idea of rectilinear progress,[8] is belied by the realities of the Islamic world and other non-Western civilizations, where science and technology are adopted quite without regard to the views of a global civilization. Western civilization seems in fact to be unique in having been deeply affected by secular standards of cultural modernity, specifically by the Renaissance, the Reformation, and the Enlightenment. And although Christianity, too, has been touched by the ongoing politicization of religion, Western civilization might not be as susceptible to the appeal of religious fundamentalism. In the West, fundamentalist groups have been peripheral to date, but Eastern unreformed Christianity is already gathering around orthodox beliefs preparatory to confronting both Islam and the West.[9] The support of the atrocities committed by the Serbs in Bosnia, offered not only by the Orthodox Slavic civilization but also by the Greek Orthodox Church, provides a clear example for this contention. The politicization of the Orthodox Church in the Balkans lays the groundwork for a marriage of religious fundamentalism and ethnic nationalism, for which I have coined the term "ethnofundamentalism."[10]

The violent clashes between Muslims and Serbs during the war in Bosnia, between Azeris and Armenians in the Caucasus, between Muslims, Hindus, and Sikhs in India as well as in Sri Lanka, and between the ethnically diverse Muslims themselves (be it within Afghanistan or in the guerrilla war within Karachi, Pakistan) are signs of a terrifying future. Basically, these ethnic clashes have been incited by religious fundamentalists. Ethnicity can bolster fundamentalism but can as easily become a divisive factor that contributes to undermining the unity of the religious community so earnestly sought. Afghanistan is a case in point.

Religious fundamentalism employs religious *symbols* and fills them with new meaning. In this venue, symbols are a good deal less than *belief,* in being abused as a vehicle for the articulation of sociopolitical, economic, and cultural claims. We cannot, however, equate the global ideology of religious fundamentalism with such secular ideologies as communism, nationalism, and liberalism. Religious appeals override all other appeals, and religious ties are unlike political commitments. Religion as a cultural system gives meaning as no ideology can. Religious fundamentalism, by politicizing religion, is thus an ideology of a special caliber.

CULTURAL MODERNITY IN REVERSE: BACK TO COLLECTIVITIES

Fundamentalisms are highly affected by modernity, and indeed they constitute a strategy avowedly directed against cultural modernity itself. Democracy and the political culture of pluralism, human rights, and liberal tolerance are basic products of cultural modernity.[11] As early as the Renaissance, we find Machiavelli departing from the concept of divine order in establishing the idea that man can govern himself.[12] The notion of government of the people by the people (that is, popular sovereignty) later served as a basis for the legitimacy of the secular nation-state, and some believe that techno-scientific advancements have contributed to a global civilization that will unite all of humanity.

But is this true? Clearly, religious fundamentalisms are challenging these assumptions. Modernity has fostered the idea of man/woman as an individual; fundamentalism is returning the individuals to the collectivity of which each person is considered to be but an appendage. Thus, the organic bonding to a civilization, not the free will to be a participating member of a democratic body politic, is the alternative view of man presented by fundamentalism.

As I will show in Chapter 4, modernity has two dimensions: cultural and institutional-structural. By *cultural modernity* I mean, with reference to the work of Jürgen Habermas (see note 11), the "principle of subjectivity" according to which a person is defined as an individual of free will, capable of determining his/her own destiny and changing the social and natural environment. *Institutional modernity*[13] takes science and technology as its instrumental achievements. That this constitutes a dichotomy, with intricate links between its two members, is demonstrated by its reception in non-Western civilizations, where institutional *but not cultural* modernity can take structural root.

In the Islamic part of the Middle East and in most other non-Western civilizations, people have been exposed to modernity primarily on institutional grounds (in the form of the hegemony and technical and military superiority of the West) and less on cultural grounds (the project of cultural modernity). The ongoing structural decline of Western power has been matched by a process of de-Westernization, expressed in the contesting of Western values and norms. Religious fundamentalism, then, is the ideology of this burgeoning revolt against the West, in the sense of mounting a conflict among civilizations on a global scale.[14] This process of de-Westernization sees culture as a process of local social production of meaning, and bears little reference to the American consumptive patterns called by some "American public culture" (and characterized by the coinage "MacWorld"). Culture is something more than "McDonaldization," the drinking of Coca-Cola, or the watching of soap operas on television.

Those who question the contention of an increasingly de-Westernizing world by citing the wide spread of what I call the "Coca-Cola culture" are misled. The deeper dimensions of religious fundamentalism must be addressed by more appropriate frameworks. Unlike the minority of Protestant fundamentalists in North America, the Islamic, Hindu, Orthodox Christian, and other non-Western fundamentalists can address an entire civilization as a collectivity and count on a powerful response, one definitely not constrained to the likes of "Coca-Cola" as a pattern of consumptive public culture! Responding to naive questions by two German journalists writing for *Der Spiegel*, the Malaysian prime minister, Mahathir bin Mohammad, renowned for his contempt of the West, answered rightly that "When I eat a hamburger I certainly do not change my values overnight."[15] The Western belief in the impact of this sort of mass culture hampers a proper understanding of the simultaneity of structural globalization and cultural fragmentation.

ANTAGONIZING DEMOCRACY
AND CREATING DISORDER

Modernity is thought to be expressed in the framework and dynamics of a democratic order. Democracies are secular nation-states based on popular sovereignty. This Western model has come to serve as a basis for the unity of humanity, despite manifold differences of religion and ethnicity. On the contrary, the idea of the "Government of God," as a divine order (*hakimiyyat Allah*), which is presented by Islamic fundamentalists as a global alternative to the secular state, exacerbates the division of humanity into civilizations. Fundamentalist politics also tear the populations of existing multireligious and multiethnic states—like Sudan under the rule of Muslim Brothers under the conditions of civil war—into gerrymandered agglomerations. The sundering of the population of Bosnia-Herzegovina into three collectivities, each belonging to a distinct civilization, is another topical case in point. No prudent observer can preclude such a destiny for India or other such states, if fundamentalists continue to draw the fault lines of conflict that they have publicly announced. The clash between Muslims and Hindus in Ayodhya in December 1992 was just a warning. The global character of religious fundamentalism heralds an age of disorder and open strife, on both the state level and the level of the global international system.

In quoting the leading Algerian fundamentalist Ali Benhaj, I have shown that Islamic fundamentalists perceive democracy as a *kufr*/heresy (see note 38, Chapter 1). In their view the idea of *hakimiyyat Allah*/God's rule is the imperative alternative to democracy, which they dismiss as a valid pattern for organizing public life. From this example it follows that there is a profound conflict between fundamentalism and democracy. Having read the pamphleteerings of Islamic fundamentalists and talked to them in different parts of the World of Islam, I have great difficulty in understanding the contention of some Western students of contemporary Islam that political Islam is aimed at an "Islamization of democracy."[16] My findings rather support the warning that Islamic fundamentalists constitute the most serious challenge to democracy in our age. To be sure, I believe that Islam can be compatible with democracy, if interpreted with an open-minded spirit. Fundamentalists, however, emphasize the contrary (see note 26). For them, democracy is a *hall mustawrad*/imported solution[17] and, as such, to be rejected.

Fundamentalists do not restrict themselves to antagonizing democracy within their own countries. They do this as migrants in the West, as well. In November 1993 a nationwide confrontation erupted when Muslim fundamentalists sought to establish a logistics base in France for their underground activities in Algeria. In the Parisian journal *Le Figaro*, an eminent Imam argued that "Allah's law stands above French law." The French, proud of their *laïcité*—secularity as regards separation of religion and politics, a cultural heritage of the French Revolution—responded strongly that only secular law, precisely French positive law, is valid in their country. In contrast to divine law, positive law is crafted by humans, in democratic institutions. This is the pattern of law to be complied with in France. These events seemed to create a precedent in France,[18] and comparable problems have arisen in the United Kingdom[19] and in Germany[20] with respect to Muslim communities living there. Fundamentalists are thus at pains to hijack diaspora Islamic communities. In this regard, fundamentalism has become an issue affecting Western societies in the search for models for the Islamic migrant communities: communitarianism or integration as individual citizens / *citoyens*.

In short, a state-centered framework is a poor basis from which to gain an understanding of fundamentalism as a source of conflict. The reader is by now familiar with the growth of the World of Islam: it comprises one-fifth of humanity (1.3 billion Muslims) living as a majority of the population in 52 states (these are the members of the OIC, or Organization of the Islamic Conference) and as considerable minorities in a number of others. In India alone, the Islamic minority amounts to 130 million. Islamic fundamentalists challenge the ruling elites in most of these states on religio-political grounds. Their avowed goal is to replace existing orders by the "Islamic State."[21] Although this alternative is based on a formula too fuzzy and elusive to be defined in straightforward terms, the mobilizational appeal of the formula is formidable for gathering force against the mostly undemocratic, mostly corrupt states in the World of Islam. I agree with Mark Juergensmeyer that the confronting of the secular state by religious ideologies, of whatever stripe, will be the hallmark of our age, or what he fearfully proposes to call the "New Cold War."[22] But again, I disagree with him in characterizing this call for a religious state, as distinct from the secular state, as "religious nationalism." At issue is a religious fundamentalism, not a nationalism. In the case of Islamic fundamentalism, no particular nationalism *can* be involved, for the simple reason that what is at issue is an alternative universal model designed for the entire world. Unconfined religious ideologies are not expressions of religious nationalism.

In some cases, such as the ethnofundamentalism of the Serbs in Bosnia, or the Hindus in India, we might find some justice in employing the notion of religious nationalism for the phenomenon in question. The presently contained irredentist vision of the Serbs is that of an Orthodox Greater Serbia, defined not simply on political-nationalist grounds but on religious grounds (see note 51, Chapter 1). Greater Serbia is believed to be religiously Orthodox Christian and ethnically Serbian, and the envisaged Hindustan in India is seen, both politically and religiously, as an exclusive state of the Hindus. Both are conspicuous expressions of ethnofundamentalism. But unlike these fundamentalists, the Muslim militants politicize the idea of *da'wa* /

Islamic mission and develop it into a concept of world order. They will not confine themselves to the existing territoriality of the World of Islam but, rather, covet the entire world as beneficiary of their vision. In their view the expansion of Western civilization[23] has been realized at the expense of Islam. And indeed, the intellectual father of Islamic revivalism, al-Afghani, calls for the restoration of Islamic dominance and the return of Islam to what it has been deprived of by the West. "We have turned to imitate the European nations and thus . . . to accept our subordination to their rule. In doing so we have given up the major character of Islam, which lies in rule (*sulta*) and dominance (*ghalab*). Instead we have become lazy peoples accommodating ourselves to the dominance of the others."[24] Replacing Western dominance by an Islamic *ghalab*/dominance cannot bring world peace, which in my view can be established only on the basis of secular international morality.

Having done extensive research on the attitudes of Islamic fundamentalists, I fail to see the vaunted power of science and technology in uniting humanity.[25] On the contrary, as I shall show in Chapter 5, the diffusion of hegemonic power is related to the spread of modern technology. Technology does not bring peace to the world, but international morality could. My aim is to shift the focus of international relations studies from the technicality of state-centered power to the normative grounds of a world order acceptable to all of humanity. I contend that the religious fundamentalisms, in particular those with a universalist outlook, not only create great obstacles to world peace but also actively contribute to a violent world disorder.

Basically, fundamentalists insist that God's rule is the only religiopolitical truth acceptable as a basis for designing world order. Aside from the clerical-totalitarian implications of the concept—already horrendous enough—any effort to determine, *specifically*, what is meant by God's rule not only leads nowhere but also creates dissent among the fundamentalists themselves, ultimately divorcing them from one another. The most prominent Pakistani fundamentalist, the late Abu al-A'la al-Mawdudi, said, in no uncertain terms, that in his view Islam and democracy are profoundly at odds, and in fact irreconcilable.[26] The other most prominent Islamic fundamentalist, the Egyptian Sayyid Qutb, indicts as heretics all humans who believe they can govern themselves by themselves. To him the notion of man's rule is megalomania, for man is created by God and can only be governed by God, within the framework of *hakimiyyat Allah*.[27]

At the outset of the modern age, when the church dominated the cultural sphere, Europe was beset by similar problems. When Machiavelli argued that men can govern themselves, the catchphrase for the response of the church was "Machiavelli in Hell" (see note 12). It is worth mentioning, curiously enough, that the Renaissance could not have come about had not the Arab Muslims assisted in introducing to European thought the basically rational-secular legacy of Greece. As Leslie Lipson puts it, "Aristotle crept back into Europe by the side door. His return was due to the Arabs."[28] Ironically, the great Muslim thinkers who developed Greek rationalism further are today despised in their own civilization. At the First International Islamic Philosophy Conference on Islam and Civilization, the Egyptian philosopher Mourad Wahba coined the term "The Paradoxon of Averroës,"[29] by which he meant that this great rational thinker of Islam has come to be revered in the West even while his renown is contested in his own civilization. The deeper meaning of this episode for the positive Islamic-Western encounters that led to the Renaissance is that civilizations seeking common grounds may find them in reason and rationality, whereas fundamentalism contributes to constraints on thought and to the "war of civilizations" (the war of rival civilizational worldviews).[30] The concept of *hakimiyyat Allah/* God's rule is a hallmark of fundamentalism, not of rationality. Religion is an *iman/*belief, and not a political system of government.

Indeed, the concept of *hakimiyyat Allah* does not exist in the Qur'an. A closer look at this more recent addition makes clear that it heralds an Islamic form of totalitarianism,[31] not one of democracy. The two contemporary examples of this form of rule in fundamentalist states—those in Iran and the Sudan—can in no way be likened to democracy.

INVENTING TRADITION: THE LEGACY OF ISLAMIC REFORMISM AND TRADITIONALISM

Fundamentalism is not traditionalism, and although fundamentalists do draw on tradition, they do so clearly within a modern context and with a nontraditional mindset. An example of this sort of expedient thinking is the *shura/*consultation, which is offered as a substitute for secular democracy. In touching on the alleged link between the political strategies of Islamic fundamentalism and the need for what is called "Islamization of democracy"—whatever that may mean—the debate on the *shura* is pertinent.

Unlike secular democracy, the wholly invented tradition[32] of the *shura* promises to deliver freedom without "falling into the trap of secularism," as the fundamentalists argue.

Shura thinking virtually reflects the tribal tradition of pre-Islamic history, a tradition adopted in the formative years of the Islamic polity. The Qur'an honors this pre-Islamic tradition in stipulating that the Prophet must "take counsel with them in the conduct of affairs / *wa shawiruhum fi al-amr*" (Qur'an: Surat 'Imran, 3/159). The only other passage in the Qur'an that addresses this issue makes reference to "[those] who avoid gross sins and indecencies and, when angered, are willing to forgive, [those] who obey their Lord, attend to their prayers, and conduct their affairs by mutual consent / *wa amruhum shura baynahum*" (Qur'an: Surat *al-Shura*, 42/37–38). In fact, these commandments are the basis for the highly honorable political ethics of Islam. Islamic fundamentalists, however, draw on this concept and present it as a truly Islamic alternative to democracy,[33] not as an "Islamization of democracy."[34]

In Saudi Arabia, one of the two Islamic traditional monarchies legitimized by Islam, we find another reference to the *shura*, but one that makes no claim to be either an Islamic substitute for democracy or an Islamization of democracy. In the *shura* decree of King Fahd of Saudi Arabia, issued in August 1993, one finds that all reference to democracy is carefully avoided. Indeed, the *shura* council in Saudi Arabia has absolutely no power.[35] *Shura* means consultation; it is by no means binding. Not even for this imputed function does this traditional gathering in Saudi Arabia yield ground; the king and his tribal family are the only source of power and decision making. This is an old Islamic tradition, definitely not fundamentalism; the tradition upon which Islamic fundamentalists draw is an invented one.

We need now to place Islamic fundamentalism, as a politicization of religion, into the larger Islamic context. Having just argued that fundamentalism[36] and traditionalism are diverging lines of thought in Islam, I must pay heed to a third current in modern Islamic thought: Islamic reformism, or modernism.[37] The foremost Islamic reformer, Muhammad 'Abduh, sought to embrace modernity in Islamic ways.[38] He was definitely not a fundamentalist, nor does he function today as a precursor of fundamentalism, after the fashion of his contemporary, al-Afghani.

Islamic modernism attempted to espouse cultural and institutional modernity by seeking a synthesis between these concepts and Islam, but doing so without rethinking the traditional Islamic theocentric worldview.

But no Islamic reformer or modernist went so far as to shift from the theo-centric to the man-centered view of the world, as did, for instance, the Christian Jesuit René Descartes.

I must make clear that the *Menschenbild* of cultural modernity (that is, the man-centered view of the world) is not tantamount to atheism, for the acknowledgment of man's capabilities and responsibilities need not result in denying the existence of God. Islamic fundamentalists, as semi-modernists of sorts, also seek to embrace modernity, but only on instrumental grounds, that is, by confining the effort to the adoption of techno-scientific achievements. They vehemently refuse the rational worldview that has produced modern science and technology, and they accuse the early Islamic reformists/modernists of facilitating the cultural impact of modernity on Islam. True, the Islamic modernists tried this and failed, but they failed not because they were wrong but because they stopped short of finding solutions that might have succeeded. As regards the cultural accommodation of modernity, the Islamic fundamentalists lag far behind even the very slight achievements of Islamic reformism.

Among the three currents in contemporary Islam—fundamentalism, traditionalism, and modernism/reformism—the third is the weakest. The last significant Islamic reformer of our time, the Sudanese sheikh Mahmoud Taha,[39] was executed in 1985 without trial by the then dictator of Sudan, Ja'far al-Numairi. Those intellectually significant Muslims, who, like Abdullahi A. An-Na'im and Mohammed Arkoun, still hope to apply reason to Islamic reform, had better do so in their Western exile, be it Paris or London or Washington. Their ideas are discussed in Scandinavia,[40] but not in the Islamic world.

Only in Saudi Arabia does one find evidence of traditionalism, and it exists there only superficially. Because Wahhabism is considered a traditionalism, and because it is the source of the religiopolitical legitimacy of the Saudi oil kingdom, the Saudi monarchy can be said to be traditional (see note 35). It is certainly not fundamentalist. (Wahhabism stems from the thought of Ibn Abd al-Wahhab, 1703–1797.)

Except for the largely apolitical Sufi (mystic) orders in various Islamic countries, one cannot point to any other genuine traditionalisms in our time. Not even Saudi Arabia is a truly traditionalist country today, despite the fact that its legitimacy has been cast essentially along these lines.

We can add still a fourth category for identifying the Islamic currents of the present time: conformism. Most Muslims, beginning with their political leaders, do embrace modernity, on grounds of conformism. Conformism is a way of dealing with realities that do not accord with Islamic precepts, short of rethinking the inherited Islamic concepts and worldview. Because no effort is made to reconcile the tension between professed belief and deviant action, Islamic conformism is characterized by behavioral lag. In a debate with John Piscatori carried out in publications[41] about the nation-state I argued that conformism is an ill-fated effort to deal with modernity. I juxtapose conformism to what I call the "cultural accommodation of social change" (see note 2) and conclude that these are two distinctly different things.

Let me explain the distinction I make through an example. The need to pay the interest on loans—a fact of life in a modern society—compels one to deal with the prohibition of collecting interest in Islam, which is called *riba*. To raise interest under some rubric other than *riba* while in fact doing the same thing is to circumvent the prohibition. In fact, you raise *riba* interest, perceive your action differently, and so continue to believe in the prohibition you are violating. This is behavioral lag—true conformism—but not an accommodation of change. Nor is the conformism of Islamic states to the world order of nation-states—without rethinking the inherited Islamic dichotomy of the world between *dar al-Islam*/house of Islam and *dar al-harb*/house of war—an accommodation either. On the contrary, cultural accommodation implies the ability and willingness to revise longstanding beliefs, and the norms and values related to them, when they become obsolete and create obstacles for daily life. Cultural modernity can be summarized in one phrase: all knowledge is open to revision!

To sum up: Islamic traditionalism either is past history or it exists in greatly modified form, with little public notice, on the periphery, in the religious enclaves of Sufi orders. As a way of dealing with modernity on cultural and institutional grounds, Islamic modernism/reformism is a failed project. And Islamic conformism, by default, is the attitude of most Islamic authorities and institutions in the realities of our time. Scriptural Islamic fundamentalism, then, is a revolt against all of these currents. In recent history, it has been an effort to Islamize modernity, rather than an effort to come to terms with modernity by accommodating it culturally into Islam.

THE STRUCTURE OF THIS INQUIRY

The major thesis of this book is that fundamentalism, of whatever stripe, is part of a global phenomenon. The Islamic version of the phenomenon is unique in being basically a claim for an alternative world order based on Islamic tenets, as interpreted in a modern context. This claim is peculiar to Islamic fundamentalism in that it is equally an effort to overthrow the existing world order and to de-Westernize the pillars (for example, the body of law) on which the world order rests. Fundamentalists are incapable of materializing the announced claim; but they *are* able to unleash considerable fragmentation. The result is likely to be a new world disorder. Prior to the shrinking of the globe in the context of the networking unleashed by processes of globalization, each civilization had its own historical "time." In the time of global history there exists only one world time.

In fact, the predicament of modernity is a key issue for understanding Islamic fundamentalism, because the latter is virtually a response to the mapping of the World of Islam into alien global structures. Modernity has been the framework for the globalization of Western structures, and the present world order has been created by the expansion of Western civilization, on grounds of modernity, throughout the world. Islamic fundamentalism is not, as some would argue, a neo-traditionalism,[42] nor is it aimed at a retraditionalization of Islamic societies, regardless of what Islamic fundamentalists themselves contend, directly or rhetorically. The empirical study of fundamentalism itself reveals abundantly how this new phenomenon has become embedded in the context of world time. In other words, fundamentalism is a sort of response to world time that has been shaped by modernity itself.

A closer look at the political concepts of Islamic fundamentalism, seen as an expression of the repoliticization of Islam for nonreligious ends, shows that we are dealing with a modern phenomenon dressed up in traditional symbols. The *turath* / Islamic heritage includes no concept of world order, as Muslim fundamentalists prefer to believe. Their quest for an Islamic world order is simply a reading of modern thinking into classical Islamic concepts. Most fundamentalists have in fact engaged their lives in the modern sector, and most grew up in modern educational institutions.

The context of the rise of fundamentalism in the Middle East has been a context of wars. The Gulf War gave Islamic fundamentalism a great boost, but the movement itself had been growing continuously since the Arab defeat in the Six-Day War of 1967. In much of the Arab world today, the Balkan War was perceived to be an extension of the West's war on Islam. The effects of these wars have led to the contesting of the prevailing world order dominated by the West. For Islamic fundamentalists, combat against the present world order is paramount, and leads naturally to their presenting an Islamic alternative. One can find such views—that is, an Islamic claim to an Islamic world order—as far back as the writings of Sayyid Qutb, who was executed in 1966. At that time, these views were not an issue, even though Qutb and Abu al-A'la al-Mawdudi are today among the authors most often translated and read in the entire World of Islam, not just in the Arabic-speaking part of it. It is only with the coming of the Gulf War that this claim became pivotal in the political thought and policy preferences of Islamic fundamentalism. I join John Kelsay in addressing this as "the Saddam Hussein legacy."[43] In my many German newspaper articles during the Gulf War, published primarily in *Frankfurter Allgemeine Zeitung,* and in my comments in the mass media throughout Europe I have addressed these issues from precisely this vantage point, and I have continued to do so while observing and covering the repercussions of the Balkan War in the World of Islam. I believe, however, that Kelsay should be credited for introducing this formula to North American thought.

The breeding ground for Islamic fundamentalism has been the perennial Islamic predicament with modernity. Islam's encounter with modernity began with the painful defeats suffered by Islamic armies trying to inject the World of Islam into Europe itself.[44] Islamic defeats led to various efforts by Muslim rulers to emulate the West by importing the European form of army.[45] No civilization, however, could limit its embracing of modernity to the instrumental adoption of the technology of War, which the West had by then elevated to industrial standards. For embracing industrialized warfare[46] means embracing modernity itself.

These ramifications of the Islamic predicament with modernity are my point of departure. They are dealt with in the following two chapters, 3 and 4. Then, in Chapter 5, I shall deal with the world order itself, and with the historical context of contesting this order, not only by Islamic fundamentalists. The latter contest this order not only because it is based on Western dominance but also, and foremost, because they reject the norms and values it is based on. The divine order that Islamic fundamentalists look forward to achieving stands in all respects in conflict with the secular order of the world as an order of sovereign nation-states.[47] Algeria and Egypt, so long entrenched in modernity but increasingly confronting uprisings from within, are cases in point.

Dealing with the crumbling nominal nation-state in the World of Islam (as I shall in Chapter 6) means dealing with the challenges directed toward it by the Islamic fundamentalists. While examining the crisis itself, I shall ask whether religion in its politicized guise of fundamentalism can be the solution. Political religion is here a uniting factor against the West, but becomes, when mixed with ethnicity, a divisive factor within and among the very societies involved. These intra-Islamic, basically ethnic conflicts tend to incapacitate Islamic fundamentalists and to give to their world order challenge a rhetorical character. These conflicts do have, however, a global impact, for although I do not believe there is a global "Islamic threat" in the offing, I do foresee, in fundamentalism's destabilizing effects, an emerging world disorder.

In chapters 7 and 8, I introduce the writings and thinking of Islamic fundamentalists. Basically, the ideology of Islamic fundamentalism is embedded in the concepts of *nizam Islami* / Islamic order as opposed to secular order; *shari'a* / Islamic law as opposed to human, positive law; and, above all, in the idea of *hakimiyyat Allah* / God's rule.

I subscribe to religious tolerance and believe that religion must remain a faith. If it is politicized, then we have Muslim, Jewish, Hindu, or Orthodox Christian fundamentalists slaying one another while legitimating their atrocities in the name of religion. This concern underlies my search for an international morality shared by all civilizations and religious communities. In my view the elements of this international morality are democracy and human rights.[48] My inquiry thus ends, in chapters 9 and 10, with an examination of these two pillars of international morality, as they might be applied to Islamic civilization. As an Arab Muslim who has become a European citizen, I see my task as bridging this gap of understanding between civilizations, and I view the idea of international morality as the needed consensus.

What is more, I believe the idea of international morality to be compatible with the ethics of Islam and the ethics of most other world religions. Conversely, I contend that hatred and the ignoring of religious ethics are common failings of fundamentalists of all religions. Fundamentalism as a politicization of religion in the pursuit of nonreligious ends incites hatred among peoples of different religious communities and civilizations. The study of fundamentalism thus becomes an inquiry into the obstacles confronting the search for peace among civilizations and their religions.

—⚅—

THREE

World Order and the Legacy of Saddam Hussein

Islamic fundamentalism is a universalism—it believes that its tenets speak to all of humanity. Among fundamentalisms it is the most significant variety in the world. We shall be focusing on this variety, while bearing in mind that there is another universalism, in the Christian West, and that there are other fundamentalisms elsewhere.[1]

Fundamentalism can be said to be the major trend of political opposition in the Islamic part of the world, which numbers about 1.3 billion people living as a majority in 52 states and as substantial minorities in countries and regions like the United States, Canada, Western Europe, the Balkans, Russia, India, and even China (not only in Xinjiang).[2] The Islamic brand of fundamentalism is a phenomenon that can be grasped neither in traditional Islamic terms nor with reference to the religion of Islam itself. Although it presents itself as a challenge, it is in fact a defensive-cultural response to global issues;[3] it cannot be understood if we fail to place it in the global context of the modern world it is embedded in. To understand fundamentalism in its global-historical context, we must examine two basic concepts: *world order* and *cultural modernity*. My focus in this chapter is on the first, and in Chapter 4 I take up the second.

The vocabulary of *al-usuliyya*/fundamentalism is a recent addition to Middle Eastern languages, primarily to Arabic, the foremost Islamic language and the language of the Qur'an. What we choose to call the phenomenon of Islamic fundamentalism can be debated. Call it political Islam,

Islamism, *al-sahwa al-Islamiyya*/Islamic Awakening, or, simply, *inté-grisme*, as the French do. What is meant and what matters is the *mobilization of religion for political ends*. Moreover, the phenomenon is not restricted to Islam; religious fundamentalism can also be observed in other civilizations, Western and non-Western alike (see note 1). What distinguishes the politicization of religion in non-Western civilizations, particularly in Islam, is its prevailing anti-Western outlook. Those who interpret it simply as a variety of xenophobic anti-Americanism fail to grasp the deeper roots of this phenomenon, which first caught the attention of the international community through the events of the Islamic Revolution in Iran and, more fiercely, on a global level, in the course of the Gulf crisis and its repercussions. The calls for *jihad* made the fact of an extensive anti-Western constituency most clear. The fundamentalist "revolt against the West" is not simply a revolt against Western hegemony, for it is underpinned by a civilizational attitude: it is primarily a revolt against Western norms and values. For many Muslims, globalization is perceived as an expression of evangelical Christianity, as a crusade, and the concrete manifestations of this perception are the wars believed to have been fought against Islam, from the Gulf War to Bosnia and Chechnya. Islamic fundamentalists view *jihad* to be the proper means for facing the perceived crusaders.

For a deeper understanding of Islamic fundamentalism, then, we need to look beyond the obsession with terrorism and anti-Americanism. We need to ask: What are the aspects of the wars in the Gulf, as well as in Bosnia and Chechnya, that lie beneath the day-to-day events? What is the civilizational legacy of the Gulf War? What has it unleashed? And why do Muslims perceive a link between the Gulf War and the war in the Balkans? In this chapter I seek answers to these and analogous questions.

THE LEGACY OF THE GULF WAR

The dispute over world order in international politics is the most important single legacy of the Gulf War. But by "world order" I do not mean to invoke then President George Bush's vague formula of a "New World Order," for not only is the concept of world order much older than the president's formula but its meaning is different from the one he had in mind. The international order of sovereign states fashioned after the Peace of Westphalia in 1648, and then expanded to a mapping of the entire world, is the substance of world order.[4] Because the expansion of this international society[5] has been based on Western universalism, it has posed a potential conflict with Islam as another civilization that had made universal claims—long before the rise of the West or the emergence of contemporary fundamentalism. The Gulf War[6] and the Bush vision of a "New World Order" simply reactivated this conflict potential. As an important fundamentalist book published in Algeria during the year of the Gulf War suggests, the issue following the defeat of Iraq is how Islam should confront this "New World Order": "*L'Islam face au nouvel ordre mondial.*"[7]

The conflict between these two civilizations lies in the fact that this world order—comprising, as it does, all parts of the World of Islam and the worlds beyond—stands in contradiction to Islamic universalism and its vision of a world organized along lines of its own choosing. The prevailing world order is based on commitments by its sovereign states to interact peacefully with one another while honoring clear boundaries recognized mutually by all, but this delineation of state boundaries is at odds with the tradition of Islam, which recognizes no boundaries and claims to be a *da'wa*/universal mission for all of humanity.

The Western understanding of the nation-state as the sovereign unit of action in the world order and "a bordered power-container" (Giddens) is based on the principle that each state, and in turn the world order itself, *is a secular, not divine, institution.* This is the point of departure for understanding the collision of popular sovereignty with the traditional Islamic view that admits only God as the sovereign. The classical Muslim jurist Ibn Taimiyya dismisses "human rule" as *ta'til,* the suspension of God's rule.[8] This is a traditional legacy. After the abolition of the Islamic caliphate in 1924 Muslims adopted the idea of popular sovereignty underpinning the institution of the nation-state, but the idea never quite took root, and the current crisis of the nation-state has led to the politicization of the classical Islamic doctrine, within the new confines of Islamic fundamentalism. It should come as no surprise that the writings of Ibn Taimiyya are among the most basic readings of contemporary Islamic fundamentalists.

From the beginning, the ideology of political Islam has been focused on the view that the institution of the nation-state denies Islam's claim to a universal Islamic order constructed along the lines of the *shari'a*/Islamic law. Thus, all oppositional Islamic fundamentalist groups challenge the extant nation-states in the World of Islam and claim to replace them by a universal divine order based on the *shari'a.* This order is perceived to be *hakimiyyat Allah*/God's rule.[9] The next step in this program is to challenge world order itself, for world order is not only the global umbrella of these secular states but also an impediment to Islam's putting its own views into effect on a universal scale.

World order, again, is simply the system of peaceful international inter-action among sovereign states. *Global order* is the shape that this system assumes in particular historical periods. Until the First World War, global order was sustained by the prevailing system of balance of power. In the aftermath of the Second World War, bipolarity became the determining con-figuration of world order. As early as 1962, no less an authority than the late Jewish-French sociologist Raymond Aron, in his study on war and peace in world politics, argued that bipolarity veils the real conflict potential. In his view the "heterogeneity among civilizations" is the real conflict pend-ing in world politics. And with the end of the Cold War, the predicted po-tential conflict is bubbling to the surface and provoking disorder and global turmoil.[10] Current uncertainties, in fact, seem to suggest a transitional pe-riod to a world order of some new character. The irregular wars in the Balkans, the Caucasus, Central Asia, and Somalia, in all of which Islam is involved, are, however, more an indication of unfolding disorder than of any new world order. The Gulf War did not lead to the promised new order. In the West, it is perceived to be a closed issue, an event encapsulated in the recent past, but in terms of world order its repercussions are with us still and will remain with us for years to come. Regional conflicts in the age of fundamentalism differ markedly from those of the old Cold War. Unlike the Gulf War, future regional conflicts are not likely to be based on inter-state wars. Irregular wars in the tradition of Islam[11] are more likely to be the sce-nario of the future.

When Saddam Hussein invoked Islamic principles as legitimization of his invasion of Kuwait, he clearly was exploiting a pretext. Nevertheless, it is the symbolic meaning of his references to these principles that matters. Saddam not only denied the sovereignty of Kuwait, by dusting off the ar-gument that it belongs to Iraq, but he did so basically through reference to the historical fact that the existing boundaries were drawn by Western colo-nial powers and, therefore, in the World of Islam, lack all cultural legitimacy. Indeed, Islam does not recognize such boundaries of nation-states; and those who deny a conflict between Islam and the idea of the nation-state confuse imperial and territorial states with the modern nation-state.

Pan-Arabism, a secular movement sustained in some quarters through much of this century, stretches the notion of *al-dawla al-qawmiyya* / the

nation-state to the vast pan-Arab state aspired to in the course of dismissing the several extant Arab nation-states as *dawla qitriyya* / territorial
states. These Islamic and pan-Arab concepts, buttressed by the fundamentalists' rejection of the nation-state, were consciously mixed in the ideological legitimizations presented by Saddam Hussein. It is ironic, in fact, that
the person presenting these arguments is himself not a fundamentalist but
a pan-Arab nationalist, that is, one who subscribes to the idea of the nation-
state but in the pan-Arab version of an entity stretching "from the Atlantic
Ocean to the Gulf." These shifting and conflicting currents show how weak
the cultural underpinning of the secular nation-state is in the World of
Islam. We shall return to this issue further in Chapter 6.

In the West today, the Gulf War is no more than a pale memory. The un-
deniable inheritance of that war, however, is the situation addressed earlier
as "the legacy of Saddam Hussein" (see note 11). To this legacy belong both
the symbolic references he employed and the power of the religious symbols he revived in the consciousness of most Muslims. Even Halliday, who
(as we saw in Chapter 1) dismisses the debate on the "clash of civilizations,"
acknowledges that these references "served to mobilize Islamist sentiment
in a range of countries in support of Saddam Hussein."[12] The growing power
of these religious symbols to mobilize is becoming an essential part of the
emerging civilization-consciousness in world politics. Those in the West
who no longer pay heed to the mobilizing power of symbols, playing them
down as simply rhetoric, understand neither the "clash of civilizations"[13]
nor the meaning of symbols in politics in an age characterized by a growing politicization of religions. The Gulf War was not only a real war, during which Iraq was reduced to a "pre-industrial condition" (*The New York
Times*), it was also a perceptual war of symbols and worldviews. The war of
the armies is over, but the perceptual war implied by the "legacy of Saddam
Hussein" persists. John Kelsay has written that "[t]he Gulf War was not just
about oil, or markets, or even territory, pure and simple. It was a struggle
over values; or more precisely, part of an ongoing struggle over who will
define the direction and limits of appropriate political behavior in the modern world."[14]

My recent work in a number of countries of the World of Islam leads me
to the same conclusion. Moreover, in my comments in the media and in my
articles during and after the Gulf War I maintained that one should not be
too quick to ridicule those fundamentalists summoned to Baghdad in January 1991 who called for installing Saddam Hussein as the new Caliph for

all of Islam (see the report by Tony Walker, "Muslim Militants Want Saddam as Caliph," in *Financial Times,* January 10, 1991, p. 2; behind the summoning, certainly, stood Saddam's *mukhabarat* [intelligence service], which at that point worked closely with leading fundamentalist groups). When Saddam reminded the Arabs and Muslims of their past glory, while indicting the West for having "entered Arab lands, . . . divided Arabs and established weak states"[15] to facilitate the imposition of Western supremacy, he not only evoked sentiments of nostalgia but also expressed a widely felt outrage over the subordination of Muslims to Western dominance. Westerners who do not understand the meaning of these sentiments fail to understand politics in the Middle East.

In recalling the days of Muslim supremacy, "when Baghdad was the center of Islamic rule and civilization,"[16] Saddam Hussein raised at least a rhetorical claim to establishing Muslim power anew. Needless to say, no Muslim state or alliance disposes sufficient capabilities for pursuing this end, but again, we ought not to underestimate the mobilizing power of religious symbols in politics. Since the Gulf War there has arisen a steadily growing and increasingly anti-Western civilization-consciousness among Muslims. I have seen this in North Africa, Central Asia, Egypt, and the Occupied Territories during many periods of research in these states and regions. This consciousness has been related to an Islamic *jihad*-oriented revolt against Western views on world order. When the West talks about world order, Muslims feel an unease, for "there is a double standard in world politics. For the West and its friends, the present international order provides freedom, security, dignity. But for Arabs, Muslims, and developing nations, there is only oppression, exploitation, and dishonor."[17]

In the course of their revival, religious symbols have been used to denounce these very double standards of the West. In this context, Islamic fundamentalists further politicize their own religion by exploiting its power to further the alternative promised by their political strategies. Their alternative is *al-nizam al-Islami*/the Islamic order; it is their *hall Islami*/Islamic solution for the crisis. The Islamic system of government, they insist, should replace what they view as *hulul mustawrada*/imported solutions (see note 17, Chapter 2). In the pursuit of this goal, Islamic fundamentalists operate on two levels, domestic and international. Domestically, they strive to topple most of the existing governments in the World of Islam in pursuit of the divine order they seek. Internationally, they challenge both the long-standing world order and the vague new one called the "New World

Order" (see note 7 above). In contemporary history the Gulf War has been
the context of the conflict, but the larger and more timeless context is a conflict between two civilizations on what a world order should be.

THE SEARCH FOR A NEW WORLD ORDER

At the height of the Gulf crisis, then President George Bush, in his speeches
of September 1990, rhetorically coined the term "New World Order." In his
chronicles of the Gulf War the journalist Rick Atkinson found it appropriate to name his own accounts "Crusade," in due course using the word as
the title for his book. He ends these accounts by stating that "the 'New
World Order'... proved an empty slogan.... The Persian Gulf War was
neither the greatest moral challenge facing America since 1945 ... nor [a]
pointless exercise in gunboat diplomacy.... The truth lay somewhere ...
awaiting discovery."[18] The current state of fragmentation and disorder I
posit would seem to be the truth that awaited discovery. Having so grandly
trumpeted his formula, shortly after the Gulf War even Bush stepped back
to the day-to-day business of international and Middle Eastern politics. Accordingly, since the Gulf War the Western powers have moved from an effort at the global level to a more modest one dealing with regional politics
in the Middle East, in the context of an envisaged Middle Eastern order.

Inherently, the struggle has been to decide who will determine order not
only in that part of the world we call the Middle East[19] but also across the
globe. Those experts in world politics who confine their perspectives to matters of military security believe that with the overwhelming victory over
Saddam Hussein the power of the West was demonstrated and the main
issues were basically solved. In so doing, they overlook the response of Muslims, a response that assumed the shape of a political claim. These public
preferences, which were revived during the war and continue to be with us,
are addressed today as the "Saddam Hussein legacy." Again, the Iraqi dictator has never been a fundamentalist, and his references to the Islamic
jihad/holy war and the supremacy of Islam were simply expedient, offered
aloft in an obviously desperate situation. Historically, however, Saddam unleashed attitudes and aspirations in a manner that will continue to determine political thinking in the World of Islam past the turn of the century.
Those who are familiar with the writings of the intellectual fathers of
Islamic fundamentalism, Sayyid Qutb and Abu al-A'la al-Mawdudi, are
cognizant of political Islam's claim on the leadership of the world, replac-

ing the West in that role. Prior to the Gulf War, these views were as widely known and popular as they are today, but in my view they were not yet identified as an expression of a civilization-consciousness.

Well, the already dated formula of a "New World Order" was not inherently less rhetorical than that of the more topical *nizam Islami* / Islamic order. In each, however, is the implication of a concrete worldview and a particular understanding of world politics. Seen in a more positive light, the West's concept of a "New World Order" underlines the need of humanity to establish some commonalities among its diverse civilizations with regard to international morality, that is, for shared norms, values, and procedures for conflict resolution. Concomitantly, there is a need to reach agreement on means to enforce these standards of international morality. There are competing views on what those commonalities and means might be.

The concept of *nizam Islami* presents the claim of Islamic global supremacy based on the *da'wa* as the universal Islamic mission. This *da'wa* / mission, Islamic fundamentalists maintain, is especially to be pursued against the irreligious, morally bankrupt, but dominant West. It follows that the anti-Western sentiments are clearly *not* anti-Christian. Sayyid Qutb once dismissed secular world order as the return to the *jahiliyya* / pre-Islamic age of heedlessness, as I shall show later. The notion of *jahiliyya* as grounds for rejecting the postulates and conditions of the modern world was revived by Sayyid Qutb. He saw cultural modernity as a new variety of *jahiliyya* (*jahiliyya jadidah* / neo-*jahiliyya*), and this reference leads us to questions well beyond the Gulf War, beyond the vision of a "New World Order." At issue are not current topical developments, but rather the fundamental differences between the Islamic and Western worldviews. At issue is also the place of Muslims in a world order dominated by the West and by its civilizational standards.

Again, the present international system of nation-states grew from the globalization of the European system. As Charles Tilly put it: "Over the next three hundred years [after the Treaty of Westphalia], the Europeans and their descendants managed to impose that system on the entire world. The recent wave of decolonization has almost completed the mapping of the globe into that system."[20]

Given the American preponderance in contemporary Western civilization, we face here the claim of a *pax americana* competing with that of a *pax islamica*. Certainly, Muslims of today lack the power needed to see their claim realized. Still, the fact is that the claim exists. It is also a fact that this

mode of thinking not only is popular in one of the largest religious communities in our world (1.3 billion Muslims out of a world population of 5.7
billion) but also presents its own distinct civilization-consciousness. These
facts urge us to deal with such claims seriously and not to rudely dismiss
them as mere rhetoric. Following the dissolution of the Soviet Union, which
had been the other superpower, the United States is the only remaining superpower. But *pax americana* is a claim, not a reality, even though it derives
from the manifold capabilities of a major world power. Nevertheless, the
United States is clearly losing influence in international politics. Many
Western scholars have rightly observed the decline, not only of Western
power but also of Western civilization. In focusing on the rise of religious
fundamentalisms throughout the world I would add that the major trend
in post-Cold War international politics is the de-Westernization resulting
from the challenges hurled by other civilizations, the Islamic challenge foremost among them. It is not a bloc of states, but rather a civilization, that is
posing this challenge to the West. Again, this new current cannot be properly understood within the old framework of inter-state relations.

Unlike Huntington, who views the relations among civilizations in terms
of conflict, I had proposed in my earlier book *The Crisis of Modern Islam* to
view world politics in terms of "international cultural communication." In my
later work I have observed an increasing cultural fragmentation that parallels
the intensifying of structural globalization in our world.[21] This idea of the
simultaneity of cultural fragmentation and structural globalization is taken
up in Chapter 5. The simultaneity addressed continues to produce contradic-
tory results: conflicting civilizations moving closer to one another in their
levels of interaction while drifting apart because of their irreconcilable views
on world order and, in general, their worldviews on life, religion, law, and other
human conditions. The idea of a Western-style universalism becomes increasingly disputed in an age of the growth of civilization-consciousness.

To be sure, I do not subscribe to any of the fashionable multicultural or
postmodern views according to which universally valid standards are no
longer tenable. I maintain that common standards of human rights,[22]
democracy, and mutual recognition of secular sovereignty in relations
among states should command attention as a basis of international morality. Certainly, the idea of international morality needs to be developed for
establishing cross-cultural international standards. Only if these standards
are honored by all participating states in the international system can
humanity live in peace and dignity (see chapters 9 and 10). But given that

most of these principles of world order are still basically Western in their origin, some modest compromises seem inevitable in our age of global de-Westernization. The well-known Swiss theologian Hans Küng has suggested a "*Weltethos*/World Ethics" that combines all religions of the world on ethical grounds. The idea is appealing, but it does not move beyond a vague ascertaining of the need while ignoring the realities of the international system. To put it bluntly, it is no more than the daydreaming of a theologian. A more professional approach would establish norms and values on cross-cultural, not universalistic, grounds.

An international morality will need not only to be shared by all religions on a secular basis but also to be institutionally upheld. In my view, separate codes of religious ethics exclusive to each civilization would continue to separate the divergent religious communities from one another. Given that the "clash of civilizations" is being intensified through the political interpretation of religion, along lines of civilization-consciousness, any intrusion of a particular religion into world politics would lead only to a further intensification of the conflict potential emanating from this clash. As much as I may discard the universalization of "the American way of life" as the "pursuit of happiness" for people everywhere, as some politicians in Washington envisage, I equally reject the claim of Muslim fundamentalists to be morally responsible for the broad panoply of humanity on which they aim to impose their *da'wa*/mission of Islam. There is a need for a genuinely pluralist world order, not a single-source "New World Order." Divergent civilizations need to agree on common terms for living in peace with one another. The consensus that emerges cannot be in line with either a *pax americana* or a *pax islamica*. Most crucially, such a consensus cannot be imposed, but must be accepted freely.

As a rationally thinking Muslim living in the West, I dislike some Western foreign policy behavior but fail to see the "crusade mentality" in Western policies that Muslim fundamentalists believe they perceive. American hegemony is power politics and has nothing to do with Christianity, and the large-scale secularization of the West long ago began to shift it away from Christian toward secular universalist views. The Gulf War can be criticized as an act in the pursuit of political hegemony, but not as a "crusade of the West,"[23] as Muslim fundamentalists are wont to argue in their pamphleteering. The world order favored by Muslim fundamentalists is the only religious concept, in this competition over who will determine the character of the world, that I can see.

The war in Bosnia is a different matter. That war nourished Islamic fundamentalist ideology. Professedly, the impact of religion needs to be considered in this case. Orthodox Christian Serbs themselves claim to wage a "crusade against Islam in Europe."[24] Orthodox Eastern Christianity never went through the stages of reformation and secularization that have so deeply affected Western Christianity. The end of the war fostered by the decisive bombardments by NATO against the Serbs does not mean that the conflict has been resolved. It will be with us for years to come. The end of the atrocities notwithstanding, Islamic fundamentalists continue to believe they see in the Balkans a concerted Christian effort against Islam. The perception that Orthodox Eastern Christianity along with Roman Catholicism and Protestantism—nowadays a secularized Western Christianity—are united against Islam is mistaken, perhaps knowingly mistaken, but nonetheless serves to inflame anti-Western sentiments. Moreover, Western policies in the Balkans, flawed as they were in many ways, unwittingly contributed to supporting these sentiments.

THE CONCEPT OF ORDER BETWEEN CULTURAL RELATIVISM AND NEO-ABSOLUTISM

In our age of the "clash of civilizations," as religion-based consciousness continues to grow, the cultural dialogue between the conflicting civilizations becomes an important instrument of peaceful conflict resolution or, to put it more realistically, a means toward crisis management. The challenge of religious fundamentalisms in non-Western civilizations should be taken seriously by the secular West in the search for a true and mutually accepted new world order. One need not be a multiculturalist to understand other cultures and civilizations. As non-Western peoples proudly develop strong commitments to their particular civilizational standards, the West comes under pressure to defend its own civilization. Certainly among the fashionable postmodernists and multiculturalists in the West, I fail to see a commitment to Western civilization. In denying objectivity and global standards in general, they deprive their own civilization of its basic virtues and elements.[25] In this framework, owing to the spread of cultural relativism, it seems no longer possible, for instance, to defend human rights as universal rights. It was once considered progress when sociologists—along the lines of the *sociology of knowledge* developed by Karl Mannheim—determined knowledge to be embedded in the social conditions from which it grew. But it is a setback to the sociology of knowledge to apply this very approach to cultures, as some anthropologists do in speaking of an *anthropology of knowledge.* These anthropologists prematurely conclude that there is no universally valid knowledge, since each body of knowledge is valid only in its own culture[26] or, as in our age they might say, in its own civilization. The application of these fashionable approaches to international politics would mean giving up the idea of a world order valid for all civilizations. This would be a momentous turn of events, very likely yielding, as the title of one of my recent books warns, a *War of Civilizations / Krieg der Zivilisationen.*[27]

Most intriguing here is the convergence between Muslim fundamentalists, who are neo-absolutists, and postmodernists, who are cultural relativists. Clearly the concerns of the two are different. By their notion of de-Westernization of knowledge, Islamic fundamentalists mean reestablishing Islamic knowledge, as based on the Qur'an and *hadith,* as the absolute, that is, the only, valid standard and source of knowledge. For this reason they contest Western knowledge. For quite different reasons, European and American postmodernists, multiculturalists, and cultural relativists alike are today abandoning the secular standards of knowledge established by the Renaissance and the Enlightenment, that is, by cultural modernity (see Chapter 4). Though this troublesome pursuit is no part of the consciousness of most citizens of the West, it does serve to encourage the de-Westernizationist drive of the Islamic fundamentalists. As I shall show in the next chapter, secular cultural modernity is worth defending against the predations of religious fundamentalisms, and I join Ernest Gellner[28] in the conviction that reason and enlightenment need also to be protected from the intellectual adventures of postmodernism.

Among the values and norms favored by the post-Cold War world order are individual and secular human rights, as determined by natural law. If these rights can be moved to center stage, not simply as a foreign policy instrument, their acceptance will go far toward vitiating the "crusade" demagogy of Islamic fundamentalists. Until recently, the Western policies in Bosnia have been unwittingly supporting the propaganda of the Islamic fundamentalists, who argue that what is taking place there is a Christian crusade against Bosnian Muslims (see note 24).

Some distinguished victims of the Holocaust and Jewish humanists like Henry Siegman have warned of ignoring "Bosnia's parallels with the Holocaust,"[29] and have compared the crimes of the Third Reich with the atrocities committed by the Serbs in their pursuit of Greater Serbia. Many Western governments run the risk of losing all legitimacy for their defense of human rights, owing to their silence about the most inhumane violations of human rights in Bosnia by "Serbian crusaders" (Lerch; see note 24). This is a lasting and burdensome legacy of the war in Bosnia, no matter that the West was instrumental in bringing it to an end. The delegitimization of Western values, even while they remain a major source for international morality, is contributing to the process identified earlier as a simultaneity of cultural fragmentation and structural globalization. Their de-legitimization would surely accelerate the ongoing process of de-Westernization.

Though I will occasionally make other references, for example to India and Bosnia, my focus will continue to be on the Middle East, and Islamic civilization will remain the more general scope of my inquiry. This choice is not due to any Arabo-centric inclination devolving from my ethnic origin. As I have shown in my earlier books (see note 21), Arab culture was the environment of the birth of Islam and the foundation of its civilization. The Qur'an was revealed in Arabic, and the text of this holy book itself is replete with references to the Arabs' having been chosen by God, who revealed the Qur'an to one of them—*an-nabi*/the messenger, the Prophet Muhammad—in their language. I am aware that these grounds ought not be stretched to the extent of identifying Islam with Arabness, which Saddam Hussein, standing in line with other secular prophets of Arab nationalism, has attempted to do. This unseemly pride is wrong and, moreover, Arabo-centric, and I believe myself to be free of this bias. I confess, in fact, that I am more sympathetic to Southeast Asian Islam than to Arab Islam. My encounter with Islam in Indonesia and Malaysia aroused in me great admiration for the tolerance, pluralism, and open-mindedness of Southeast Asian Muslims. But it is the Islam of the heartland that determines the mainstream of Islamic civilization.

In giving this Arabo-centric view of Islam a fundamentalist shape, Arab fundamentalists not only have denied the "Islamic Revolution"[30] in Iran (a non-Arab country) a legitimate claim to lead the *umma*/universal Islamic community but are also applying their neo-absolutism to Islamic civilization itself. Clearly, Islamic civilization is characterized by great cultural diversity. During my visit to Indonesia and Malaysia in spring 1995 I encountered Arab Muslims and even local Muslims who had studied at al-Azhar in Cairo or at Saudi universities and had thus become scripture-oriented fundamentalists. In disdaining the local cultures as not truly Islamic because they are not inspired by the scripture in its original tongue, these zealots spread views infringing upon local cultures in an effort to impose upon them a neo-absolutist understanding of scriptural Arabo-centric Islam. Happily, these fundamentalists in Southeast Asia are no more than an irritant at the periphery of society, and not, as their counterparts in the Middle East, a force at the center of politics.

In Indonesia[31] the concept of the *Pancasila* (panca = five, sila = principles), once coined by former president Ahmed Sukarno, is established in the constitution, and has been adopted by the current New Order regime. The five principles of the Pancasila are equality of monotheisms, humanism, national unity, democracy, and justice. These five principles guarantee a more secular and pluralist character of state and society. The Pancasila concept provides the grounds for unity among the 193 million Indonesians belonging to 300 cultures and five religions, though the Muslims are a majority of 85 percent. If the new Western fashion of cultural relativism were to prevail in Indonesia, the result would be turmoil and chaos. And if the neo-absolutist view of political Islam, as promoted in Indonesia by a few Islamic parties and underground groups, were to become a public preference, the result would be civil war. In being both constitutionally binding and pluralist in outlook, the Pancasila forestalls this scenario. (In this depiction of Islam in Indonesia I do not overlook the much publicized human-rights violations perpetrated by that Islamic state, in particular the invasion of East Timor in December 1975 and the annexation of this former Portuguese colony in July 1976, against the will of its people and in defiance of the resolutions of the UN General Assembly and Security Council; but this deplorable incident must be examined separately from the evaluation of Islam in Indonesia.)

This is precisely the morality on which I hope a new order might come to be founded, both in the world at large and in the Middle East in particular. Could the periphery of Southeast Asia emerge as a model for the civilization of Islam?[32] Unlike the core of Islamic civilization in the Middle East, Southeast Asia has been successful in coping with the challenge of economic growth and in achieving some prosperity. Moreover, in multiethnic and multireligious Southeast Asia, Islam coexists peacefully with other religions on pluralist grounds. There, the peace among the diverse religious communities is not a vision but a reality. For this reason my deliberations on an international morality (in chapters 9 and 10) focus on this issue. Some of these thoughts were offered to my Indonesian audience in the course of lectures in March 1995. I have in mind a cross-cultural validation of democracy and human rights as unifying factors. Both principles more or less prosper in Indonesia, as compared with other parts of the Islamic world.

These illustrations would seem to support the reservations elucidated above vis-à-vis both the cultural-relativist mind of postmodernism and the fundamentalist intolerance of neo-absolutism.

With the exception of the Pakistani Abu al-A'la al-Mawdudi, most leading ideologues of Islamic fundamentalism are Arab writers. Moreover, the challenge of an Islamic world order evolved first in the Arab Middle East. There is a link between this challenge and the debate ensuing since the Gulf War on how to establish a Middle Eastern order. Islamic fundamentalists have envisaged a new order based on Islamic civilization, as opposed to one based on Western civilization, on whose principles the contemporary world order is laid.

A popular book published in Arabic and distributed throughout the Arab World (see note 23) indicates the incursion of the West into the World of Islam: the former Egyptian general Sa'duldin al-Shadhli, hero of the October 1973 war, published a best-selling book on the Gulf War under the title *The Eighth Christian Crusade.* I encountered this book in most of the Arab cities I visited in 1992–94. I was exposed to anti-Western attitudes similar to those expressed in al-Shadhli's book after my tour of lectures at many universities throughout the Maghreb in Algeria, Tunisia, and Morocco, and during my visits to Egypt and the Palestinian Territories in that period. What I found most troubling was the equation of "Westerners" and "Crusaders." This sentiment is among the repercussions of the Gulf War, as expressed by the general's book. The establishment of a stable new order in the Middle East, integrated into a post-Cold War world order, would run counter to the fundamentalist vision of decoupling the Middle East from the current world order. The global fragmentation I speak of can be observed on both local and regional grounds in the Middle East, and, again, it is fundamentalism that poses one of the major forces of fragmentation.

THE REGIONALIZATION OF WORLD POLITICS AND THE POLITICIZATION OF MIDDLE EASTERN ISLAM

Violence has been endemic in the Middle East. The contemporary history of the region has been one of wars.[33] But unlike the earlier wars—even the Six-Day War, which was the most shattering among them—the Gulf War has linked the Middle East to the greater civilization of Islam, inasmuch as this war was viewed by virtually the entire Islamic community—even in Southeast Asia—as a "crusade of the Christian West" against Islamic civilization (see notes 18 and 23). Some Western commentators choose to downplay the meaning of this observation by pointing out that the foremost Islamic country, Saudi Arabia, as well as other significant nations like Syria, Egypt, and Pakistan, participated in the war on the side of the West. Indeed, the general populace of these four countries *disagreed* with the idea of their battling on the side of the West; most people there were *regretful* that Iraq lost the war. As I noted in Chapter 1, the approach of this book is not state-centered. Rather, I relate Islamic fundamentalism to public choices. These are determined through the attitudes of the people belonging to a civilization, not to governmental policies, and in the case of the Gulf War, the perceptual war was between the West and Islamic civilization.

In keeping with this approach, and by way of illustrating it on a lighter note, I want to tell two jokes that are widespread among the Egyptians, whose president chose to participate in the Gulf War on the side of the Western alliance. One of these is that the Saudi king no longer holds the Islamic holy title *khadim al-haramayn al-sharifayn* (custodian of the holy shrines of Mecca and Medina), because President Bush has delegated this title to himself. The other joke relates how a *Sa'idi* / Upper Egyptian peasant who— even though illiterate in Arabic—learns English; he explains to his fellow villagers that he wants to use his life's savings for the *hajj* / pilgrimage to Mecca, and therefore needs to learn English to find his way after the Americans have established themselves there. To be sure, it is impossible to translate the Egyptian manner of telling jokes, nor can English convey the cultural nuances. These jokes may not seem funny in the West; in the Middle East, they do!

The Gulf War showed that Islam, perceived as a civilization, can serve as a referent for a political identity in an "imagined community." The Gulf War engaged Islam, on the one hand, to a degree unprecedented in modern history, pushing it to the fore in world politics. On the other hand, however, the war showed that people belonging to Islamic civilization are *dis*organized; their member states do *not* have a strong consensus.

One of the consequences of the end of the Cold War and of the Gulf War itself is the increasing trend toward regionalization in world politics. This trend could be seen long before the end of the Cold War and contributed to "a more regionalized world system," as Hedley Bull[34] had put it as early as 1977. Regionalization can also be seen in Islamic civilization. There are disparate regions within Islam: that in the Middle East differs markedly from that in Southeast Asia. From this point of view, Islamic unity is perceptual; it lacks structural underpinning. Globalists in the academic discipline of international relations who have no grasp of these regional conjointures can have but little understanding of attitudes and events in the Middle East, or in other regions of Islamic civilization. Regions are related, among other things, to local cultures and to their grouping in civilizations. The patterns and mechanisms of regionalization affect political developments in all non-Western regions of the world,[35] and the ongoing de-Westernization and regionalization of the world require one to rid oneself of the prevailing Eurocentric globalist approaches to understanding these issues. In no way, however, does my recognizing these forces contradict my subscribing to the virtues of universal knowledge (see note 26) and international standards, as drawn from the program of cultural modernity, that I have expressed here.

What we can conclude from observing an increasing regionalization in world politics is that we need to find ways to combine regional study of the Middle East and other regions of Islamic civilization with the new conceptual approaches of international studies. By contrast, the schools of thought that have focused on the globalist approach in international relations have become obsolete.

Claims have been made for forming a world bloc based on Islamic civilization, but such claims are heedless of the significant regional differences within that civilization. The recent efforts to establish a new stable order in the Middle East in cooperation with the West (for example, the Mediterranean Summit in Barcelona, in November 1995) are thus sorely lacking in legitimacy. Not even the regional participants of the Western-dominated alliance during the Gulf War were on good terms with each other, and Islamic fundamentalists fiercely oppose projects of this kind as simply components of a Western-dominated world order.

The phenomenon of regionalization in world politics also arises from cultural self-assertion and an increasing self-awareness, a process for which religious fundamentalists might serve as a vehicle. Islamic fundamentalism surfaced in the 1970s; clearly, the phenomenon addressed is older than the Gulf War, older even than the Six-Day War of 1967, and these wars have in fact contributed to the unfolding and strengthening of Islamic fundamentalism. Historically speaking, Islamic fundamentalism has been a reality since the 1920s (note for example the Muslim Brothers, founded in 1928). As a mass movement, however, the phenomenon began to take shape in the aftermath of the Six-Day War, in which the two pillars of secular Arab nationalism, Ba'thism and Nasserism, had challenged Israel. Syria and Egypt were, however, defeated in disastrous fashion.[36] In the early 1970s one could observe new movements gathering around the concept of *al-sahwa al-Islamiyya* / Islamic awakening,[37] but it was only in the 1980s that supporters and members of these movements began to be referred to as *usuliyyun* / fundamentalists. *Usuliyya* / fundamentalism is a neo-Arabic term for describing political Islam.

Usul means, in Arabic, fundamentals, and *din* means religion; an important discipline of Islamic jurisprudence is *usul al-din.* The fundamentalists themselves adopted the title in adding an *ism* (in Arabic *iyya*) to *usul* / fundamentals to make clear that their goal is to make Islamic fundamentals the bottom line of Muslim public life.[38] For this reason it is abundantly clear that to identify those who politicize the religion of Islam as fundamentalists does not constitute imposing the term "fundamentalism" on them, nor does it arise from Eurocentric bias. Rather, the term is an established one in contemporary Arabic. Readers of Arab newspapers are familiar with this identification while reading about the deeds of the *usuliyyun* (slaying intellectuals in Algeria, Turkey, and Egypt, for example) almost every morning. It would be a grave mistake, however, to reduce the meaning of *usuliyya* / fundamentalism to *al-tatarruf* / extremism. Despite much justified criticism, not every fundamentalist is an extremist.

To the politicization of the religion of Islam belongs the interpretation of Islamic *umma* as an international political community. In this political usage *umma* is not simply restricted to a religious community of believers. Interestingly enough, it was the secular Arab nationalists who had previously given the term *umma* a political meaning in rendering it as *umma 'Arabiyya* / Arab nation. Rendered thus, the national *umma* comprises Arab Muslims and Arab Christians alike, while excluding non-Arab Muslims, like Iranians and Turks, from the definition of the *umma.*[39] Fundamentalists reverse this usage, returning to the true Islamic notion of the universal *umma,* which cannot be interpreted as nation. For this reason, the identification of Muslim fundamentalists as "religious nationalists" is mistaken, because it is a contradiction in terms. Not only do they return the term *umma* to its primeval meaning but they also develop a new internationalist political outlook based on the concept of a universal Islamic world order.

The *umma* is envisaged by primordial Islam (*din al-fitra* / the natural religion of humanity) as embracing all of humanity. Thus a world order of border-contained nation-states, or the security-oriented Middle East regional order proposed following the Gulf War, does not accord with the traditional understanding of order in Islamic civilization now being politically revived, albeit in a modern shape. The Islamic worldview is a universalism and cannot be accommodated to other, competing universalisms unless it is first secularized. By this I mean that there must be a separation between religion and politics so as to establish grounds for peaceful coexistence with other worldviews in a pluralist manner.

THE FUNDAMENTALIST WORLD REVOLUTION: *JIHAD* BETWEEN PEACE AND MILITANCY

In Islamic understanding, Islam is the religion of peace. The Qur'an is based on a verbal inspiration passed to the Prophet as the final revelation of God to all mankind. In *dar al-Islam* / the territoriality of Islamic civilization, Allah's rules are expected to be strictly followed, and *dar al-Islam* is thus identical with *dar al-salam* / the abode of peace. Muslims are expected to spread their religion through *da'wa* / mission, which entails the obligation to enhance their territoriality as the abode of peace. This effort in the pursuit of peace, that is, spreading the true religion of peace all over the world, is called *jihad*,[40] which literally means "exertion," in contrast to the usual translation into Western languages as "holy war."[41] It is simply an opening (*futuhat*) of the world to Islam aimed at encompassing all of humanity, and the effort is based on the belief that the message the Prophet Muhammad received from Allah constitutes the true religion for all of humanity.

It is difficult to convey to Western readers the Islamic meaning of *jihad*, not as war, but rather as a peaceful undertaking for the sake of humanity. In this meaning *jihad* is simply a religious duty Muslims must fulfill in carrying out Allah's message. The *da'wa* / call to Islam, like Christian evangelism, is supposed to be peaceful. But if the peoples to whom Muslims bring the message of Islam do not submit to it voluntarily ("Islam" means "submission to God"), Muslims are entitled to use force in defending the *da'wa* against the resistance of the unbelievers. This struggle is called *qital* / defense. Again, Muslims' use of force is not considered to be a *harb* / war, but rather a righteous reaction to the unbelievers' hindering of the spread of the *da'wa* as call to Islam.

In Islamic understanding, Muslims by definition do not fight *hurub* / wars. Islamic *jihad* is never an aggression but rather an effort to spread Islam as the true religion through the enhancing of *dar al-Islam* / Islamic civilization by *futuhat*, understood as an opening of the world to *dar al-salam* / the abode of peace. Only unbelievers fight *hurub* / wars in the conventional sense of the word as an unjust aggression.

In a contribution to a comparative project on the ethics of war and peace run by the Ethikon Institute and published by Princeton University Press (see note 40), I attempted to explain these intricate issues to Western readers. My attempt can be summarized in this manner: Islam's image of itself is to be the religion of peace. Muslims are obliged to carry out this *da'wa* / mission worldwide. The *da'wa* as call to Islam is conceived to be a peaceful mission, but the non-Muslims hinder the peaceful spread of this mission. For Western observers the *futuhat* of Sunni Islam are wars, and resisting the spread of Islam may to them seem a just war, but Muslims view these issues in a different manner. In the classical doctrine, the use of force for the spread of Islam is not war but rather *jihad*, in the worst case a "defensive war," for *jihad* is never an aggression. In modern interpretations (e.g., al-Azhar sheikh Jadulhaq), the use of force has been swept out by fresh interpretation.

Professedly, this argumentation is difficult for Westerners to understand, but it clearly reveals how people of different civilizations fill concepts with different meanings. In our age of the heterogeneity of civilizations and their conflicting worldviews, the claim of de-Westernization of thought is pivotal, and the Islamic perception of *jihad* is a case in point. Again, the Western translation of *jihad* as "holy war" is misleading, because Muslims do not see it this way. But notwithstanding how Muslims may see their own actions, it is broadly understood, in the East and the West and elsewhere, that every substantial use of armed force is by all reasonable standards an act of war. The contradiction lies in the classical doctrine itself: it forbids the use of force as simply aggression but allows it as legitimate if it serves the spread of Islam.

In the revival of the concept of *jihad*, the only *significant difference between Shi'i and Sunni religious fundamentalisms* is the approval of suicidal terrorism by Shi'is and its disapproval by Sunnis. In the case of the Palestinian self-bombers (the terrorist actions between February 26 and March 4, 1996) there is clear evidence that the Sunni terrorists involved were trained by Hizbullah Shi'i fundamentalists in southern Lebanon, after they were deported to Marj al-Zuhur by Israel, from December 1992 to summer 1993.

In contemporary fundamentalism we find a new understanding of *jihad* as an expression of "Islamic world revolution."[42] This concept can be traced back to Sayyid Qutb, the Egyptian political preacher who is seen as the intellectual father of Islamic fundamentalism. He began his career as a teacher, came to the United States (1948–50) for further academic training,[43] and then returned to Egypt as a furious anti-American and anti-Western Muslim intent on laying the groundwork for a vision of Islam that would offer an alternative to that of the West. During his New York years Qutb had read the book *L'homme cet inconnu*, by the Nobel Prize winner Alexis Carrel, in which this French scholar described, in most pathetic terms, the alienation of man in modern industrial societies. Qutb felt lost in the West and projected onto New York City his vision of the decline of Western civilization and its replacement by Islam.

In his numerous writings Qutb argued forcefully that the West is morally bankrupt and about to crumble.[44] In his view, only Islam is prepared to assume the world leadership that the West is about to relinquish. This idea can be found in his major pamphlets:[45] *The Future Belongs to This Religion*, and *Signposts*. Qutb was convicted of subversion, sentenced to death, and executed in 1966, under Nasser's rule. With no exaggeration his pamphlets can be compared, in terms of spread and influence, with the Communist Manifesto in the period of the early worker's movements in Europe and later under communism. His basic missionary message was that world peace can be achieved only under the banner of Islam, within the framework of *jihad* as an expression of "world revolution" (see note 42).

The Gulf War and the Western efforts to reorder the Middle East as the heartland of the World of Islam, within the constraints of Western security policies, gave a great boost to efforts to revive Sayyid Qutb's indictments of the West as the "ferocious enemy of Islam." Qutb viewed Western civilization with contempt as an expression of *jahiliyya jadidah* / neo-*jahiliyya*, that is, the heedlessness of pre-Islamic times manifested in a new "crusader design." Scholars who contest the concept of the "clash of civilizations" are advised to read his "Problems of Civilization" so that they might understand that he was the precursor of that clash. The novelty is simply that the concept is only now being added to the agenda of international relations.

For Qutb, man-centered cultural modernity is the cause of the deadly disease that has befallen the West and is now turning to infect Islam. For this reason he was at pains to replace modernity with an unrestrained theocentrism that leaves no room for democracy in the sense of rule of the people by the people. Only Allah, the supreme sovereign, rules. Humans can have no sovereignty, and Islamic revelation takes precedence over the reason-centered view of the world. The exposure of the World of Islam to modernity and to its rational worldview is, since Qutb, the point of departure in the political and social thought of Islamic fundamentalism. The principle of subjectivity of man/woman and his/her self-determination as a free individual, entitled to certain rights, is the major achievement of cultural modernity. Qutb sought to return the individual to the community as simply one element in a collectivity.

Qutb extended his assault on modernity to Muslims themselves in arguing that they have let themselves be infected by the West and by modernity. In his view, Muslims have forgotten *al-taghallub*/superiority, the hallmark of Islam, in allowing the West to advance itself at the expense of Islam. He concludes that Muslims themselves have begun to return to the *jahiliyya*/pre-Islamic age of heedlessness.

Following in the footsteps of Qutb, current fundamentalists consider the struggle against Muslim governments and against those individual Muslims who have fallen into *jahiliyya* (recall the slaying of intellectuals in Algeria, Egypt, and Turkey) to be their hitherto "neglected duty."[46] Only *jihad* can lead to reestablishing the *nizam Islami*/Islamic order, even in Islam's heartland.

The efforts of Western policies to reorder the Middle East along the lines of Western notions of security after the Gulf War were fiercely opposed by Muslim fundamentalists. So also was the peace process that got under way in Madrid (October 30 to November 4, 1991) and reached its height in Washington on September 13, 1993, when the PLO and Israel, following the Oslo accords, agreed to recognize each other.[47] The continued struggle against the "New World Order" and the peace process became, in this context, part of the fundamentalist strategy, and the Islamic fundamentalist movements *Hamas* and *Jihad Islami*,[48] acting in the Palestinian Autonomy Zones, try to obstruct the peace process through terrorist actions justified as *jihad*. To understand these issues properly, we must look into their background.

At the heart of fundamentalist policies stands the reinterpretation of Islamic *jihad*. In the latter half of the twentieth century many sheikhs of the al-Azhar University, which is authoritative for the Sunni part of the World of Islam, were at pains, in their modern interpretation, to combat reference to *jihad* as justification of violent acts, and did so in the name of combating terrorism. They argue that *jihad* is a peaceful concept that entails the struggle of Islam against poverty, illiteracy, and disease—in effect, against underdevelopment. They plead for the spread of Islam by peaceful, not violent, means. The late sheikh of al-Azhar, Jadulhaq, has contributed to this modern interpretation; he has made clear that a distinction must be drawn between Islamic *jihad*, as exertion for worthy purposes, and *jihad musallah*, as resort to violence. This Azhar sheikh, the late Jadulhaq Ali Jadulhaq, discarded the resort to violence in the name of Islam and underlined the peaceful character of the Islamic message.[49] The successor of Jadulhaq continues this commitment today. As this distinction makes clear, Islam is a religious belief. In contrast, Islamic fundamentalism is a political ideology, and the two are different issues.

Long before Jadulhaq advanced his argument against terrorism—on the basis of a modern interpretation—one of the earliest and most influential Islamic fundamentalists contested such peaceful views. In his essay on *jihad*, Hassan al-Banna ridiculed those Muslims who deny that *jihad* implies the use of force. For al-Banna there are two patterns of *jihad*, the lesser one (*al-jihad al-asghar*) and the greater one (*al-jihad al-akbar*). The latter, for him the true Islamic *jihad*, is a distinctly violent one.[50] Qutb stretched this violent understanding of *jihad* to empower an "Islamic world revolution" (see note 42) based on religious legitimacy and the use of force in the form of irregular war. By international legal standards today, this kind of violence qualifies unequivocally as "terrorism."[51]

Within the framework of *jihad*-oriented Islamic revolution the opposition of fundamentalist groups to current nation-state policies, which are qualified by fundamentalists on both regional and global grounds as neo-*jahiliyya*, is legitimated. Though interpreted anew and filled with new meaning, the new legitimacy is expressed in classical Islamic terms. The fundamentalists accuse their fellow Muslims not only of being infected by secular modernity and thus to have lapsed into the pre-Islamic *jahiliyya*, but also of *kufr*/heresy. These accusations are sufficient to justify the slaying of intellectuals, journalists, artists, lawyers, and other "infidel" Muslims. In the classical doctrine, there *is* no justification for the slaying of individuals. The Qur'an forbids assassination and ambush attacks (see note 40).

In the fundamentalist view, current Islamic societies are generally characterized as a mix of *jahiliyya* and *kufr*. True Muslims retreat from these societies, and in so doing emulate the Prophet, who retreated from Mecca and set out for Medina in 622 (the *hijra*). Going underground to battle the extant regional and world orders becomes a modern variety of *hijra*, that is, retreat. *Hijra*, however, is coupled with *jihad*, and they become interlocked. Translated into contemporary language, then, *hijra* means going underground; *jihad* becomes terrorism. Those Muslims who question and resist these arbitrary interpretations, like the earlier quoted sheikh of al-Azhar, are renounced as "infidel Muslims." Egyptian fundamentalists ridicule even the dignified late Sheikh Jadulhaq.[52]

In 1990, during the Gulf crisis, Saddam Hussein gambled that Middle Eastern Muslims would sanction his appropriating these views for his own policies. On August 7 he called for the *jihad*, and repeated the call on September 5, using the formula *darb al-kufr kullahu bi al-iman kullahu*/to combat total heresy by means of total belief (the call was broadcast by, among others, Radio Baghdad).[53] Hundreds of thousands of Muslims followed his call by taking to the streets of Amman, Rabat, San'a, Algiers, Tunis, Cairo, and even remote Indonesian towns to demonstrate their support. I was in India during that period (August–September 1990) and was stunned to see that it was not only Muslims who were shouting their support for Saddam Hussein. Indian newspapers, trumpeting anti-American slogans, celebrated Saddam as a "Third World Hero," and even the Hindu community—not generally thought to be favorable to Islam—took warmly to Saddam's call. He had become the symbol of anti-Western attitudes and of the phenomenon addressed as the "revolt against the West." In January 1991 the leaders of the major fundamentalist movements were summoned to Baghdad, where the Jordanian fundamentalist al-Tamimi called for installing Saddam as the new Caliph of all Muslims. By then, some Westerners had begun ridiculing this event and considered it to be a "joke" related to Islam's forgotten better days. In so doing, they overlooked and encouraged the coming legacy of the Gulf War.

To be sure, it is not this crude oriental despot who is of interest to us here, but rather the concepts he appealed to. Saddam Hussein did not invent the Islamic notions he used, and they did not disappear after his shattering defeat. Nor, even, will they disappear if he is someday toppled. Some observers raised the question why the actions the Islamic fundamentalists had been expected to undertake during the Gulf War did not take place. One explanation is that this movement has no real center; it is extremely various in both approach and action, and is schism-ridden.[54] These facts underlie my view that Islamic fundamentalists are quite capable of destabilizing regimes and fomenting disorder, but are not globally organized. This should be small consolation for the West, however, for despite the nonappearance of the global fundamentalist uprising that had been expected during the Gulf War, Islamic fundamentalism is still the legitimate expression of a challenge to both world and regional orders. The challenge is expressed concretely through both energetic mobilization schemes and the resort to violence, that is, to irregular war.

AN ISLAMIC WORLD ORDER?

Sayyid Qutb proclaimed that the days of the West's dominance over the world are numbered, and that the time has come for Islam to claim its world leadership.[55] These words have provided the framework for the perception of world politics by Muslim activists in the late twentieth century while unfolding their civilization-consciousness.

The claims cited, though not feasible, as well as the use of Islam for legitimizing concrete policies not necessarily consonant with Islamic precepts, must be seen in the light of the miserable social conditions under which fundamentalists mobilize their adherents and take action. Conditions in the World of Islam, particularly in its heartland, the Middle East, are by all accounts devastatingly desperate: economic crises, ruthless dictatorships, delegitimization and decay of political rule, and a monumental crisis of meaning—all leading to dislocation, disruption, and violence. Some observers have used the term "Saddam Hussein generation" to allude to the underlying concerns that led the desperate to pin their hopes on the unpredictable moves of a ruthless dictator. The Iraqi writer Samir al-Khalil, alias Kanan Makiya, denounced the Arab intellectuals on moral grounds for having applauded Saddam as an Arab Bismarck without, however, fully appreciating the truly desperate social conditions under which Arab peoples were living.[56]

When the dictator is gone, the desperation will remain. The path will then be free for another hero, and the Saddam legacy will drive events as before. Saddam did not create the needs; he simply gave them voice. The frustration that ensued following his defeat has led to greater frustration, and the rhetoric—of the claim to lead the world while establishing an Islamic order—moves to greater heights.

Unlike those in the West who observe the World of Islam from the bias of orientalism, I look at Islamic fundamentalism—and its revolt against both the "New World Order" and the efforts to reorder the Middle East—within the framework of peaceful conflict resolution. To crack down on fundamentalists in an oppressive manner is no solution. Peace can be lasting only if the political, economic, and social conditions underlying the rise of fundamentalism[57] were to improve rather than deteriorate further. The component of this revolt arising from the forced incorporation of the World of Islam into globalized modernity, in both its cultural and its institutional dimensions, will be dealt with in the next chapter. Nevertheless, one cannot understand the attitudes of Muslims in general and Islamic fundamentalists in particular if one does not examine closely their responses to the existing conditions in the overall global context.

The pains arising from the globalization of the European-Western system are suffered most among Muslims. Like peoples in non-Western civilizations, Muslims suffer the concrete effects of disruption and dislocation, but unlike the others they have a worldview that entitles them to dominate. But to the contrary, they are dominated by others, to whom they feel—thanks to their divine revelation—superior. If this point is missed, Western observers will fail to grasp how Muslims feel about the current world order.

Rabbaniyya/theocentrism and *tawhid*/unity of God are classical Islamic concepts that lie at the core of Islamic faith. A Muslim is a religious, not necessarily a political, man. As a Muslim I believe in *rabbaniyya* and *tawhid*, but as a liberal Muslim I do not infer from this belief the claim that Islam must govern the world within the framework of an Islamic world order. The concept of the *nizam Islami*/Islamic order does not exist in the Qur'an, nor does it in the *hadith* of the Prophet. The regional needs of the Middle East are related to a comprehensive peace settlement,[58] not to establishing an Islamic order.

What hurts Muslims most is the fact that the international system they are subordinated to, and the world order that gives this system its design, are purported to be universal in nature, whereas in reality they stem from the standards of Western civilization. This state of affairs stands utterly in conflict with the Muslims' claim to determine these standards by the terms of their own civilization. This is not a religious, but a civilizational, issue; the clash is between two universalisms—one secular, one divine—each claiming global validity. In most Islamic writings on the West one finds a preoccupation with the conviction that the West is not only morally corrupt but also preordained to decay. Is the classical Ibn Khaldunian philosophy of history at work here? In his *Muqaddimah*/Prolegomena, in the fourteenth century, Ibn Khaldun taught that civilizations, including the Islamic, reach heights, but then must decline. Islamic fundamentalists feel that only their own civilization is eligible to succeed the decaying West in dominance. They believe this to be predetermined, owing to the ranking of Islamic monotheism as the final creed among all, and to its superiority to all other religions. Thus the religious belief of a universal Islamic mission almost imperceptibly becomes a political vision of an Islamic world order. One of the very few Western scholars who seems to understand this phenomenon intimately is the scholar of religion John Kelsay:

> Much of the contemporary return to Islam is driven by the perception of Muslims as a community [with] a mission to fulfill. That this perception sometimes leads to conflict is not surprising. In encounters between the West and Islam, the struggle is over *who will provide the primary definition to world order* [italics mine]. Will it be the West, with its notions of territorial boundaries, market economies, private religiosity, and the priority of individual rights? Or will it be Islam, with its emphasis on the universal mission of a transtribal community called to build a social order founded on the pure monotheism natural to humanity? . . . The very question suggests a competition between cultural traditions with distinctive notions of peace, order, and justice. It thus implies pessimism concerning the call for a world order based on notions of common humanity.[59]

The idea of a *sahwa Islamiyya* / Islamic awakening is much older than the Gulf War, but the context of the war has given fundamentalism a great boost. The issue is a competition between Islam and the West as civilizations, and the arena of competition is world politics. The Gulf War ended in a disastrous defeat for the Iraqi military regime, but unwittingly left a powerful legacy: an Islamic challenge to both the existing world order and the regional order in the Middle East, a challenge that will be with us long after Saddam Hussein is gone—be he toppled or assassinated.

Inherent in that legacy is a challenge to the existing boundaries in the World of Islam, boundaries drawn by the European powers long ago. Muslim fundamentalists do not honor these state circumscriptions, nor do they recognize the separate sovereignties of the nation-states thus circumscribed. They also reject the universality of Western values and norms, as was clear for all to see during the United Nations Conference on Human Rights in Vienna in June 1993. Those who were there—I was one—were witness to one area of dispute in particular: the nature of rights. In Islamic civilization there exist no individual rights, but only those of the *umma* / universal Islamic community, which impose *fara'id* / duties on the believers. This stands in contrast to what Westerners perceive as rights.[60] Muslims who spoke in Vienna were addressing the uniquely Islamic concept of human rights, as a challenge to the Western concept of individual rights, but what they had in mind were duties, not rights.

In short, the issue at stake in the civilizational conflict we see today is not faith and a belief in the oneness of God. Had it been so, there would have been no "clash of civilizations." Basically, the conflict is between cultural modernity, on the one hand, and premodern local cultures, grouped as a regional civilization, on the other. I envisage an international morality, secular in its outlook, able to unite all humanity (see chapters 9 and 10). The Enlightenment project remains intellectually powerful, albeit it deemed by some to be overrun in time by the power of religious appeal that regional civilizations hold to, or undermined by the postmodern and cultural-relativist fashions at work in its own kitchen. The next step in our inquiry here will be to ask questions about fundamentalism and modernity and to seek answers to them.

—∞—

FOUR

The Sociocultural Background

and the Exposure to Cultural Modernity

The Cold War was an "Imaginary War,"[1] in the sense that scholars and journalists at times greatly exaggerated the communist threat. The international paranoia and dissent that defined that period were provoked more by the challenge that communism presented than by communism itself. International relations scholars were often culture-blind in failing to recognize the cultural fragmentation that accompanied the ongoing processes of structural globalization. Following the Cold War there was a sense of triumph in the West, coupled with the misperception that the major source of international tension had been overcome. These observers of world politics were not prepared to see local and regional conflicts erupting as never before. With the restraining power of bipolarity no longer maintaining a global order of checks and balances, the aspirations of ethnicities and religiopolitical ideologies that had lain low during the Cold War now boiled to the surface. It was only after the Cold War that the factors underlying these conflicts came to be perceived. Previously, ethnicity, religion, and culture were considered to be the terrain of anthropologists, and of little interest to students of international politics. That situation has changed: cultures and civilizations and the ethnic subdivisions within these entities are moving to center stage.

CULTURE IN WORLD POLITICS: GLOBALIZED
STRUCTURES AND CULTURAL FRAGMENTATION

A congenital problem for Western writers not familiar with non-Western civilizations is that they take for granted the universality of Western values and
norms, and the particular view of the world that these values and norms tend
to construct. Thus communism was thought to be the only obstacle to
establishing secular democracy on a global scale. Only a few cultural anthropologists recognized that democracy, individual human rights, and secularity
are products of Western civilization and of the project of modernity that gives
this civilization its imprint. The corollary of this West-centrism has been the
inability of most Western writers to see that these products are alien to non-
Western civilizations. This fact, it seems, did not come to the attention of those
scholars and journalists preoccupied with communism, and for many of these
observers it has been a shock to see that the breakdown of communism did
not bring about a great era of peace and accord.

Moreover, the attainments of structural globalization and cultural modernity have harbored a great confusion. What has been globalized through the
European expansion and the ensuing mapping of the world into a Westernized international system was what Anthony Giddens called "the institutional dimension of modernity."[2] This dimension of modernity is related
to science, technology, and the achievements (that is, the modern institutions and instruments) resulting from them; it is not related to Western values and norms, and the latter are the real substance of cultural modernity.
Clearly, the ongoing process of globalization has not universalized the cultural modernity that Habermas described in his masterpiece *The Philosophical Discourse of Modernity.*[3] Cultural modernity has remained distinctly European, restricted largely to its heartland and the North American
societies linked to it. Cultural modernity is based on the principle of subjectivity, that is, on the view that man (or woman) is an autonomous sub-
ject/individual free to discover and master nature and place it at the service
of one's own society for fulfilling human needs. This worldview is both
secular and man-centered, and as such required the replacing of the cosmological views of the world by a rational worldview based on modern
science. To be sure, the more tangible and more useful products of modernity—in particular, science and technology—were transmitted to other
civilizations as well, but were instrumentally confined; that is, they were
adopted by the recipient civilizations without the cultural underpinning of

the worldview they sprang from. In this sense, the more structurally globalized our world has become, the more culturally fragmented it has come to
be. In this regard I coined the phrase "simultaneity of structural globalization and cultural fragmentation."[4]

The project of modernization was driven by the almost missionary zeal
of the universalist modernization approach[5] that dominated American
thought and Western approaches in general in the postcolonial period. The
failure of modernization to travel beyond its original confines is the background for the ongoing process of cultural revival in non-Western civilizations. Although this spreading sentiment had been strong before the onset
of the Cold War, it had not yet been internationally felt, and the end of
the Cold War gave this sentiment its first great boost. As early as 1962 the
great French sociologist Raymond Aron noted that the "heterogeneity of
civilizations" is the major source of conflict in international politics. He
added that the bipolar atmosphere of the Cold War contributed to "veil-
ing" this source and predicted its unveiling in the aftermath of bipolarity.[6]
This is the historical background and the content of the de-Westernization
of the world we are now witnessing; the process has moved to center
stage. The issue is then no longer modernization, which had been proposed
mainly by American social scientists, but de-Westernization. Western social
scientists had been enlisted to address developments that would have the
effect of promoting Westernization as modernization. In contrast, non-
Westerners sought to promote modernization without Westernization.
Fundamentalism is in fact not a traditionalism but rather a propensity to
de-Westernization in the sense of dismissing cultural modernity while embracing instrumental modernization. I have depicted this propensity as an
"Islamic dream of semi-modernity."[7]

Going back to the roots means returning to the sources of one's own local culture, and in today's world that is the definition of de-Westernization.
Culture, in the terms of Clifford Geertz' cultural anthropology, is the expression of a social production of meaning, a process that is always local,
never global.[8] Local cultures that are related to one another, like the great
variety of Islamic cultures stretching from Southeast Asia to the Balkans
and West Africa, form a particular sort of loose unity that I address as a civilization. Many scholars and journalists confuse culture and civilization, and
at times use them interchangeably.[9]

In the current resurgence against the West, cultural references are
becoming politically instrumental, serving as grist for a civilization-

consciousness and a regional cross-cultural unity created for political ends. Religious fundamentalism is thus the political expression of the "Revolt against the West,"[10] but unlike the process of decolonization of past decades, this revolt is not purely political. Non-Western civilizations are increasingly exposed to a global matrix that projects cultural modernity as well as communication. For this reason the contemporary anti-Western revolt entails projecting, on political grounds, a cultural worldview. In other words, religious fundamentalism cannot be conceived properly as simply a political phenomenon—without reference, that is, to its sociocultural background. Nor is it simply a cultural revival. For despite their anti-modernity rhetoric, the fundamentalists are basically not traditionalists, but rather a product of modernity themselves. They seek to confront modern and secular institutions by reviving the worldviews of their own civilizations, all the while imprisoned in modernity and openly subscribing to its instruments.

This is the historical context of the phenomenon of religious fundamentalism that we encounter in most civilizations—most prominently, however, in Islam. Bearing this context in mind we are better able to realize how simplistic is the use of fundamentalism as a label synonymous with terrorism. To be sure, adherents of political Islam do undertake murder and other horrifying terrorist acts, as they have, for example, in Algeria, Turkey, Egypt, the Occupied Territories, Afghanistan, and Somalia. But these acts are only the surface manifestation of a historical phenomenon that cannot be grasped or explained by such primitive catchphrases as "Warriors of Allah" or "Islamic Terrorism." Terrorism reflects only a minor dimension of the global and all-encompassing phenomenon of fundamentalism.

What, then, are the real constraints underlying the rise of fundamentalist ideology? I ask my readers to free themselves from the habit of associating fundamentalism with the media-driven image of bearded and screaming "fanatics." During my sabbatical in 1995–96, spent partly in Egypt, I encountered Islamic fundamentalists in Cairo as handsome lawyers and medical doctors leading their professional associations while calling for the Islamic system of government as "God's rule." As regards the "unwashed faces" as a Western media image of the fundamentalists, one ought to bear in mind that as practicing Muslims Islamic fundamentalists do wash themselves five times daily, in compliance with the ritual precepts for their daily prayers. In their rhetoric, fundamentalists might glorify the achievements of Islam during the height of Islamic civilization, but today they stand in the context of modernity and the "world time" related to it. (By "world time" I mean the context of contemporary global history.) It is only in this context that the fundamentalists can be properly understood. True, they take scripturalist recourse to religious texts to undergird their views and actions, but the religious text they consider to be the only authoritative basis, as *sola scriptura*, in reality is not only drawn upon selectively but also elaborated with meanings related specifically to the context of our contemporary world. They use the language of modernity to contest the evils of modernity, and their plan is to adopt the instruments of modernity to beat it at its own game. They are torn between their selective use of tradition and the fragmentation brought on by modernity; some of the fundamentalists operate in an intellectually schizoid program.

In short, religious fundamentalists seek to disentangle the instruments of modernity they want to adopt from the worldview that has produced them. They aim at modernization while dismissing the worldview of cultural modernity, as I have shown in work that grew from the Fundamentalism Project of the American Academy of Arts and Sciences.[11] This is exactly the fundamentalist dream, earlier addressed as semi-modernity (see note 7), of an Islamic modernity devoid of modernity's secular and rational worldview.

ISLAMIC FUNDAMENTALISM AS A SEMI-MODERN, BACKWARD-ORIENTED UTOPIA CONTESTING CULTURAL MODERNITY

Cultural modernity (see note 3), the ongoing project of modern Western civilization, is based upon a rational, man-centered worldview. Individual human rights and secular democracy, the political culture of pluralism, and the private religiosity determined by secularity are some of the basic components of the project. The French refer to *laïcité*, that is, the political culture of the separation of religion and public life, to circumscribe the politicocultural substance of modernity.

Islamic fundamentalism is the contemporary outgrowth of tensions between the secular worldview of cultural modernity and the cosmological worldview of Islamic monotheism. These tensions become the source of international political conflict. Muslims did not encounter the West in the mantle of Enlightenment, but rather as a belligerent force militarily superior to them. The West did not so much aim to enlighten Muslims as to subject them to Western political rule. This is the history of European expansion.

In the wake of structural globalization, the economic and political structures of Western industrial societies became the framework of our larger world. The rise of the West was linked to the process the historian Geoffrey Parker has called "The Military Revolution."[12] The technological superiority of the West, in particular in the waging of war, facilitated the European expansion and the mapping of the world into the European system. To emulate this superiority, non-Western civilizations sought to "import the European Army."[13] Learning from Europe became tantamount to adopting Western technology, in particular the technology of war. Ottoman rulers, for example, sent their emissaries to Paris to inquire into the sources of Western military superiority.[14] The answer was clear: technology. But technology is not a neutral tool. The unfolding of the technological revolution in Europe has been part and parcel of the radical changes in Western worldview. The sociologist Franz Borkenau, of the German Frankfurt School, inquiring into the constraints that determined the change of the *Weltbild*/worldview of the Europeans, found that the key was modern science, which facilitated the modern scientific view of the world.[15] Edgar Zilsel concluded that modern science originates from the interplay of the humanities with the practical knowledge of craftsmen/artisans as prescientific technicians.[16] Modern science and the scientific mode of thinking facilitated the progression in the instruments of warfare from tools to machines and, ultimately, the industrialization of war.[17]

The World of Islam and other non-Western civilizations encountered the West on the field of military superiority, not in the gentler reaches of Habermas's Project of Cultural Modernity, and the processes of globalization exposed Muslims primarily to the instrumental and institutional dimensions of modernity. Only tangentially were Muslims exposed to cultural modernity's new ways of viewing the world. The Ottoman rulers did not send their emissaries to France to study the political philosophy of the French Revolution, nor did the founder of modern Egypt, Muhammad Ali, send the imam Rifa'a Rafi' al-Tahtawi and his students to Paris to read Rousseau and Montesquieu.[18] The encounter with cultural modernity was, however, inevitable, if only as a by-product. The modernism of Tahtawi, the Islamic reformism of Muhammad 'Abduh, and Islamic liberalism in general must be seen in the context of these early encounters with Europe.[19] Finally, the nation-centered idea of nationalism that Muslims borrowed from the West contributed to their adopting the European idea of separation of church and state. But because the cultural and institutional underpinnings of the nation-states they formed were missing, the borrowed institution has been doomed to be no more than nominally a nation-state in the Western sense.[20]

A proper understanding of the rise of fundamentalism in Islamic civilization, as a religious alternative to cultural modernity, requires a deep understanding of European-Islamic encounters with globalization in modern times. Unlike cultural historians, who restrict their views to normative grounds, I conceptualize the geopolitical area of the World of Islam as an Islamic civilization, and view the encounter between Islam and the West on the basis of a multilevel analysis. The Muslims' encounter with the militarily superior West humiliated them and shattered their image of themselves as a congregation of believers superior to all others, the Qur'anic verse decreeing them *khair umma ukhrijat li al-nas* (the finest community in all of humanity; Qur'an: Surat 'Imran, 3/110). The economic and political penetration of the World of Islam by European powers, in the context of structural globalization, has created all manner of hardships, from disruption and disorientation to dislocation.

Islam's exposure to cultural modernity has a parallel in classical Islamic history: the encounter with Hellenism. Then, however, the context was much different. The ordained superiority of Muslims allowed them to study this remarkable Greek legacy not within the context of domination and global subjugation, but as a stimulating element of a truly cultural encounter. Integrating the Greek legacy into Islamic tradition in that period was a great deal easier than giving cultural modernity an Islamic face today. But as much as I despise simplistic one-level analyses, I also dismiss monocausal explanations. Thus, the context of domination does not entirely suffice as an interpretation of the tension between contemporary Islam and cultural modernity. As it happens, in classical Islam, Islamic philosophers who subscribed to rational Greek knowledge were contested by the proponents of Islamic orthodoxy, who would not accept reason, in preference to scripture, as a point of departure in the pursuit of knowledge about society and nature. The two most influential medieval jurists, Ibn Taimiyya (1263–1328) and al-Mawardi (974–1058), made it clear in their stand against a rational Islamic philosophy that only divine revelation, not reason, should be admitted as a primary source of knowledge.[21] Similarly, the fundamentalists of our time—on the ruins of a failed cultural accommodation—contest modernity not only in its institutional dimension (perceived as Western dominance) but also as the cultural project of a rational, man-centered view of the world. In both cases, classical and contemporary Islam, there has been a clash between the divine and rational views of the world, a clash that complicates, even blocks, a cultural accommodation of social change. Without smacking of essentialism my analysis sees herein an Islamic cultural predicament.[22]

Europe's voyage to modernity began in the Renaissance, with the discovery of classic Greek knowledge and thought. As Leslie Lipson, in his global history of civilizations, puts it, "Aristotle crept back into Europe by the side door. His return was due to the Arabs. . . . The main inspiration of Europe shifted from Christianity back to Greece, from Jerusalem to Athens. Socrates, not Jesus, has been the mentor of the civilization that in modern times has influenced or dominated most of the planet."[23] Because rational disciplines had not been institutionalized in classical Islam,[24] the adoption of the Greek legacy had no lasting effect on Islamic civilization, as it has in Europe. What matters here is that Europe and Islamic civilization in that period found common grounds and a greater closeness via the mediation of the classical Greek legacy. When, however, both civilizations chose to define themselves in terms of religion, they encountered one another in terms of *jihad* and crusades, that is, as enemies. In his address to the Western Islamic Dialogue Forum established by the Euro-Islamic Institute at the European Academy of Arts and Sciences, the Jordanian Crown Prince Hassan, a Hashimite and thus a descendant of the family of the Prophet, characterized Islamic-Western relations aptly in the following manner: "The historical relationship between Europe and the Muslim world has ranged from cordial to brutal; but it has always been a significant relationship, not least in shaping each other's identities. . . . Muslims and Europeans have been at their worst when they sought to dominate each other; and at their best when they looked to learn from each other." (This speech was given in Salzburg, June 1, 1996, when I was appointed director of the aforementioned Euro-Islamic Institute.) It is correct to criticize Western hegemony; but the reversal of this hegemony by an Islamic dominance, as envisaged by Islamic fundamentalism, is no way out.

Crown Prince Hassan's comments help us return to the present: cultural modernity's worldview and its idea of progress would be inconceivable without the Greek legacy passed to Europe through the Arabs. Today, however, contemporary Islamic fundamentalists denounce not only cultural modernity, but even the Islamic rationalism of Averroës and Avicenna, scholars who had defined the heights of Islamic civilization. Not surprisingly, contemporary fundamentalists draw upon the teachings of Ibn Taimiyya, the unyielding foe of Islamic rationalism, in their politicization of Islam. Classical *fiqh*, as a political doctrine put at the service of fundamentalist ideology, is being revived under conditions of exposure to cultural modernity and structural globalization. In Islamic tradition *fiqh* is the Arabic word for knowledge par excellence, the more general term for knowledge being *'ilm*. Unlike Christianity, Islam is based on *fiqh*/jurisprudence rather than on *kalam*/theology. In the foremost contribution to the study of Islamic law, by Joseph Schacht, we read on the first page that "the very term *fiqh*, 'knowledge,' shows that early Islam regarded knowledge of the sacred law as the knowledge par excellence . . . only mysticism was strong enough to challenge the ascendancy of the law over the minds of the Muslims. . . . Apart from this . . . it is impossible to understand Islam without understanding Islamic law."[25] Nevertheless, *fiqh*—albeit knowledge about sacred law—is in itself not divine, for the simple reason that *fiqh*, unlike the *shari'a*, is human knowledge. Islamic jurists, the *fuqaha'* (plural of *faqih*, a scholar of *fiqh*), interpret the Qur'an and *hadith*/legacy of the Prophet as sources of the *shari'a;* the result is human reasoning, that is, *fiqh*. Unlike Islamic tradition, contemporary fundamentalists willingly confuse *fiqh* and *shari'a* in order to render to their human views a divine character. The result is to declare every opponent a *kafir*/unbeliever and thus to smooth the way for slaughtering non-fundamentalist Muslims. At the height of classical Islam, Islamic rationalists were also victims of *takfir*/declaration as unbelievers by their foes; thus the intolerance of the *takfir* is not wholly new, but new is rather its fundamentalist shape.

Politically, economically, and culturally, the encounter with the West has shattered Islamic civilization. In decades past, Muslims tried earnestly to accommodate to changing situations, in a number of ways; Islamic reformism and secular nationalism, though completely different approaches, can both be seen as efforts to embrace cultural modernity. But when all had failed, a new movement, antithetical to cultural modernity, began establishing itself. The result is religious fundamentalism.

Whatever else might be said about it, Islamic fundamentalism addresses the double crisis[26] under which Muslims suffer: first, the socioeconomic and political crisis deriving from the imposed integration of Islamic civilization into a world system dominated by the West; second, the identity crisis, or crisis of meaning, brought on by exposure to cultural modernity. Any handling of these (1) *structural* and (2) *interactional* constraints on analytically separate levels must lead to equally simplistic and biased views, for the interplay between the two crises must also be honored. Books published in the United States, such as Daniel Pipes's *In the Path of God*,[27] relate the growth of political Islam to the oil boom. But with the sinking of oil prices, the oil boom is gone, and Saudi donations to fundamentalists are subsiding, whereas religious fundamentalism remains, more powerful than ever! Oil sheikhs and fundamentalists, after all, are different people with different backgrounds and very different views and agendas.

Basically, religious fundamentalists denounce cultural modernity as a virus that has befallen Islam and contributed to the weakening of Islamic civilization. Political Islam purports to reverse this condition. Confronting cultural modernity thus becomes a struggle against the West, in particular a struggle against "the intellectual invasion of the World of Islam."[28] This denouncing of the West is extended to encompass not only the secular Muslims despised as *al-mutagharibun* / the Westernized but also the early Islamic modernists like Tahtawi (1801–73) and even the most honorable Muhammad 'Abduh (1849–1905), as well.

I have dismissed the oil boom interpretation of political Islam, but in so doing I must acknowledge the financial support that Islamic fundamentalists received from Saudi Arabia prior to the Gulf crisis. For reasons of expediency the Islamically legitimized monarchy of Saudi Arabia granted vast sums of money to various Islamic fundamentalist movements, seemingly not understanding that their political ideology is directed against the traditional Saudi legitimacy, as well. Though these funds were most supportive, they were not the roots of the phenomenon; Islamic fundamentalism is a social and political phenomenon, not the outcome of a Saudi conspiracy. The Saudis evidently needed the anguish of the Gulf crisis, during which the fundamentalists denounced them as instruments of the infidel West,[29] to come to a realization of how the land lies. The Mufti of Saudi Arabia, 'Abdulaziz al-Baz, publicly attacked the fundamentalists—an indication of the deepening rift between traditional Wahhabi Islam, as represented by the Saudis, and religious fundamentalism, as a distinctly anti-Western protest movement. Here we have clear evidence, then, that fundamentalism is not a neo-traditionalism, as some scholars claim, much less a pan-Islam conspiracy. It is unfortunate that the anguish of the Gulf War has not been sufficient to deter the Saudis from offering further donations to fundamentalist movements, in particular among the European diaspora of Islam. Clearly, they do this for political expediency.

In my work I have had occasion to study the attitudes of Sunni Arab fundamentalists toward modern science and technology,[30] and to study the responses of these people to the larger panoply of cultural modernity. Unlike traditionalists, Muslim fundamentalists very much favor the adoption of modern science and technology by contemporary Islam. But they restrict what may be adopted to selected instruments, that is, to the *products* of science and technology, while fiercely rebuffing the rational worldview that made these achievements possible. The late great Berkeley scholar Reinhard Bendix showed that "modernization in some sphere of life may occur without resulting in [a full measure of] modernity," and added that "more or less ad hoc adoption of items of modernity [actually] produces obstacles standing in the way of successful modernization."[31] The experience of Islamic fundamentalism offers strong support for this statement.

Islamic fundamentalists fail to understand that the worldview that drives modernity is essential to its capacity for producing modern science and technology. In a way, the dismissing of the scientific mind by the fundamentalists qualifies their views as "anti-science."[32] They dream of a semi-modernity (see note 7), a hybrid outlook restricted to instrumental borrowing, thus incapable of creativity and doomed to failure. For Islamic fundamentalists, man can never be creator, for he himself is created *makhluq*, that is, a creature of God. Only God can be *al-khaliq*/the Creator. The German historian Christian Meier coined the term *Könnens-Bewusstsein*[33] for the classical Greek synthesis of *episteme* (knowledge) and *techne* (technical skills), that is, the consciousness of man of his own ability to be creative and to change human conditions. Humanity's awareness of its *Könnens-Bewusstsein* is an awareness of the possibilities of combining "knowledge" and skills in the pursuit of fulfilling one's needs. Cultural modernity—including the whole realm of science and technology—cannot be conceived properly if this intellectual background of determining man as a creative agent is ignored.

In my inquiry into the attitudes and worldview of Islamic fundamentalists toward modern science and technology (see note 30), an inquiry based on reading their writings and on direct observation and interplay during my field work, I came to the conclusion that their approval of modern science and technology does not, and can never, amount to embracing the notion of *Könnens-Bewusstsein*, which for them would inherently constitute heresy.

Ironically, the fundamentalists seem not to be aware of the fact that they are themselves nothing but a response to modernity. As Bruce Lawrence so nicely puts it,

> Fundamentalists oppose modernism. . . . Modernity . . . is the key category to consider when interpreting fundamentalism. It becomes and remains the enveloping context. Without modernity there are no fundamentalists, just as there are no modernists. The identity of fundamentalism, as both a psychological mindset and a historical movement, is shaped by the modern world. Fundamentalists . . . are at once the consequence of modernity and the antithesis of modernism.[34]

In short, fundamentalism is powerfully affected by modernity even though militantly oriented against it. The politicization of religion is the response of the fundamentalists to the crisis, and their means for dealing with it. Islam is, then, no longer restricted to the role of religious faith; rather, it becomes a political ideology aimed at reconstituting the secular world as a divine order. In projecting an ideology of salvation, and in promising a better world, Islamic fundamentalists attract a broad constituency; the Front Islamique du Salut (FIS) in Algeria incorporates *al-inqadh* / salvation even into its name.

BETWEEN PRIVATE RELIGIOSITY AND
THE POLITICIZATION OF RELIGIOUS BELIEFS

By paving the way for self-awareness, cultural modernity has helped unfetter humanity from the cosmological worldview, in time establishing a rational worldview that enables us to explore our own creativity and thus to affect, through our actions, our own destiny. Max Weber described this achievement as "disenchantment/*Entzauberung* with the World." In achieving this goal the Enlightenment disentangled religion from politics, but did not require that secularization be anti-religious. And although the anti-religious attitudes of many early Enlightenment philosophers cannot be denied,[35] it is utterly wrong to interpret the secular character of modernity as being anti-religious. In sociological terms, secularization is manifested basically in processes of structural and institutional differentiations in society. These processes affect the system of life by dividing it into subsystems like science, politics, economics, and, in this context, religion, as well. (In a paper presented and published in Cairo at the First International Islamic Philosophy Conference on Islam and Civilization, I introduced this concept of secularization as it might relate to Islam; see note 26, pp. 127–48.) Secularization affects religion by encouraging it to develop as a separate system. Consequently, religion becomes private religiosity; it may express its tenets, but it may not force them on others.

The conference mentioned was held in November 1979, when Islamic fundamentalism was already a reality, but was not yet so robust that

presenting such views publicly meant risking one's life. The killing of the
Egyptian writer Faraj Fuda in June 1992 for having publicly avowed secular views, and the prosecution of the Cairo professor Nasr Hamid Abu-Zaid
in 1995, are dramatic demonstration of the deterioration of the situation,
and also of how far the fundamentalists have risen in the halls of power. But
despite this evidence of religious intolerance I ask my readers to bear in
mind the importance of the distinction between terrorism[36] and religious
fundamentalism. Fundamentalism is a defensive-cultural worldview related
to the disruptive effects and dislocations growing from modernization
processes, whereas terrorism simply reflects a pattern of violent political action. The continued slaying and threatening of coreligionists with whom
the fundamentalists do not agree is clearly terrorism, but we ought not allow our focus on the constraints of the phenomenon and its diagnosis to be
blurred by its superficial manifestations, so dispiriting as the killing is. I am
familiar with these terrorist threats from my own experience, but I try to
separate them from clear analytical thinking about the forces and the thinking behind them.

Some scholars choose to define religious fundamentalism as a renaissance of religious belief, but my research does not support this contention.
The fundamentalist is primarily an activist and a political man, *homo politi-
cus*, not a man of religion or of beliefs, not a *homo religiosus*. Islam is a cultural system with its own religious symbols, and Islamic fundamentalists
simply invoke these symbols to further their political goals. Still, there is a
difference between religion as a belief and cultural system and religion as
a tool for establishing political legitimacy, be this for people in power (like
the Saudi and Moroccan kings[37]) or for the political opposition of a wide
range of fundamentalist movements. Unlike political ideologies, religious
beliefs employed politically can command such overriding power that no
secular political ideology can compete with them. As the German-Jewish
philosopher Ernst Bloch puts it, in his book on Thomas Müntzer, one of the
leaders of religious revolution in the age of Reformation, religious movements can be described "as the ecstasy of walking upright, as the chafing,
rebellious, most ardent will to paradise." In "religiously agitated times"[38]
these movements could become powerful indeed. But does this observation
on Christian history apply to Islam, too?

Despite the condemnations of the fundamentalists by the nominal political leaders of the World of Islam, one can observe the great sympathy
these movements enjoy among the populace, their proclivities for terror-

ism notwithstanding. The explanation is simple: Arab nationalists, secular democrats, and socialists of whatever stripe, as well as others in the Arab world, speak a modern language alien to the average Muslim. Modern elites are as strange as their Westernized thoughts, for the bulk of the Muslim people have other concerns. A leading fundamentalist ideologue, Yusuf al-Qaradawi, alludes with contempt to these secular ideologies, calling them "*hulul mustawrada*/imported solutions."[39] Contrary to pan-Arabists, secular-liberal democrats, and socialists, who employ a political language alien to most Muslims, Islamic fundamentalists can count on a powerful response when they make reference to traditional Islamic symbols, albeit in a distinct context.

In the United States, Islamic fundamentalism as a politicization of religion is most often referred to as a phenomenon of Islamic resurgence or of Islamic reassertion, mostly on unspecified grounds—Islam itself is not being introduced anew. In continental Europe the term "re-Islamization," though utterly inappropriate, has taken hold. In the aftermath of the abolition of the caliphate and the dissolution of the Islamic order of the Ottoman Empire, Islam as a political ideology was forced to give way to secular ideologies, largely in the form of secular nationalism.[40] But Islam, as a cultural system for all Muslims, a system that affects their everyday lives, has always been there. What makes the difference today is that Islam is again assuming a political shape, but under conditions not known in earlier Islamic history. Thus, we can speak of a repoliticization of Islam, but not its return as a religion, for it has not been somewhere in limbo. The proponents of the new movement, looking to the past, contest the interpretation of Islam as simply a religious belief restricted to private religiosity, and the formula that Islam is a "*din wa dawla*/unity of religion and state" becomes once more a sweeping political belief. It is clear that this formula, as thus attributed to Islam, exists neither in the Qur'an nor in the tradition of the Prophet (the *hadith*), nor is it to be found in any of the authoritative classical writings. The same can be said of the fundamentalist concepts of the "Islamic state,"[41] and of "*hakimiyyat Allah*/God's rule." Both are recent additions to Islamic thought, and both are distinctly fundamentalist in character.

Even though one of the fathers of Islamic fundamentalism, the Pakistani Abu al-A'la al-Mawdudi (1903–79), stated in no uncertain terms that his political interpretation of Islam is at odds with democracy, some Western experts on Islam contend that political Islam is an effort to "Islamize democracy." A closer look shows that the fundamentalist notion of *din wa dawla* and the concept of the Islamic state point clearly to totalitarian political rule.[42] Thus I agree with Jean François Revel that Islamic fundamentalism is a major threat to democracy.[43]

The formula *din wa dawla* includes a political strategy: the toppling of the several formally and avowedly secular regimes in the World of Islam and their replacement by Islamic "governments of God" committed to the concept of *nizam Islami*. This too is a recent concept, another that cannot be found in the authoritative Islamic sources (see Chapter 7). As I argued when quoting Sayyid Qutb, this concept of *nizam Islami* also becomes the basis for the Islamic fundamentalist claims on the international stage, that is, for an international *nizam Islami*/Islamic order to be materialized through an "Islamic world revolution" (Qutb).

One can trace fundamentalist movements through earlier periods of contemporary history throughout the Muslim world. The most prominent of these were The Movement of the Muslim Brotherhood established in Egypt in 1928[44] and, later, the Tahrir Party in Jordan. But it was not until the disastrous defeat of the Arab armies in the Six-Day War in June 1967 that one could speak of an overarching fundamentalist drive, first in the Arab world and then throughout the World of Islam. I have already quoted the Egyptian Muslim Brothers' fundamentalist Yusuf al-Qaradawi, who as early as 1970 called for the discarding of what he characterized as "imported solutions." The alternative to the de-legitimized Arab regimes that were defeated in June 1967 in a most humiliating manner is the "*hall al-Islami* / the Islamic solution." But to argue that the assertion of a *hall Islami* first occurred in the heart of the Sunni Arab world, and not in Iran, to be spread then throughout the Islamic world, does not imply an Arabo-centric outlook.

Even though Islamic fundamentalism is, in my view at least, the major collective choice in the World of Islam at present, one cannot gainsay the fact that the organized fundamentalists, as political activists, are still a minority among Muslims, if indeed a terrifying and energetic minority. These are people who view themselves as challengers of modernity, not as products of it. But it is a fact that, in the main, politically active Islamic fundamentalists are to be discerned in major urban areas, the very heartland of creeping modernity. They are products of the modern sector, some of them with a full or interrupted university training and perhaps professional careers, viz. the lawyers and medical doctors in Cairo. In other words, we are dealing with people who are *themselves* dislocated and suffering the disruptions of the failed introduction of modernity into Islamic societies. Their greater familiarity with the West makes their angst all the more formidable.

Islamic fundamentalists offer an ideology of salvation, an ideology that promises to deal successfully with all problems resulting from uncontrolled demographic growth and concomitant economic stagnation or even decline. The promise is a legitimate Islamic government, one that complies with the *shari'a*, that will bring wonder and magical solutions into this desperate, crisis-ridden world. Fundamentalists in power, however, such as those in Sudan and Iran, have proved to be quite unable to deal with any of the pending problems, and their poor performance cannot be explained simply by reference to the obstacles put in their way by the West. It is seemingly remarkable that these fundamentalist regimes so effectively sustain their appeal: the consistency of their failures with domestic problems should take the bloom off the rose, but they deflect disillusionment by their successful presentation of a Western conspiracy (*mu'amarah*) directed against Islam, and by focusing on Iran and Sudan as "true" Islamic states.

CONCLUSIONS

The World of Islam is large and diverse, and the forces of Islamic fundamentalism that aim to unite all Muslims are powerfully constrained by this very diversity. Divisive sectarian and ethnic elements fragment the Muslim community as a whole and split the fundamentalist movements in particular. The Hobbesian *bellum omnium contra omnes* / the war of all against all best describes the warring Afghani *mujahidin*, who after seeing the departure of the external enemy, the former Soviet Union that had unwittingly become a force uniting the Afghans, now turn to fighting one another, most brutally. This realization obliges us to pursue our analysis of the power of fundamentalists on a dual basis: pinpointing their fixation on an external enemy who will serve as a uniting factor while at the same time not losing sight of the inner divisions in Islamic civilization.

The legacy of the Gulf War lies in the revival of the classical dichotomy between the abode of Islam and the abode of the external enemy. Appeals to this tradition deepen the trenches between Islam and the West. The legacy lies also in the revival of the Islamic claim for the "*ghalab* / dominance" (a term of the early Islamic revivalist al-Afghani) that has been denied by Western hegemony. The perception of the Gulf War as a "Christian Crusade" is being kept vividly alive among Muslims, and the recent genocidal attack against the Muslims in Bosnia has given that perception a great boost. Wolfgang G. Lerch, who writes on Islamic politics at the major German daily *Frankfurter Allgemeine Zeitung*, is to my knowledge the first journalist working in the Western media to inform his readers about the linkage being forged in Muslim public opinion between the crusades and the Bosnian war.[45] In the Balkan case, ironically, it is the Serbs, not the Bosnian Muslims, who are the fundamentalists.[46] Outside the Balkans, during the war, Muslim fundamentalists made full use of the agonies and hardships of the Bosnian Muslims in assailing the West for the fecklessness of its policies in the Balkans, and in fact accusing the West of being a party to the genocide. These accusations continue even in the aftermath of the war in Bosnia, and despite the role of the West in bringing the bloodshed to a halt.

No other civilization in the world feels so bitterly that the European expansion has taken place at its expense. For unlike Hinduism or Confucianism, but like Christianity, Islam is a universalism. The Muslims, just as peoples of other civilizations, did not gather, in their encounter with the West, the fruits of the Enlightenment, did not partake of the cultural dimensions of modernity. Rather, they were confronted by the ugly face of institutional modernity manifested in military superiority and political domination. It is true that in their separate histories these non-Western civilizations did not pursue the processes of building a democratic civil society and ensuring individual freedoms that led Europe ultimately to the establishment of a basic code of human rights. And the West did little to aid the introduction of democracy into the Islamic world. It is wrong, however, to blame only the West for this failure of democratization, for Western policies are the one constraint, local preconditions and predispositions the other.

As Habermas[47] has argued, the implications of cultural modernity are (1) individualism, (2) the freedom and ability to subject traditions to critical reasoning, (3) autonomy of individual action, and (4) the philosophy of man that resulted in a man-centered view of the world. This is the European pattern of modernity. Non-Western civilizations, however, did not encounter this pattern of modernity when they were exposed to European expansion but, rather, faced colonizing armies brutally manifesting the superiority of industrial technology. Still, in the earlier colonial and even postcolonial periods, non-Western peoples, the Muslims among them, were at pains to emulate the West, despite these humiliations. They even employed such Western concepts as the right to sovereignty and self-rule in their struggle against colonialism. But after a few decades of living in nominal nation-states that failed to meet the challenge of modernization, and failed, as well, to devise a beneficial strategy for emulating the West, the non-Western peoples rediscovered an awareness of their own civilizations, a need to search for other alternatives, basically to grow from one's own heritage. Religious fundamentalism has been the salient progeny of these processes.

Fundamentalists thus believe they present a genuine and feasible alternative. I have my doubts. Accordingly, in chapters 9 and 10 I shall introduce a new cross-cultural understanding of human rights and democracy that may yield an alternative to both Westernization and the challenge of fundamentalism.

The revival of the call for the *turath*/heritage among Muslims has become a major component of a strategy of de-Westernization that aspires to cover all domains of Islam. But the revival cannot be mobilized in isolation, for *our present time is "world time,"* and no Muslim can escape the "consequences of modernity." Islamic fundamentalists nonetheless believe that they can defeat the West with its own armaments and technologies. They view modernity in a way that favors their own purposes, expecting to adopt its techno-scientific achievements while dismissing its "corrupt" worldview. For Islamic fundamentalists the West is evil incarnate, and the historical background of the West's domination of the Islamic world underlies their resentment. Compounding their resentment is the fact that the expansion of the West has led to the denial of Islam's universalist claims.

Discovering oneself, one's own identity, necessarily means, in this case, drawing clear lines between "we" and the "others." It is not Samuel P. Huntington but the Islamic fundamentalists themselves who draw these fault lines of conflict between civilizations. Their "we"-awareness is assuming the shape of a civilization-consciousness claiming the unity of all Muslims against all others. But in light of the divisiveness inherent in a long roster of sectarian and ethnic forces, one must question the unity they expound. If an external enemy can be made the rallying point, these centrifugal forces may subside, but they do not cease movement. The intolerably ineffectual policies of the West vis-à-vis the genocide brought down upon the Bosnian Muslims by the Serbs have been a deadly mistake. I share the view of Wolfgang G. Lerch (see note 45) that the "Serbian Crusade" will affect Muslim-Western relations "deep into the next century." It fuels Islamic fundamentalism's fiery rhetoric and unwittingly unites and empowers the "revolt against the West."

—ᴍ—

Cultural Fragmentation, the Decline in Consensus, and the Diffusion of Power in World Politics

Islamic fundamentalists gain their notoriety in world politics and the world's press in part from their perception that the West has been pursuing fresh new crusades against Islam, from the Gulf War to the Balkan War. But the phenomenon of fundamentalism is not simply reducible to such day-to-day events. Rather, it demonstrates that basic structural changes are taking place both in Islamic countries and in the international system. Fundamentalism, the religiopolitical response to these changes, will be with us for years, perhaps decades, to come. The Islamic breed of fundamentalism is in fact a sociopolitical revolt against regional order and the overarching world order.

In the preceding chapters we have seen how the competing worldviews of the major civilizations contest one another in the design of a new world order in the aftermath of the Cold War. True, the Islamic claim for a specifically Islamic world order as an alternative to the existing world order is rather a flight of rhetoric, since the capabilities for realizing this claim are clearly lacking. Moreover, the power fragmentation in political Islam diminishes its efficacy. Nonetheless, I take the claim more seriously than those scholars do who discuss the issue at the level of the alleged "Islamic threat" (that is, terrorism) or simply ridicule Islamic fundamentalist rhetoric. In my view, it is imperative that we examine the phenomenon that lies beneath the surface events and the attendant sensational news coverage, and beyond the incessant polemical debates.

If we are to understand Islamic fundamentalism, we must look beyond a fixation on the nation-state. Traditional international relations scholars ask first, when confronted with religious fundamentalism, in what way can fundamentalist ideologies affect policies or even be embodied in state policy? Thus from the outset these scholars limit their access to the phenomenon at issue. In Chapter 1 I argued that the major trend in current international politics is the simultaneity of structural globalization and cultural fragmentation—the latter a phenomenon not confined to the state or to inter-state relations. To understand this trend we must grapple with the phenomenon on multiple levels. To begin with, few fundamentalists are now in power; basically, they belong to the underground opposition. Given this fact, that is, that they are not policymakers, some traditional international relations scholars would deny these groups any further significance. In my view, such an approach is dangerously lacking in the insights needed for understanding fundamentalism and its growing political presence. The crisis of the nation-state, an entity alien to the World of Islam, needs also to be subjected to sober scrutiny, for this crisis generates developments that can be counted among the major sources of the fundamentalist challenge.

Following the arguments of Hedley Bull in his "Revolt against the West,"[1] I emphasize the radical changes taking place in the world as we move toward the turn of the century. The challenges arising in this volatile age compel scholars and practitioners of international relations to rethink their frameworks and envisage new ways for gaining a grasp of future developments. The prevailing approach in international relations—little changed in a century or more—focuses almost exclusively on "the state" and the use or threat of military force. This approach fails to provide an explanatory framework for interpreting the current politicization of cultural fragmentation in international society. In my view, religiocultural fundamentalism, especially as illustrated by the case of Islam, is an active agent in the spread of international cultural fragmentation and the hitherto unprecedented decline in international consensus. I do not believe that the "clash of civilizations"[2] is inevitable, because an international morality,[3] if earnestly pursued among nations, can bridge the gap between civilizations. (I shall elaborate on this concept in the final two chapters.) I do believe, however, that religious fundamentalism contributes to this clash by disputing an international morality that must be secular in nature if it is to establish cross-civilizational approaches.

In our efforts to understand undemocratic societies, which are characteristic of the Middle East and most other parts of the World of Islam, we must distinguish between public choices and state policies. Political Islam, nourished by recent events, is moving to the fore, rapidly becoming the major source of public choices among Muslims. State policies in Islamic countries do not yet necessarily reflect these public choices, but in the ongoing crisis there are many fundamentalism-ridden states like Tunisia, Algeria, Jordan, and Egypt whose nonfundamentalist governments are pressed by their own populations to honor these new choices. Worldwide, Islamic fundamentalism is the most widespread and most potent variety of the "revolt against the West." Nevertheless, the phenomenon can be observed elsewhere, as well. The victory of the Hindu fundamentalists of the Bharatiya Janata Party (BJP) in India in the summer 1996 election, now the strongest faction in the Indian parliament, is another case in point.

It is safe to say that the Saddam Hussein legacy addressed in Chapter 3 has been the Middle East's rebuttal to the prevailing international norms and rules. Fueling the rebuttal is the awareness that these norms are Western in origin, and that they have been imposed on the Muslims by the West. Positing that legacy is not inconsistent with acknowledging Saddam's profoundly weakened position in 1996, and such breakdown as might yet befall his regime will not deny the force of his legacy.

Saddam's assertion of a "revolt against the West" during the Gulf War ensured his appeal to Muslim fundamentalists, but we need to depersonalize his claim, since it is related to issues, not persons. Saddam will be gone one day, but his legacy will remain. In my view, Charles Krauthammer, in his article "The Issue Is World Order, Not Just Oil," captured the situation well: "In 1973 and 1979 the only thing at stake was oil. . . . Today there is another value at stake in the Gulf. It is even more important than oil. It is world order. . . . Saddam Hussein's Iraq presents a challenge to that order."[4]

The "revolt against the West" is in substance a revolt against the dominant world order. A comment by the prominent Tunisian professor Hisham Djaït, president of the Tunisian Committee for the Support of Iraq during the Gulf War, makes this point clear: "In . . . the Arab countries . . . the frontiers have been drawn by the colonizers. . . . In my opinion the moral justification for the annexation of Kuwait far outweighs, in this case, the rule of international law."[5]

To contest legally existing boundaries and thus to refute the principle of sovereignty and territoriality is to rebel against the West. Following Joseph

Nye's distinction between the challengers (states) and the challenges (structural and otherwise) facing the current power structure in world politics,[6] I propose to view the current "revolt against the West" as one of these new challenges, even though the revolt still lies in the stadium of public choices, not yet in the arena of state politics.

Non-Western, politicized religious fundamentalisms, of which the Islamic variety is "the most prolific,"[7] have become the vehicle for articulating this revolt against Western values. An international relations approach not restricted to the analysis of state actors and their policies would interpret the rise of fundamentalism as a sign of cultural fragmentation in international society. When fundamentalist outlooks manifested as public choices succeed in affecting policy choices, they precipitate a disquieting decline in the international consensus on norms and rules—and it is around those norms and rules that the interaction among states ought to be organized.

CULTURAL FRAGMENTATION AND
THE INTERNATIONAL DIFFUSION OF POWER

Political Islam, interpreted as a religious fundamentalism, is a factor of increasing importance in a world characterized by cultural fragmentation and a growing diffusion of power, on both domestic and international levels. On the international level the diffusion of power is indicated by the great powers' increasing inability to control their global environment. The arms race in the World of Islam demonstrates how easily "weak states" can gain access to modern mechanisms of power, even as they crumble internally.[8]

Ethnic strife and rapid, uncoordinated change are undermining the basis of the already structurally weak new states. And just as there is an international diffusion of power among states, the rapid pace of social change in the weak states is channeling power from the central state to private actors and to subnational groups such as ethnoreligious communities. In the World of Islam these private actors are primarily the fundamentalists, acting as "soldiers without portfolio" in reviving the pattern of "irregular war in the tradition of Islam."[9] *Jihad*, in the meaning of *qital*, that is, use of force by warriors, is an example of the "irregular war." The two Katyusha wars, in July 1993 and April 1996, carried out by Hizbullah against Israel in South Lebanon, are a case in point. As the two Katyusha wars reveal, the most sophisticated weaponry of the dominant states proves incapable of dealing with the challenge of irregular wars, and a single-minded preoccupation with the state can lead analysts to overlook the growing role of these private actors.

In the non-Western countries in general and the Islamic world in particular, we may speak of "strong societies and weak states" (see note 8). The strengthening of the Islamic fundamentalist underground groups as irregular warriors, for example in Algeria and Egypt, demonstrates this process. On both international and domestic levels, political Islam is a destabilizing factor in the diffusion of power, and as such contributes to weakening state order and provoking world disorder. Because of the spread of the modern technology of war, many Muslim states are strengthening internationally; but the same states are weakening domestically, owing to their conspicuous internal disintegration and the channeling of funds into arms purchases rather than into development projects. The growth of armed fundamentalist groups in this deteriorating situation can be overlooked only by negligent or myopic observers. In other words, the growth of military capabilities is manifested both by weak states and by irregular warriors.

Nye has observed "a general diffusion of power." He then qualifies the traditional instruments of power as "rarely sufficient to deal with the changing issues in world politics. New power resources, such as the capacity of effective communication and for developing and using multilateral institutions, may prove more relevant."[10] For this reason, Nye shifts the focus in the study of world politics to the need for more robust international institutions. These institutions require broadly accepted common rules and shared patterns if they are to communicate and adjudicate effectively. Do these criteria exist? Are they broadly shared?

To answer these pivotal questions properly we need to cast a retrospective glance at the prevailing world order. As the ideals of the French Revolution swept the continent, European sovereign states became nation-states based on popular sovereignty (see note 42). Now globalized, the nation-state is no longer an exclusively European institution. It is rather a global unit of action. Globalization and the concomitant extension of the originally European system of states to a global system create what has come to be called "world time."[11]

The new non-Western states are organized along the lines of the European nation-state, even though they lack the substance of sovereignty and are thus more or less nominally nation-states; in the Middle East, they are tribes with flags, and fundamentalism challenges this veneer of orthodoxy.

According to Bull, "[t]he idea of international society identifies the relationship between the states as that of members of a society bound by common rules and committed to common institutions."[12] The problem of the expanded international society is that the European norms and rules essential to international interaction are not shared by all civilizations. But in the Islamic civilization there is no idea of a state with clearly delineated boundaries, no concept of the political sovereignty of the state. To most Muslims, Saddam Hussein's violation of Kuwaiti sovereignty was not a violation of Islamic rules, for the boundaries involved were imposed by the West. Of course, the other depredations of Iraqi occupation troops in Kuwait were clear violations of Islamic rules as well as international rules.

During the formative periods of its history, the international system was identical with the system ordering the European society of states. But unlike the international *system* of states, which is based on formal interaction, a *society* of states "exists when a group of states, conscious of certain common interests and common values, form a society . . . bound by a common set of rules in their relations with one another. . . . An international society in this sense presupposes an international system, but an international system may exist that is not an international society."[13] In this understanding, the pre-World War I balance of power in Europe and the post-World War II system of bipolarity in the world were a mixture of "system" and "society," in the sense that they have marked the continuation of the dominance of the norms and rules established long ago by the European powers and their North American progeny. In the course of decolonization, new, non-Western states came into being and joined this international system. But the system itself did not change its character, even as it was becoming no longer an exclusively European society. The late Oxford law professor H. L. A. Hart showed clearly how European law in this process became a template for international law, through imposition: "It has never been doubted that when a new, independent state emerges into existence . . . it is bound by general obligations of international law. . . . Here the attempt to rest the new state's international obligations on a 'tacit' or 'inferred' consent seems wholly threadbare."[14] This very kind of consent is now being challenged by fundamentalism.

Because the globally extended European system has been so clearly based on Western norms and rules, it has been only in a limited sense an international society. For through expansion the system forfeited its original cultural homogeneity. Non-Western states, often described as quasi-states,[15] may formally subscribe to these "international" norms and values, yet these norms and values neither affect the outlooks of non-Western people nor determine their public choices.

Herein lies the root of the cultural fragmentation that currently besets world politics. When linked to the ongoing processes of diffusion of power on international and domestic levels, the fragmentation leads to disorder. Order in world politics, just as in international institutions, requires the acceptance of common norms and rules for international interaction. But cultural fragmentation may—and does—lead to the rejection of this general requirement and thus to the creation of disorder. If each civilization were uncompromisingly to claim the exclusivity and universality of its own norms and values, be they based on secular ideas, as they are in the West, or on religious ideas, as they are for Islamic fundamentalism, there could be no consensus on international morality. The result would be, inescapably, international disorder.

If it is true that our world, on the brink of the twenty-first century, is characterized by "a general diffusion of power" (Nye), then we may well wonder about the order (the norms and rules) that is defined by this changing situation, a situation in which the great powers are no longer able to control their international environment or to impose sanctions on deviant practices. We need think only about the recent domestic non-state wars, of which Bosnia, Afghanistan, Somalia, and Liberia are prominent cases. Because of the diffusion of power, the great powers lose much of their leverage over the more complex system, and the irregulars acquire a more significant standing. This has clearly been the case since the end of the Cold War. According to Bull, order is maintained primarily by the very existence of "rules which spell out the kind of behaviour that is orderly."[16] In our culturally diverse world it is becoming increasingly difficult to maintain global consent to international law as a source of common rules, since those rules stem from a civilization (the West) that is alien to most parts of the international community. Under these circumstances, the revitalization of particular non-European cultural rules—such as those of Islam—on the grounds of rejecting the globally dominant rules contributes to the politicization of the ongoing cultural fragmentation. The result is the raising of politically exclusive claims rather than the harmless, even perhaps fruitful, articulation and discussion of divergent cultural options.

The adherents of Islamic fundamentalism not only reject the existing world order, because it is based on Western norms and rules, they basically claim to replace it by an Islamic order based on Islamic rules. The leading authority on the ideological source of Islamic fundamentalism, Sayyid Qutb, blatantly declares that "the end of Western rule lies ahead" and hastens to add that "only Islam is eligible to assume the leadership of the world."[17] When Islamic fundamentalists address Islam's new role in world politics, this is exactly what they have in mind.

The greatest obstacle to maintaining order by multilateral institutions, as Nye points out, had already been observed by Bull: "There has been a decline in the consensus about common interests and values within the state system."[18] The spread of modern technology, communication, and transportation networks has led to a shrinking of the globe, bringing societies of different cultures and civilizations to an unprecedented degree of mutual awareness and interaction. But this shrinking of the globe, as Bull continues, "does not in itself create a unity of outlook and has not in fact done so."[19] Rather, the result of the globalization processes, as Zbigniew Brzezinski puts it, is a "simultaneously more unified and more fragmented humanity."[20] The structural mapping of the world is among the significant "consequences of modernity,"[21] but the other side of the coin is a culturally "fragmented humanity," with its implications for a decline in international consensus. This is the historical background of all non-Western varieties of religious fundamentalism.

ISLAMIC FUNDAMENTALISM AS THE EXPRESSION OF A REVOLT AGAINST THE WEST

The present world order came about as a product of European dominance. (In this interpretation, the United States is considered to be an appendage of Europe and its civilizing processes.) European hegemony has not always been merely economic and political in nature; it has also included the "cultural project of modernity" (which we dealt with in Chapter 4). The earlier revolt of non-Western peoples against the West, in the course of decolonization, drew its force from the adoption of such Western ideas as freedom, the "nation," popular sovereignty, and self-determination.[22] But the current revolt against the West, as the Muslim and Hindu cases plainly demonstrate, no longer leans on European values, and today's fundamentalist movements are drawing upon homegrown values to ward off the West. As Bull notes, "the reassertion by . . . non-Western peoples of their traditional and indigenous cultures, as exemplified in Islamic fundamentalism . . . is . . . a revolt against Western values as such."[23] This development marks not only a challenge to the existing legal order but also a "deep division between the Western powers and Third World states about a wide range of normative issues."[24]

On both national and regional levels, Muslim fundamentalists challenge the nation-state as a non-Muslim, European institution imposed on them, and they see pan-Arab nationalism as another Western plot against Islam.[25] The acclaimed alternative is the *nizam Islami* / Islamic order, and the call for an Islamic government is seen as a step underpinning Islam's claim to supremacy in international relations.[26] Religious fundamentalism in its Islamic guise is a sign of cultural fragmentation in world politics, inasmuch as it seeks to establish new norms and rules on exclusively Islamic grounds. In being a universalism, political Islam envisages the validity of these new norms and rules for the entire world. As a first step, fundamentalists plead for the decoupling, or de-Westernizing, of Muslims from "international society" (Bull, see note 13), but in the long run the Islamic domestic order is to be the international order. As mentioned earlier, the Egyptian Sayyid Qutb contended that "only Islam" is capable of overtaking the lead from the "sick West" and therefore called for a "*jihad* world revolution."[27] Another authority on Islamic fundamentalism, the late Pakistani Abu al-A'la al-Mawdudi, held that only Islam "is eligible to overtake the lead of the modern age."[28]

Such radical and all-encompassing normative dissent not only diminishes international consensus but also affects ways of communicating and negotiating the existing differences. The spread of communication technology brought culturally different peoples to an unprecedented degree of mutual awareness and interaction, but this technical closeness is greatly overshadowed by the radically different outlooks of the same peoples. Communication is not simply words and technology but, foremost, *discourse*. If free discourse is not honored, then there can be no effective communication. Likewise, the work of international institutions cannot succeed if no mutually accepted grounds for discourse exist on which to base international interaction. Without a common discourse, international institutions would be reduced to a dialogue of the deaf. A pertinent illustration of such a pattern of "communication" is the "dialogue" between countries of non-Western civilizations and Western (as well as some newly democratized Eastern) states on the occasion of the United Nations Conference on Human Rights held in Vienna in June 1993. Western representatives addressed the issue of the increasing violations of individual human rights in most of the Islamic

and other formerly "Third World" countries. The response was an accusa-
tion of "cultural imperialism." I was in Vienna during that conference and
have reason to believe that the conflict over the universality of individual
human rights is in fact an example of the "clash of civilizations."[29]

Given that individual human rights are based on the "principle of subjectivity" that "determines the forms of modern culture,"[30] to quote Habermas, it becomes clear that the conflict they so easily provoke revolves around
the universality of the morality espoused by cultural modernity. That
morality constitutes much of the substance of the European project of cultural modernity. In Islam there is no cultural understanding of individua-
tion, and thus no concept of individual rights. In Islam the individual is conceived to be no more than a part of a collective, be it the universal Islamic
umma / community or any of the other collectivities opposed to it (the enemies of Islam). In Vienna, an anti-Western coalition of non-Western civilizations, including the Islamic one, was formed to oppose the elevation of
individual human rights to a basis of international morality.[31] From an ethical point of view, however, there can be no compromise on the universal
validity of individual human rights in international relations[32]—despite all
cultural and civilizational differences.

The European philosopher who so long ago laid the foundation for the
modern worldview, and whose name has become synonymous with modern discourse, René Descartes (he of Cartesianism), insisted on calling his
major piece of work a "discourse" rather than a "treatise." To him, discourse
was something debatable: "I do not have the inclination to teach, but to communicate."[33] If discourse in this sense were to be accepted worldwide, the
adherents of diverse outlooks could communicate rationally about the differences that separate them from one another. But fundamentalism, being
a neo-absolutism, is contrary to Cartesian discourse, for if religious fundamentalism (Islamic or otherwise) becomes the ground on which arguments
are set forth, then there can *be* no substantive communication between divergent civilizations. Islamic fundamentalists, for example, do not offer a
culturally varying vision for world politics to debate. Rather, they claim to
have an immutable, absolute, divine message they must deliver to and—if
situations permit—impose on all of humanity. The Islamic law, the *shari'a*,
is the content of this message, for all of humanity. As the Muslim fundamentalist Sabir Tu'ayma puts it, the Islamic *shari'a* is the grand design not
only for Muslims but for mankind as a whole: "Islamic rules are not
restricted to Muslims and to their societies. They are designed to organize

all human relations and thus are assigned for the entire humanity, be it Islamic or not yet Islamized, be it in peace or in a state of war; for Islamic rules create an international law."[34] In the preceding chapter I showed how Islamic fundamentalists confuse *shari'a*, which is divine, with *fiqh* (jurisprudence), which is human, to render to their political views a divine character.

Unlike the Cartesian worldview, this Islamic worldview is not debatable, because it is based on scripture (the Qur'an) that is considered to be absolute and divine. It becomes clear, then, that for Muslim fundamentalists there can be no other platform for international interaction and communication than their own religious belief, established as a political formula. The effects of the fundamentalists' collective choices on policy options are therefore significant for the decline in international consensus. Furthermore, these choices could have an impact on decision-making procedures, which are "practices for making and implementing collective choices," as we know from the debate on "international regimes."[35]

The policy options of current Islamic fundamentalists who are not yet in power, in particular "restoring the global rule of Islam,"[36] are gradually and conspicuously becoming the expression of collective choices in the World of Islam. As early as the writings of the nineteenth-century Islamic revivalist Afghani we encounter allusions to the notion of *"raf' rayat al-sulta/*supremacy" and *"ghalab/*dominance" as the basic features of Islam.[37] The editor of Afghani's works, the American Nikki Keddie, points out that many topical themes of the contemporary revival of political Islam go back to Afghani because of "his stress on Islam as a force to ward off the West and to strengthen Muslim peoples through unity."[38] The unity of concern here is the unity of Muslims as a civilization opposed to the civilization of the West. Seen from this perspective, modernization becomes not a goal of development but rather an instrument by which to reverse the balance of world power to the benefit of Islam. A contemporary Muslim fundamentalist, Hasan al-Sharqawi, argues along similar lines, in stating plainly, "[w]hen Kemal Atatürk called [on Muslims] to emulate the West he had nothing [more] in his mind than to be in line with the West. . . . This is not our intention. Our goal is to learn how to use modern arms and, more than this, how to produce them and further develop them in order to [defeat] our enemies."[39] These remarks make clear the implications of the worldview of Islamic fundamentalists[40] and also the link between the diffusion of power and the growth of cultural fragmentation. The statement sheds light on the consequences of these processes, as well. Joseph Nye relates the diffusion of power to the spread of technology, which enhances the military capabilities of non-Western states. The politicization of cultural fragmentation, then, not only contributes to a further decline in international consensus; if linked to the diffusion of military technology, it becomes, foremost, a source of disorder and confrontation in the existing global power structure.

THE POLITICAL CLAIMS OF RELIGIOUS OPTIONS IN A SECULAR WORLD ORDER

Politically, the Peace of Westphalia in 1648 marked the beginning of the decay of the ancient divine order and the emergence of the modern international system of states.[41] The cultural framework for this system has been the project of modernity, which meant the cultural dismantling of the "world of the divine" (Habermas; see note 30). The basic historical events in this unfolding were the Renaissance, the Reformation, the Enlightenment, and the French and American revolutions. At its outset, this shift from the divine to the secular was restricted to Europe, but in the aftermath of the French Revolution popular sovereignty emerged as the legitimating device of *all* states participating in the modern international system, which, as we have seen, was identical with the system of the European society of states. The path of development was from sovereign state to nation-state. In the three hundred years following the Peace of Westphalia, Europeans imposed this system of states, each unit enjoying internal and external sovereignty, on the rest of the world. In "the mapping of the globe into that system,"[42] the World of Islam was no exception.

In our age, Muslim fundamentalists (and many others in the Arab world) discern these events as the birth of the international, Western-dominated order that continues to prevail at the expense of Islam. In this, they are right. But they insist (as they do in most other issues) that Islam was the first civilization to create a set of norms and rules for international interaction.[43] They infer from this contention that it has been Western dominance in the modern age that has deprived Islam of its rightful place of precedence in determining the basis for international order. Qutb blames Muslims themselves for having allowed the West to push Islam into the margins of the international system, where it has little influence in determining the framework of world politics. Because the ascendancy of the West has been based (in the view of Muslims) on technology-based military superiority,[44]

Muslim fundamentalists—who are, as we have seen, by no means traditionalists but truly bizarre modernists—aspire to an "Islamization of modern technology."[45] The diffusion of power in terms of the spread of technology thus constitutes a crucial issue on the fundamentalist agenda. Although
Muslim fundamentalists are quite prepared to adopt Western technology
while claiming to Islamize it, they envisage a "de-Westernization of knowledge"[46] in order to free themselves from—what they perceive as—the "epis-
temological imperialism of the West."[47] This means of course that they want
simultaneously to acquire Western technology and to reject the Cartesian
rational worldview that fostered it. Nor do they want to adopt the *philosophical* discourse of modernity. For them only "the holy Qur'an is the complete and final revelation . . . and there is no other knowledge—except [that]
based upon it and pointing to it—that can guide and save man."[48]

The effort to understand Islamic fundamentalism and to place it in a
broader context might be further facilitated by a brief review of some basic
historical events. The breakdown of the decaying Ottoman Empire[49] in
World War I marked the end of the long epoch of divine universal orders in
the world. Following the abolition of the Muslim order of the caliphate in
1924, the Arabs adopted the Western idea of the nation for pursuing political action, but they were reluctant to restrict it to any of the existing nation-states whose boundaries had been drawn by the Western powers. The
Arab dream of a vast pan-Arab state within the framework of the existing
international order of nation-states for a time superseded the universalist
dream of the unity of all Muslims, Arab and otherwise, in a universal Islamic caliphate. At the same time, however, pan-Arab nationalism has not
been simply an *idea*, as is the Islamic concept of *umma*. Rather, the option
of a pan-Arab nation is related to a real-world structure, the modern international system of nation-states. Arab nationalists have all along acknowledged the new order; their minds have been imprisoned by the European
idea of the "nation-state" for the simple reason that they have aspired to
the larger goal of an overarching Arab nation-state, a construct at odds with
the universal claim of Islam.[50]

The idea of an Arab nation antagonized the political consciousness of Islam for two reasons: first, because it excluded all non-Arab Muslims from
this entity, and second, because it included Arab Christians—and prior to
the creation of Israel also Arab Jews—as citizens. For the purposes of Arab
nationalism Arab Christians and Jews were no longer viewed as *dhimmi* (a

protected religious minority), but as full members of the Arab *umma*. The then influential writings of Sati' al-Husri,[51] the intellectual father of secular pan-Arabism, are a literary manifestation of that period, which began in the early 1920s and lasted until the late 1960s. The exiled Iraqi Samir al-Khalil (alias Kanan Makiya) has shown that al-Husri's Arabism greatly affected Saddam Hussein's "Republic of Fear."[52] But Saddam's rather pragmatic resort to Islamic fundamentalism during the Gulf War did not reverse this quasi-religious belief in Arabism. It aimed, rather, at combining Arabism with an idiosyncratic understanding of Islamic fundamentalism. For this reason, Shi'i Iranians make no secret of their disdain for Saddam's peculiar ideological amalgam. (They have, of course, their own amalgam.)

The turning point, however, was the Six-Day War of 1967, because it humiliated the secular Arab regimes and contributed powerfully to their delegitimization.[53] The years since have been a period of intensifying crisis that has spawned the current varieties of Sunni Arab fundamentalism. At the outset of the post-1967 period, many Arab writers hoped that the defeat would have its positive side, in the sense that the Arabs would stop living in a world of poetry and illusory dreams and start confronting the reality that stands beyond the deceptions of wishful thinking. The years 1967–70 witnessed a process of anguished self-criticism, in which I participated.[54] This hopeful period was, however, short-lived, for in the early 1970s the voices of millenarian dreams, often called the "voices of resurgent Islam,"[55] began drowning out the voices of reason and self-examination. Most significantly, the dream of a pan-Arab nation-state taking its rightful place in the world order came to an end.[56] That idea has been superseded in the political literature by the revival of the classical division of the world into the *dar al-Islam*/abode of Islam and the *dar al-harb*/abode of the unbelievers. In the language of political Islam, the terms coined for a contemporary description of this distinction are *al-sharq al-Islami*/the Islamic orient[57] and *al-gharb al-isti'mari*/the imperialist West. The revival of political Islam is directed against the "conspiracy of Westernization of the Islamic world,"[58] and the secular nation-state is taken to be the contemporary outcome of this *mu'amarah*/conspiracy.

In the course of the post-1967 developments, secular pan-Arab nationalism has thus given way to political Islam. Even Saddam Hussein, who waged war against the export of Khomeinism's Islamic Revolution from Iran to the neighboring Arab countries, and for this reason was seen as the last survivor of secular pan-Arabism, later made his own way to fundamentalism. During the Gulf War the Islamic fundamentalists cheered him as their hero, and, though he lost the war, he left a seemingly lasting legacy.

By taking the political literature published in Arabic as the appropriate window for viewing current issues and values, we can avoid the typical Western habit—one may call it orientalism—of talking about people without knowing much about them. It should come as no surprise that the concerns of political Islam dominate this literature. One of the politically pioneering ideological works of Islamic fundamentalism of the 1970s—not generally known in the West—is that by the leading Egyptian Muslim Brother Yusuf al-Qaradawi. In a wide-ranging, influential, three-volume work, he declares *al-hall al-Islami farida wa darura*/the Islamic solution is an obligation and a necessity. In Qaradawi's view, the return to the true "Islamic solution"—as he heralds it in his first volume—requires a virtual dismantling of *al-hulul al-mustawrada*/imported solutions, such as liberalism, secular nationalism, and socialism. In the third volume of this work, published in 1988, he wages war against "Westernized and secular Muslims."[59] This is the core of the argument that has been articulated in the new language of politicized Islam: a repoliticization, not the alleged "return of Islam." When pan-Arab ideology prevailed, Islam was equally a faith and a cultural system, but not a political ideology. In those years Islam receded as a political ideology but flourished as a religious belief. Today, in the shape of fundamentalism, Islam is returning politically.[60]

One could counter by observing that Islam has *always* been political, even after the abolition of the caliphate in 1924. The birth of the Muslim Brotherhood movement in Egypt in 1928 and the emergence of *Wahhabi*-inspired Saudi Arabia could be cited as evidence against the argument of a retreat of political Islam since the 1920s. One might also recall that Islam was engaged in the struggle against French colonial rule in Algeria and Morocco. But these historical references notwithstanding, one cannot escape the observation that secular ideologies, primarily pan-Arab nationalism, emerged in the post-World War I period as the dominant political discourse, whereas Islam as a political ideology (though not as a religious belief) seems to have receded until well into the 1970s.[61] This is not to say that political dreams related to an imagined "Islamic system of government" vanished during that period. Nevertheless, political ideologies based on the idea of a secular nation exclusively uniting all Arabs, regardless of their religion, replaced the Islamic understanding of the universal *umma*, which includes all Muslims. According to Qur'anic teachings, the Arabs specifically stand at the center of the Islamic *umma*. A leading Islamic legal scholar of that period, Muhammad al-Mubarak, drew a clear political distinction between *al-umma al-'Arabiyya*/the Arab nation, uniting on an equal footing both Muslim and Christian Arabs, and *al-umma al-Islamiyya*/the Islamic community, which refers loosely to solidarity among Muslims but lacks any decisive political consequences.[62]

In Arabic there exists no particular term for the secular meaning of *la nation*, such as evolved in the context of the French Revolution. In classical Arabic, during the formative years of Islam, there was a sharp distinction between a *qawm*, the particular tribe to which an Arab belonged, and the *umma*, the supreme frame of reference for all Muslims.[63] In modern times, *la nation* has been translated into Arabic by the very term *umma*, thus woefully confusing the religious meaning of the universal political community established by the Prophet Muhammad in the seventh century with the secular meaning of the nation as a delimited community that unfolded in Europe in the eighteenth century. Since, in linguistic terms, one cannot develop an *ism/iyya* from *umma*, in the meaning of nation, Arabs coined the neo-Arabic term *qawmiyya* for secular nationalism. *Qawm* in the Qur'an means, however, tribe, not nation. That there is confusion is clear! The Muslim fundamentalists want to reverse these developments by returning to primeval Islam, which in their view is not only a religious belief but, foremost, a political order and also—since it addresses all of humanity—a world order. They despise *qawmiyya*/secular nationalism as a heretical return to the pre-Islamic notion of *qawm*/tribe, a kind of neo-tribalism and an affront to the achievements of Islam.

In interpreting Islam as a cultural system[64] I want to posit the hypothesis that Islam has always been the cultural basis of the respective worldviews of generations of Muslims, even of those pan-Arab secularists. In the Middle East, as well as in other parts of the World of Islam, there has never been a process of structural change underlying a substantive shift in worldview from a religious one to a secular one, as *did* occur in the historical process that took place in Europe. Given the continuity and dominance of the Muslims' worldview, there has never been a genuine process of secularization in the Middle East underlain by secular ideologies. The ideology of secularism is one thing; the realities of secularization are another. Even in Turkey and in the Tunisia of Bourguiba (that is, in the only two Middle Eastern states to date claiming to be secular), society cannot be characterized as secular in the substantive sociological meaning of the term. For this reason, I have referred to the various nation-states in the Islamic world as nominal nation-states, that is, as entities not yet structurally undergirded and not genuinely secular. In most of the World of Islam there has been no structural secularization in the sense of social transformation of society, but rather a stratified normative secularization emerging from the embracing of secular ideologies by Western-educated elites. This sort of normative secularization lacks the structural underpinning needed if it is to be rooted in society.[65]

On the basis of these observations, we can argue that the continuity of the Islamic worldview has facilitated the shift from thinly overlain secular ideologies to the more aggressive ideologies of political Islam in the course of the 1970s and 1980s. Considering Islam's function as a cultural system underlying an integral worldview, no serious observer of the historical development of the modern Middle East can help seeing that secular ideologies were unable to set down structural roots, and have never contributed to replacing the Islamic worldview. The worldview of most Muslims is, rather, based on a separation of the world into "*gharb* / the West" and "the abode of Islam." There are of course vast non-Islamic areas in Asia (for example, China and Japan) that do not fit into this dichotomous geography of the world that reduces the globe to Islamic East and non-Islamic West. Muslim fundamentalists argue that the West has intruded upon the World of Islam (i.e., the rest of the world) and fostered its deviation from Islamic virtues. The major concern of Muslims should ultimately be to reverse this drift by returning to Islam and warding off the "intellectual invasion of the Islamic world by the West."[66] The inevitable implications of the Muslim fundamentalist program are (1) a flat rejection of the globally valid, however only superficially shared norms and rules of the contemporary world order and (2) the establishment of a world order determined and dominated by Islam. The rhetoric of these principles received a new infusion during the Gulf War, an infusion that was repeated with the Islamic dimension of the war in Bosnia.[67]

It has become obvious, then, that the study of how contemporary Muslim fundamentalists perceive the world is important for an analysis of the changing world order. The study of their perceptions and policy preferences is important for understanding their efforts to mobilize nonfundamentalist Muslims for their fundamentalist goals. Not all of the outspoken adherents of political Islam wish, however, to see the caliphate, the classical political system of Islam, reborn. The focus of most Muslim fundamentalists is not on restoring the caliphate[68] but on establishing "the Islamic system of government." Islamic fundamentalists view the effort to build this system as the first step in their plan to remake the world along Islamic lines.

THE ISLAMIC STATE AS THE NUCLEUS OF AN ISLAMIC WORLD ORDER

In a way, the political ideology of Islamic fundamentalism reflects continuity with the classical tradition of Islamic orthodox thought, in which politics is not a discipline in its own right. As *fiqh* scholars, Islamic jurists inseparably linked politics with the *shari'a*/Islamic law. Islamic *fiqh*/ jurisprudence is the human interpretation of divine *shari'a* (see Chapter 4). In this tradition the political ideas of Islamic fundamentalism are convictional in their attitude and selectively scriptural in their orientation. Enlightened reasoning and, above all, a rational political discourse—both of them established in medieval Islamic rationalism— are missing in contemporary Islamic fundamentalist thought. The merest glimpse of the fundamentalists' pamphleteering reveals that it neither provides a political analysis of the current state of affairs nor offers serious ways for dealing with the ongoing crisis it helps to sustain.

The notion of *al-nizam al-Islami*/Islamic order, which is presented as a solution for all problems, is more or less a conviction lying beyond evidence. Those who share it are true Muslims, and those who question it or, worse, doubt it are deviates from the Islamic *umma*—and therefore should be killed, as is happening today in Algeria, Egypt, Afghanistan, and Turkey. Because Islamic symbols are filled with different patterns of meaning, it is not surprising to find that among fundamentalists there exists no clear consensus on how to determine the substance of the posited concept of order. Islamic fundamentalists of various currents insist on the righteousness of their own views and deny this to their fellow Muslims—other fundamentalists included. Their ideological weapon is the *takfir* (to declare someone a "*kafir*/unbeliever"), which legitimizes the use of violence against their foes.

The scriptural references invoked by fundamentalists are both arbitrary and selective. They quote Islamic scripture to defend or disprove any specific interpretation of the notion of an Islamic system of government. Neither history, nor existing political structures, nor real institutions can serve as sources of argument in any dispute, for if their reality does not accord with the precepts alluded to by fundamentalist authorities, then the authorities simply accuse their foes of deviation from true Islam and consequently threaten their lives.

These cultural attitudes allow no room for rational discourse as a framework for the substantive communication needed in multilateral international institutions. To be sure, dialogue between Islamic civilization and the West is an instrument of peaceful conflict resolution. Liberal Muslims, but not fundamentalists, are a party of peaceful dialogue. Fundamentalists, however, can be viewed as rejectionists not only of any secular world order but even of the need for cross-cultural international institutions constructed for peaceful conflict resolution. International and interdenominational communication for a better understanding between divergent civilizations, for example the West and Islam, is a construct alien to fundamentalists of any religion. In our review of the political ideology of Islamic fundamentalism we find no notion of the plurality of humanity. Instead, we encounter an interpretation of Islam that makes exclusive claim to universal validity, a claim not confined to beliefs but extended, as well, to the notions of order and political leadership.

Islamic fundamentalists are not tolerant toward fellow Muslims who do not share their doctrines. They view liberal Muslims who regard their religion as an ethical basis for daily life rather than a political commitment to a system of government to have been "misguided" by non-Muslim, that is, Western, values. In the view of the Muslim fundamentalists Jarisha and Zaibaq, "[t]he major task of the Qur'an is to govern . . . [and] the correspondence of state and religion is the crucial part of this understanding, not such that religion is a partial dimension of the state, but on the contrary, such that religion is the major element of the state."[69] Speaking from a wholly different mindset, the late sheikh of al-Azhar, Jadulhaq, told me in an interview (September 28, 1989) that our Qur'an is a *kitab hidaya*, that is, a book of ethical orientation and guidance, not a political handbook or an encyclopedia of sciences.

As Jarisha and Zaibaq put it, a "colonial Western conspiracy" directed at Islam has culminated in an expression of Arab nationalism and in the destruction of the Muslim order of the caliphate. As part of this perceived "conspiracy"[70] they dismiss secular nationalism as a product of "missionizing crusaders." Islamic fundamentalists indict the "nation-state" as a Western institution imposed on the World of Islam by the "Western crusaders." Arab nationalists are believed to have been employed as "tools" in this Western conspiracy.[71] Clearly, Islamic fundamentalists always resort to a perception of the world as conspiracy-driven so that they might ward off what they view as alien to Islam—and so that they might attract more allies in the struggle against the common foe.

Inasmuch as the world order of our age is based on interaction among secular nation-states, it denotes, in the view of Muslim fundamentalists, a "return to the *jahiliyya*," that is, to the pre-Islamic "age of heedlessness." The return to a political Islam through the *sahwa al-Islamiyya* / the Islamic awakening opposes this tendency. The call for *al-nizam al-Islami*, the major feature of this awakening, revolves around three issues: (1) Islamic legitimacy, (2) the political interpretation of the Islamic *umma* that underpins this legitimacy, and (3) the political power necessary for advancing these concerns.

Previously, I made reference to the fact that contemporary fundamentalists no longer refer to the classical caliphate as the political system of choice. Their focus today is on the formula of Islamic legitimacy. The governance of the Islamic *umma* / community by *shari'a* / Islamic law is stipulated as a major criterion. *Umma*, however, is a community, not a state. In a major fundamentalist pamphlet we read, "[I]f political rule, first, is based on the *shari'a* of God and, second, is accepted by the Muslims, then the form matters little. We may name it caliphate, imamate, or emirate, or we may refer to whatever names [one might choose], so long as the aforementioned requirements are fulfilled. If, however, these requirements are missing, then ·no political authority can claim to have legitimacy."[72]

As we have seen from this passage, the political goal of fundamentalism is the establishment of a political system based on the *shari'a* or, more precisely, on its understanding by the currently dominant fundamentalist groups. Most of the fundamentalist agitators resort to the neo-Islamic and neo-Arabic term *al-nizam al-Islami* and plead for the absolute imposition of the Islamic *shari'a* as the incontestable frame for resolving all issues, to be applied in all times, in all places, and for all peoples. "If the *shari'a* is established in this sense and if the Islamic Law is practiced under the aforementioned conditions [that is, unlimited absolute validity], then it follows that there is an Islamic system."[73] In the view of Muslim fundamentalists, "secularization is an assault on Islam." Secular developments as by-products of social change become associated with every evil of the Satan, which is, in their perception, Western civilization.

To be sure, there are Muslims who consider Islam an ethical and a personal way of life but not a system of government based on a collective choice of political order. Needless to say, these Muslims are not fundamentalists, and their numbers are substantial. It is sad to see, however, that the mainstream of contemporary political Islam adheres to the ideological concept of *nizam Islami*. And on the general level there is no dispute among Islamic fundamentalists, particularly with regard to the basic formula defining Islam as a *din wa dawla*, that is, a unity of religion and state. In this sense we are justified in taking the words of the Tunisian writer Mahmud 'Abdulmawla to be representative of the views of Muslim fundamentalists: "Islam is a political system inasmuch as it is a religious one."[74] 'Abdulmawla has, however, but little to tell us about spelling out the nature of this avowed political system.

In the authoritative writings of Islamic fundamentalism we encounter the contention that Islam provided the first authentic legal political system in the history of mankind.[75] This view is supported by reference to the binding character of Islamic law, which leads to establishing a political system based on legitimacy rather than coercion. The Islamic system of government thus claims to subordinate both the process of governing and the political behavior of the rulers to the *shari'a*. The truth is that this argument is a modern projection into the ancient history of Islam. Max Weber's well-known typology of government outlines three patterns of rule: the traditional, the charismatic, and, in modern times, the legal. Islamic fundamentalists contend that legal rule has always been the authentic Islamic system of government, perhaps unaware that they are simply recasting a historical system by projecting modern elements into it. Islamic fundamentalists fail to acknowledge the fact that past Islamic rulers were in every case of either the charismatic or the traditional type, but never of the legal type in the modern, Weberian sense. For them, all that matters is the scripture—*sola scriptura*—not history itself. The scripture prescribes that the ruler be a *"sultan 'adil/*just ruler." The historical realities refer mostly to the pattern of *"sultan ja'r/*unjust ruler."

There have been different ways of dealing with Islamic history.[76] "The correct scientific method," the fundamentalist al-'Awwa tells us, "obliges us to agree upon the principle that we have to judge the people on the basis of their adherence to Islamic precepts and not the other way around: we should not judge Islam in terms of the behavior of Muslims, be they rulers or the ruled."[77] Such an argument leaves no room for the study of history, and historical discourse is utterly eliminated. The belief in the authority of the text replaces the need for employing the discourse of reasoning. To be sure, reasoning is involved in interpretation if the interpreted text is seen in its historical context. This is, however, not the method employed by the fundamentalists quoted. The result: Islam is seen to be immutable, regardless of history, time, culture, location, or circumstance. Muslims may change, but Islam will not, and only the Muslims are to be blamed for their deviation. Even the notion that the pattern of modern systems of government is one to which Islam could be adjusted is dismissed. As a Muslim I do share the belief that the five religious *"arkan/pillars"* of Islam are above time and space. At issue, however, is the historicity of Islamic civilization itself. Here lies the dividing line.

Islamic fundamentalists warn of the confusion between pure Islamic principles and modern political experiences, Western and Eastern alike. But they confuse their political principles with religious beliefs and present these principles without relating them to the reality they are living in. In other words, the contention of Islamic government does not go beyond a declaration of principles. We are therefore compelled to ask, what *is* the Islamic form of government? The fundamentalist answer is simple: "The call for an Islamic government in our age on the basis of a commitment to Islam is supported by millions of Muslims all over the world. This call simply means that the institutions of the government must be built up in accord with the political values of Islam. . . . As regards the details concerning the implementation of these values we must state that the Islamic *umma* has to decide upon this in each case."[78] The only condition that modern Islamic fundamentalists attach to the scope of actions of the Islamic *umma* is that legislation must be in keeping with the *shari'a*. Given the lack of division of power in Islamic doctrine, we may ask: who supervises the obedience of the ruler to the *shari'a?*

In the view of many Sunni Arab fundamentalists, the late Iranian leader Khomeini contributed substantially to closing the gap between Sunni and Shi'i Muslims. As they argue, it is now simply the turn of the Sunni Muslims to understand the writings of Khomeini properly and to act accordingly. If those who call for the unity of the Islamic *umma* succeed in understanding the message of Khomeini, and if they make full political use of his ideas, "the sons of the two great Islamic groups [*firqatayn*], the Sunna and the Shi'a, will come closer together."[79] Aside from the political content of this statement, in our age of equality between women and men as a human right, another comes to mind: and what about the "daughters"?

The views I have dealt with here represent the mainstream of contemporary political Islam. Their most concrete content is the idea that this system is legal, inasmuch as it derives its legitimacy (*shar'iyya*) from Islamic law (*shari'a*), "the only acceptable legal system on earth." The implication is that the Islamic *shari'a* is to be implemented as the basis of Islamic government. In other words, Muslim fundamentalists accept only Islamic legal norms, claim the validity of these norms for all of humanity, and dismiss all other norms and frameworks. This effort to de-Westernize legal standards is nothing but an expression of a "clash of civilizations."[80] The question that comes to mind here is whether the challenge of Islamic fundamentalists to the present world order, a challenge aimed at replacing secularity by a divine order, can be meaningful at all!

THE ISLAMIST CHALLENGE: A DIVINE GLOBAL ORDER AS AN ALTERNATIVE TO GLOBAL SECULARIZATION?

Who is challenging whom? Western secular modernity has been a challenge to Islamic civilization for centuries, but the Islamic fundamentalists, of more recent vintage, now seek to turn the tables on the West. The dichotomy between secular and divine foundations of political order is certainly at the center of concern for most Islamic fundamentalists. But aside from the rhetoric of that dichotomy, a closer look clearly reveals that the revival of political Islam is not a concern of divinities, but is, rather, related more to social, political, and economic matters than to religious issues. In the Arab Middle East, the current varieties of Islamic fundamentalism are outgrowths of a double crisis, one brought on by deteriorating socioeconomic conditions, the other by the process of state de-legitimization triggered by the crushing defeat in the Six-Day War. But the crisis is also a crisis of the moral order in Islamic civilization itself in a rational-secular and techno-scientific age.[81] In acknowledging the structural constraints underlying the rise of religious fundamentalism, I do not subscribe to whatever reductionist approach comes along, that is, to reducing the moral crisis simply to a socioeconomic and political crisis. There is an interplay between the two, and the symbolism of politicized religion needs to be studied in its own terms. To fail to understand this is equivalent to failing to understand the quest for an Islamic world order. I am reluctant to view either as simply a matter of rhetoric.

As I have argued, the revival of political Islam got under way in the Arab part of the Middle East in the early 1970s, long before the Iranian Revolution broke out. At a time when Khomeini's name and writings were, with rare exceptions, completely unknown in the Arab Middle East, the idea of unity of religion and politics (*din wa dawla*) was already being disseminated. Nevertheless, the revolution in Iran contributed, if only in its early stage, to an intensification of the ongoing crisis of legitimacy and to the concomitant strengthening of political Islam. Above all, it has been an important source of spillover effects for successful political upheaval in the neighboring countries.[82] The Iran-Iraq War of 1980 to 1988 and the turmoil of the Iranian Revolutionary Guards in the holy Islamic shrines in Mecca in 1987 greatly discredited the Iranian Revolution, and ever since then this revolution has been unable to serve as a model for political action. With respect to the claim by Islamic fundamentalists of a global Islamic order, the impact of Khomeinism is limited, and can in no way be compared with the legacy of the Gulf War of 1991.

One of the main features of the revival of political Islam is the redefining of Islamic values as political doctrines in the campaign to establish an Islamic order, on both domestic and international levels. This "redefining" clearly predates the Gulf War, but it was that war that gave this process its global framework. In fact, however, debates on these issues have never ceased in the Arab Middle East, even during the period of dominance of secular ideologies. During the 1950s and 1960s, quite influential works were published by Muhammad Dia'uddin al-Rayes, Muhammad Yusuf Musa, and 'Abdulhamid Mutawalli, among others (see note 41 to Chapter 7). Basically, these early fundamentalist writings contributed to the revival of the Islamic claim to an Islamic political order, but in terms of readership and popularity they could in no way compete with the then prevailing secular positions, such as those espoused in Khalid Muhammad Khalid's most famous work *Min huna nabda'* / Here We Start.

This book by Khalid, which was reprinted ten times between 1950 and 1963 and reached far beyond Egypt's boundaries, was the ideological hallmark of the time during which secular-liberal views dominated. Khalid's argument against what he called "*kahana Islamiyya*" (Islamic theocracy) culminates in the following clear commitment: "We should keep in mind that the religion ought to be as God wanted it to be: prophecy, not kingdom; guidance, not government; and preaching, not political rule. The best we can do to keep religion clean and pure is to separate it from politics and to place it above [politics]. The separation between religion and the state contributes to keeping religion [free of] the shortcomings of the state and . . . its arbitrariness."[83]

It must be quite amazing to some Western readers to learn that this very Khalid in the late 1980s joined the active Islamic fundamentalists. In a book published in 1989, Khalid *renounced all of his earlier positions*. In his late years (he died in March 1996) he was convinced that Islam is *din wa dawla*, unity of religion and the state, and called for declaring the message of the Prophet Muhammad the basis for an "Islamic world government" encompassing and uniting all humanity.[84] This about-face supports my view of the character of the secularization espoused by Muslim elites: it has been simply normative, lacking in structural underpinning; and it can be reversed as may be convenient, as the case of Khalid demonstrates.

Since the early 1970s, strongly worded pleas for a divine political order, for example that of the Egyptian Muslim Brother Yusuf al-Qaradawi quoted earlier, have begun to replace the secular outlooks of the liberal and nationalist Arab Muslim elites. To argue in favor of secular views has become the exclusive province of Arab Christians in their struggle for human rights, as we find in the work of the prominent Lebanese writer Joseph Mughaizil.[85] Only a handful of Muslim authors, myself included, still argue, in a few writings published in Arabic, for a disentanglement of religion from politics.[86]

With few exceptions, a closer look at the writings of Arab secularists and anti-secularists reveals a common flaw. Both groups fail to distinguish between secularism (*'ilmaniyya*) as an ideology and secularization (*'alamana*) as a social process. Thus they restrict the *linguistic* meaning of "secularization" to the institution of secular legislation, and never use the term to denote the process of functional differentiation of the elements of society that determines religion as a part of a social system. The *sociological* meaning of secularization sees religion as an institution disentangled from the societal system (see note 65).

The fundamentalists' indictments of the existing domestic order and international order are articulated in anti-secular language, and political issues are addressed with religious formulae. In this context Islamic fundamentalists use the crisis of modernity in the West to support their argument that Islam should take the lead in the world. In discussions I have had with Islamic fundamentalists I have at times been quite amazed to see them cite the postmodernist and cultural-relativist approaches posited in the West itself to sustain their conviction that modernity is on the verge of decay, and to support their neo-absolutist program. For in claiming the absolute authority of their political beliefs, these fundamentalists have nothing in common with postmodernism or cultural relativism.

A book published in 1979 illustrates the way Muslim fundamentalists perceive the crisis of modernity. The author, himself a fundamentalist, views the history of Europe as a succession of secular social movements set in motion by the French Revolution. In his view these movements failed in the past and continue to fail in the present. These predictable outcomes are what he calls *ma'sat al-'ilmaniyya* / the tragedy of secularism.[87] One of the peculiar examples he presents in support of this assessment is that the problems of contemporary New York City, the epitome of *al-day'a* / alienation, exemplify the "tragedy of secularism" and the ongoing crisis of modernity. Muslim fundamentalists infer from the example that only Islam, as they envisage it, can rescue humanity—including the benighted people of New York—from this "tragic" situation: "In seeking a way out, we find that there exists only one pattern of order [*nizam*] to which the thinkers of the West [can appeal]. This order is Islam, which . . . is consistent, sound, and able to [address] all problems of spiritual and material existence, and can thus . . . rescue contemporary civilization from its sufferings."[88]

It is unfortunate that such views about secularism and the crisis of modernity have become so popular in the Islamic world. It follows that the indictments of secularism published in Arabic have become legend.[89] Nor is this rejection of secular culture restricted to contemporary Islam; Hindu fundamentalists, for example, articulate their worldview in the familiar terms of religious fundamentalism, directing their displeasure against cultural modernity and the secular character of the state in India.

What can be done to oppose these injections of religious fundamentalism into world politics? I believe we should begin by seeking effective patterns of communication and cultural exchange between the conflicting civilizations. This first step, if even modestly successful, would provide a sound basis for the work of international institutions in the pursuit of a stable and peaceful world order. The terrifying reality is that religious fundamentalisms, wherever they may be found, are opposed to a peaceful world order—opposed even to a discussion of conciliatory possibilities—and thus contribute relentlessly to promoting conflict among civilizations in terms of clashing worldviews.[90]

THE CULTURAL BASIS OF WORLD POLITICS IN AN AGE OF INTERCIVILIZATIONAL CONFLICT

Beyond their preoccupation with terrorism, most Western observers of international political developments seem not to be prepared to deal with the rise of religious fundamentalism, or with its effects on world politics. Prior to the Gulf War, the peaceful, though radical, transformations in Eastern Europe and the concomitant dissolution of the post-World War II order—the Cold War—seemed to promise a much better world. These historic events pushed the World of Islam onto the back pages; by then nobody seemed to care any longer about the irritating practices of Islamic fundamentalism. The explosive events in the Middle East—Khomeini, the hostages, the Iran-Iraq War, the Rushdie affair, and other sensations—seemed to belong to the past. (These were of course the issues that had compelled the Western media to pay heed to Islamic civilization.) In that somnolent atmosphere, Saddam Hussein came along and proved himself able not only to reverse that neglect but also to surpass Khomeini's dark image in the Western media. And before the West could pause for breath it was confronted by the wars in Bosnia and Chechnya, which Muslim peoples steadfastly view as further steps in the West's crusade against Islamic civilization.

If observers in the West are to understand these developments, they will need new tools, tools that are to date lacking in the study of international relations. Even during the Cold War the scholars' traditional tools were ill-suited to the regional dynamics of conflict outside the West, and the approaches needed today must resonate all the more with cultures and civilizations that were beyond the scope of scholars studying international relations in earlier decades. It is also imperative that those who study non-Western civilizations take them more seriously, thus freeing Western perceptions from the preoccupation with transitory sensations that so predictably characterizes the approach of the Western media in their monitoring of non-Western civilizations.

Interest in Islam must no longer be confined to the traditional products of predominantly philologian Islamic studies; we must make an effort to place Islam and Islamic fundamentalism in the broader context of the cultural bases of world politics. As our globe continues to shrink, there is a great need to understand other civilizations. Peoples of different cultural outlooks are being brought to a far higher degree of mutual awareness and interaction but not to an appreciably improved understanding or tolerance of one another's civilizations. This context cries out for a thoroughgoing reappraisal of efforts to understand Islamic and other non-Western varieties of religious fundamentalism.

But dealing in too general a manner with Islamic fundamentalism might also lead to some false impressions. One might, for example, conclude that an Islamic monolith may emerge as a threat,[91] but no such thing is possible; the Islamic realities are too diverse, and the separate and distinct local cultures Muslims live in differ too greatly from one another. To concede this level of diversity does not, however, refute the view that unity and diversity are complementary aspects of the "Muslim world," a civilization based on the *theocentric worldview* of Islam that is shared by all Muslims. For *despite all of their cultural, sectarian, and ethnic diversity,* Muslims from West Africa to Southeast Asia share one worldview and thus one civilization, and the Arab Middle East is the hub of it: this is cultural diversity in civilizational unity.

On cultural grounds civilizations can be viewed as the major components of humanity, components that are ceaselessly borrowing, exchanging, and generally interacting with one another. On political grounds, however, the same civilizations can serve as a matrix of conflict. To view Islam, for example, as uniquely political, as Islamic fundamentalism does, serves as an organizing principle in uniting Islam's peoples against those of other civilizations.

The thesis of the simultaneity of structural globalization and cultural fragmentation[92] addresses the perennial conflict between the general need for common norms in world politics, that is, a level of international morality, and the persistence of cultural peculiarities. An international system of states can function to the benefit of all if the individual states consent to common norms and rules, honor them, and comply with them in their international behavior. Cultural fragmentation runs counter to this goal insofar as it reflects the existence of diverse cultures and civilizations, each with its own set of values and norms determining its particular brand of international behavior.

Cultural diversity is of course the normal state of affairs in a world in which no universal culture is attainable, or even desirable. Anthropologists tell us that there can *be* no universal culture, for cultures are always based on locally confined processes of the production of meaning.[93] These local cultures can group together, if sufficiently related to one another in some significant way—for example, in sharing a worldview—to create a regional civilization, such as the West or the World of Islam, but the local production of meaning underlying particular cultures can never be extended to a universal framework we may address as world culture. The question thus is, how can we combine the need for common rules and norms in international society with the reality of enormous cultural diversity? Cultural fragmentation may, but need not, be an obstacle to reconciling the tension between cultural diversity and the need for shared norms and rules. Sharing of certain basic norms and rules not only could undergird an international morality but could also—on cross-cultural grounds—sustain a global, that is, cross-cultural consensus among civilizations.

In fact, in international relations norms and rules can simply be imposed, if the requisite power structures are available, but an *imposition* is not desirable. What is needed is, rather, a cross-cultural *consent* to international norms and values, a consent to standards of international morality. The reader may recall that international law, which in its origins is European law, has in effect been imposed on the world's non-Western civilizations within the framework of an international order. That order was dominated first by Europe and later by its North American progeny. (Earlier I quoted the British legal scholar H. L. A. Hart on the entry of non-Western states into the international community "by the general obligations of international law"; see note 14.)

The link between cultural fragmentation and the current diffusion of power in the international system becomes clear in the study of the international behavior of weak non-Western states. As these states attain greater strength, their consent to international law—never offered wholeheartedly—becomes more threadbare than ever. In this situation, the politicization of international cultural fragmentation, on grounds of normative conflict between civilizations, could seriously threaten the validity of the common and shared principles of the international community. It thus becomes crucial to find new ways for dealing with the changing structure of world politics. The options presented by the religious, self-assertive reawakenings in non-Western societies seem not to be the preferable ones. The formula of an absolutist Islamic world order is a formula for conflict and world disorder rather than one of conflict resolution—let alone a basis for developing the needed international institutions and modes of communication. Nobody of a non-Islamic civilization would accede to the fundamentalist vision of an Islamic world order, and there are many Muslims, I for one, who passionately oppose this vision. To complicate the matter, the call for an Islamic world order does not come primarily from the Islamic states, as such, but from private actors (the so-called underground *imams*[94]) toiling as irregulars and resorting to the use of force in non-state wars.

In the early 1950s a prominent, farsighted scholar of international law at Yale, F. S. C. Northrop, drew the attention of his contemporaries to the need for the study of the "cultural bases of international policy." At that time, and still in our time, there was/is no sense that such a study was needed. The preoccupation with the state as the principal actor was then even stronger than it is today. According to Northrop, "[N]ations must learn how to cooperate or else they perish. . . . Collaboration requires that nations and their statesmen must learn new ways. . . . The key . . . to [the] understanding of any nation and to the specification of those of its properties which will determine its international reactions is to be found when the major common norms of its people are determined. For unless the people of a nation have a dominant ideology there is no consistent dominant response."[95]

In the book cited, published in 1952, Northrop dealt with the resurgence of Islam, with the Buddhist world, and with other non-Western civilizations in an effort to understand the "cultural bases of international policy." One of his conclusions is that "there are other political and cultural beliefs in the world than those of the liberal democratic West. . . . Buddhism, . . . Hinduism, Taoism and Confucianism, as well as Islam, are such other ways. A wise foreign policy for the democratic United States will welcome and encourage these other ways and cooperate with them."[96] The problem with this sound and even-handed advice for the conduct of world politics is that some of the systems alluded to—Islam in particular—stand firm on grounds that contradict other options for a world order. Moreover, these non-Western civilizations remain religious in their bases, that is, not yet secular.

The "revolt against the West" (Bull), as articulated for example by the religiopolitical ideology of Islamic fundamentalism, resorts precisely to the exclusivity of these religions and cultures and reactivates them in a conspicuously self-assertive manner. These exclusive ideologies thus offer no viable alternative to the present secular world order, based as it is on the cultural project of modernity, which is wholly anathema to them.

Another prominent, but contemporary, international law scholar (incidentally, a disciple of the late F. S. C. Northrop), Richard Falk of Princeton University, addresses the contemporary "religious awakening" in a fashionable manner as "verging on the postmodern." He is of the view that the modern Western secular civilization "does not inspire confidence in its capacity to respond to fundamental challenges in the contemporary world."[97] On the basis of this assessment, he infers that the "religious awakening" may develop as a source of a so-called "postmodern political sensibility" to which—though it be an extremely vague concept—he is favorably inclined. Falk is aware, however, that in non-Western civilizations this religious awakening could assume the form of religious fundamentalism: "A few islands of fundamentalist success disclose the religious revisioning of modernism. . . . Especially in the non-Western societies of Asia and Africa, the role of religious influence remains overwhelmingly reactionary."[98] The present global crisis, and the radical changes in the world to which fundamentalism is a response, thus reflect an intrinsic dilemma. On the one hand, non-Western civilizations have to be taken—in Northrop's sense—into closer consideration in order that their obligation to international consent may be stabilized. On the other, we must be aware that the fundamentalist representatives of these non-Western civilizations do not content themselves with simply being given more credit.

It is to be hoped that religious fundamentalism will not become the dominant ideology among Muslims in the World of Islam, for if this were the case fundamentalist claims would become the major source of their "consistent dominant international response" (Northrop). Policymakers preoccupied with power may ridicule the world order rhetoric of Islamic fundamentalism, secure in the knowledge that Muslim fundamentalists cannot mobilize the means necessary to put their political beliefs into effect. Nonetheless, these claims contribute to a more intensified politicization of the ongoing international cultural fragmentation and, consequently, to a further decline in international consensus. The result would be, willy-nilly, a new world disorder. Moreover, the ongoing diffusion of power and the great powers' increasing inability to maintain control over their international environment should compel us to desist from smirking at the Islamic fundamentalists' claims of superiority.

With the exception of their role in the two existing fundamentalist states, Iran and Sudan, political activists among Islamic fundamentalists operate still largely underground.[99] The illegality of these clandestine operations notwithstanding, the ideology of fundamentalism is increasingly the primary source of popular collective choice in major parts of Islamic civilization, in particular in the Middle East. The massive and overwhelmingly favorable response of Muslim fundamentalists to Saddam Hussein's aggressive call to combat in the Gulf War was a clear expression of the public choices addressed. That response also gives evidence of the broad dissemination of the fundamentalist alternative to the existing world order, an alternative that is still with us as a legacy of that war. Forgetting the Gulf War should not lead us also to forgetting these observations.

Decision makers and policy practitioners in the mostly undemocratic Islamic states cannot go on forever ignoring such popular collective choices.

In the name of greater wisdom in determining world politics, it is crucial that Islamic fundamentalism be studied more seriously than it has been heretofore. Any effort to reform Islam, in the sense of rendering it democratic and freeing it from its dysfunctional claims to absolute superiority, must be welcomed by all non-Muslim parts of the international community. The new sentiment of open-minded non-Muslim Westerners to appreciate Islamic civilization for its own sake, and as an estimable element of a pluralistic world, is a greatly welcomed attitudinal change. It is clear, however, that this burgeoning appreciation will fall well short of accepting any Islamic claim to superiority. I remind the reader that the fundamentalists believe the notion of *taghallub*/dominance to be the basic tenet of Islamic political doctrine. As a liberal Muslim I rather believe in a cultural and political pluralism that precludes the dominance of whatever civilization.

CONCLUSIONS

World peace requires that all civilizations, above all the Western and Islamic civilizations, learn to live with each other in peace, on grounds of equality. To this end, reforms in both civilizations, and a refraining from their implicit or explicit claims to universality and superiority, are sorely needed. The idea of an international morality to be shared by all civilizations requires that religion be disentangled from politics and that the secular nation-state be established or reestablished. But in the World of Islam that very institution is in grave jeopardy. The question I shall ask in the ensuing chapter, oddly enough, is whether religion can be the solution in this crisis, as its adherents are so often claiming.

Religious fundamentalism, which has emerged from the politicization of the particular worldviews and outlooks of religiously defined civilizations, cannot provide the basis for a world order in peace and justice. The proliferation of fundamentalism is in fact the ideological expression of "the Coming Anarchy"[100] or, as I put it, the new world disorder. The alternative to this grim prospect is cross-cultural consent to a secular international morality.

SIX

The Crisis of the Nation-State

Islamic, Pan-Arab, Ethnic, and Sectarian
Identities in Conflict

In the years of decolonization, most Western historians and social scientists were preoccupied with the nation-state as a vehicle for modernization.[1] Nation-building has been the magic formula for expressing and realizing that preoccupation, one that has been shared by the Westernized elites in these non-Western civilizations. The crumbling of nation-states in Asia and Africa has thus been an eye-opening process.

Even before the disintegration of the Soviet Union,[2] which was brought on in part by ethnic disunity, scholars had begun shifting their focus from nation-building to the study of ethnicity. Separatist and secessionist ethnic nationalisms, even in such seemingly benign locales as Scotland, have been a great challenge to the theoretically nonethnic nation-state, and religious fundamentalism has now become another grave challenge to the nation-state. Hindu fundamentalism in India is as surely anti-secular as Serbian ethnofundamentalism is in the Balkans. Fundamentalist movements thus seek to replace the nation-state by a divine order. For analytical purposes we may be able to separate ethnicity from fundamentalism, but in reality the two tend to form a continuum. In this chapter I want to extend my inquiry into the structural constraints underlying the emergence of fundamentalism. In my analysis I shall examine the crisis of the nation-state and relate the crisis to ethnicity and the religious salvation ideologies addressed as fundamentalisms.

UNDERSTANDING THE RESORT TO
POLITICIZED RELIGION

Crises in today's world are no longer merely domestic in range and influence, for they inevitably affect global processes and formations.[3] One response to contemporary crises has been the recourse to religion, ostensibly as a faith but basically as a political ideology. The result has been a variety of religious fundamentalisms in diverse civilizations. The interdisciplinary and cross-culturally oriented scholars engaged in the Fundamentalism Project sought to understand this resort to religion.[4] The pivotal question the project asked is, can religion be the solution to the problem or only the unwilling core of the problem?

Before turning to this perennial question, however, we must address another, more basic, question: can we pose and answer the question of religion as problem or solution *in one coherent way* for all of humanity? It turns out that we must honor the regionalized nature of our globalized but not yet unified world, and conclude that no such global answer can be given. If we accept this conclusion, how then should we view the World of Islam in particular?

Historians and social scientists have made an effort to answer this question, each in their own ways. Traditional world historians and general theorists of international relations obviously do not view each other's work favorably. Nevertheless, they share the same holistic view of the world, whether with reference to world history, or within the framework of the international system of nation-states. Area-studies scholars, or regionalists, are free from such relentless attempts to reduce the entire, very diverse world to one holistic concept, but their work tends to be characterized by the intellectual narrowness of their essentially one-dimensional inquiries, which are regularly restricted to regional confines.[5] Most regionalists resent and distrust cross-cultural comparisons that extend beyond the region they are familiar with, let alone theory-oriented studies of broad-gauged concepts.

True, our world is structurally interconnected in ways that increasingly link peoples to one another despite all of their cultural differences. Through modern means of communication, transport, and all manner of networking and interaction, our world is rapidly becoming a "global village." It follows that "the history . . . of the world since the Second World War, and more particularly, during the third quarter of the twentieth century,"[6] ought to be written in a new and novel way. Politics and society can be studied properly only in a cross-cultural and interdisciplinary manner. Eric Hobsbawm, who makes this argument, is aware of the fact that this history "cannot be written adequately yet" (ibid.). We lack the tools and outlooks for accurately and comprehensively answering impending questions about the rise of politicized religion in the crisis of the nation-state. These questions cannot be dealt with adequately by applying either the world historian's universalist vision or the ostensibly more intricate general-systems-oriented methodologies of the international relations scholars. In this inquiry I move away from the "heavy scholarship" of abstract theories and turn to the more promising approach of historical sociology[7] for answers. In our age of religious fundamentalisms, global solutions are needed, but are no longer accepted. Each civilization revives its own *Weltanschauung*, its own conception of the world, in terms of which it constructs its own solutions to crises. This process takes place on religious grounds, and religion is believed to be the solvent. The result is an ideological "war of civilizations" with conflicting *Weltanschauungen*.[8]

A closer look at global structures and globalization processes ought not lead us to overlook the unique character of each of the world's civilizational outlooks. Despite the great differences among and within civilizations they all share the fact of being globally constrained, but globalization does not create the grounds for a "world culture," nor does it standardize incompatible cultural patterns. Culture understood as a production of meaning is always specific to locales. Moreover, it is a misperception to view culture as consisting of such globally consumed items as television and Coca-Cola, or modern music and fashionable dress. These trivial exceptions to local expressions of culture do not make a world.

One of the merits of the disputed debate on the "clash of civilizations" in the discipline of international relations has been the insight that general abstract theories lead nowhere. We must not, however, conclude from this insight that we must surrender to the chaos of a global disorder. A regionally differentiated framework remains possible. In pursuing that notion, I will focus my inquiry on the Islamic, largely Arab, part of the Middle East. This narrowing of perspective is justified by the fact that all concerned see the Middle East as the cultural hub of Islamic civilization.[9]

IS POLITICAL ISLAM THE SOLUTION?

The current crisis of the nation-state in the contemporary Middle East[10] derives from the fact that this modern institution is alien to that region of the world and was virtually imposed on its parts.[11] Today, all states of that region, even Kuwait and Saudi Arabia, are—though only in a formal manner—organized along the lines of this institution. What, then, are the constraints underlying the crisis of the nation-state in the Middle East? Some scholars misinterpret this crisis in arguing, without supporting specifics, that Islamic history is quite familiar with the institution of the state. What they have in mind, of course, are the territorial, dynastic, or traditional state patterns that have long been a part of Islamic history.[12] In so arguing, these scholars seem not to understand the nature of the nation-state as a modern phenomenon. This institution is not simply a "state" in the sense of an absence of anarchy, but a modern construct based on, among other features, the organizational principle of a central government drawing its sanction from popular sovereignty.[13] When the state is defined in *this* manner, it then follows that no such institution had existed prior to this century in Islamic history. The nation-state is a recent and largely unwelcome addition to the contemporary history of Islam.

Muslim fundamentalists, as we have seen, challenge secular nationalism as an alien ideology, and the existing nation-states as imposed institutions implanted in their countries.[14] Sunni Islamic fundamentalism is clearly a response to the failure of the nation-state to take root in the Arab-Islamic region of the contemporary Middle East. These fundamentalists reject the nation-state as a *"hall mustawrad*/imported solution."[15]

The political culture of secular nationalism not only is a novelty in the Middle East[16] but also fails to penetrate below the surface of the societies involved. The political culture of Islam is more authentic in the eyes of the people in this region, since it predates nationalism and the nation-state and rests upon powerful religious tenets. Islamic tradition and the recent superimposition of the nation-state are in serious conflict.

To some extent, of course, the formation of the state system in the Middle East has facilitated the integration of that part of the world into the international system of states, as a regional subsystem.[17] Politicized religion, an expression of unrelenting opposition to the nation-state and the international system—both were of course engineered by the West—creates a great challenge and portends great conflict. Islam itself, as a premodern cultural system exposed to modernity, is also in a state of crisis.[18] Under these conditions, the politicization of religion contributes to igniting conflict and to escalating the ongoing crisis. Some observers argue that it is wrong to characterize the politicization of religion as fundamentalism, on grounds that fundamentalism is a

Western concept alien to Islam. But the characterization has not been imposed on the movement by outside forces; the Muslims who currently challenge the nation-state and international order conceive of *themselves* as fundamentalists—as *usuliyyun,* to use their own label.[19] In their view, the modern Muslim is preeminently a political man, and Islam is a *din wa dawla*/ unity of religion and state order. To be sure, the term *usuliyya* is a neo-Arabic term coined recently, and the politicization of Islam (for example, the Muslim Brethren in Egypt, established in 1928) predates the occurrence of the term.

In political Islam the image of one's self as being anti-Western is the referent for determining self-identity. The construction of an "imagined community"[20] on which to base the cultural identity of a "we"-group is integral with a perception of an inimical global environment depicted as "they," that is, "the West." The World of Islam, as a civilization, is politically seen to be engulfed by this hostile environment and constrained by the processes of globalization it generates. In this modern context, reference to the medieval Christian crusades is revived, and the projection of the crusades into the present[21] serves to reject the incorporation of the World of Islam into the globalization process—to reject, in short, this "modern crusade" of Christianity against Islam. The formation of the Middle East as a set of state systems along the lines of the modern nation-state is perceived to be the result of this imposed and unwanted incorporation. Old memories and burdens mixed with new perceptions find their way into the contemporary context.[22]

Islamic fundamentalists are themselves unwillingly reflections of the impact of modernity, for which they employ the subsuming epithet "the West." They are neither traditionalists nor nativists. To the contrary, their response to the challenge of modernity is expressed to a great extent in clearly modern terms; their thought and action are imprisoned in the world-time context designed by modernity. The predicament of Islamic fundamentalists vis-à-vis modernity has in fact become an expression of their ambiguity: on the one hand, they seek to accommodate instrumentally all or most of the material achievements of modernity (that is, science and technology) into Islamic civilization; on the other hand, they reject vehemently the adoption of the man-centered rationality that has made these achievements possible.[23] In contrast to the sovereignty of the nation-state, the fundamentalists construct the "Government of God." The *hakimiyyat Allah* is conspicuously not the traditional Islamic caliphate, and the "Islamic state"—a peculiarly modern construct—serves as an example for the fundamentalists' dream of "semi-modernity."

BETWEEN THE GOVERNMENT OF THE PEOPLE AND THE GOVERNMENT OF GOD

Muslim believers—as this author—believe that God created the universe and all therein; but for Islamic fundamentalists God also governs the world at His will, as revealed in the Qur'an. The neo-Arabic word *dustur* / constitution is used in describing the Qur'an as a "holy constitution."[24] This concept is a novelty. In the view of the fundamentalists, man is only a *makhluq* / creature of God and subject to His omnipotent will. "The principle of subjectivity / *das Subjektivitätsprinzip*" (Habermas), which determines the philosophical discourse of modernity,[25] is thus a heresy for Islamic fundamentalists. The fundamentalist politicization of the unlimited theocentric vision of Islam rejects the idea of man as a free soul, subject to his own will. Their rejection of this construct leads the adherents of this politicized religion to reject not only the normative underpinning of individual human rights but also the nation-state itself.

Bear in mind that the crisis of the nation-state in the Islamic world stems either from failed development policies (Algeria and Iran), from the effects of war and dictatorship (Iraq and Syria), or simply from local ethnic strife (Sudan) or the repercussions of foreign occupation (Afghanistan and the Occupied Palestinian Territories). To all these invalid states Islamic fundamentalists present a counterprogram based on the lessons of religion. Their counterprogram is not issue-oriented, but constitutes rather an alternative to the existing pattern of states. In their view, the "*dawla qawmiyya* / nation-state" should be replaced by the "*nizam Islami* / Islamic system,"[26] in which *hakimiyyat Allah* / God's rule, as expressed in His divine law, the *shari'a*, is the hallmark. (We shall learn more about this ideology in chapters 7 and 8.)

Despite their reference to Islam in the interpretation of "*din wa dawla* / unity of religion and state order," Islamic fundamentalists mostly avoid the term for state, *dawla*, and prefer the term *nizam*, system. This choice is in keeping with their rejection of the drawing of boundaries, for Islam acknowledges no boundaries. Politicizing the notion of God's universal sovereignty leads to the belief that the political system of Islam, as envisaged by fundamentalists, is universal, too. The ideology first addresses the

Islamic *umma*, then all of humanity. The *"umma Islamiyya*/Islamic community" is the nucleus of an Islamicized humanity and the banner of Islam.[27]

One example of the fundamentalists' rejection of the principle of subjectivity and the nation-state itself is provided in the weekly *al-Munqith*, which—before its banning—was the voice of the Algerian *al-Jabhah al-Islamiyya li al-Inqadh*/Front Islamique du Salut (FIS). *Al-Munqith* published a heated debate between Abbasi Madani, the founder of FIS, and a functionary of the dissolved Front de Liberation Nationale (FLN), the political party that emerged from the former liberation front against French colonial rule and ruled Algeria from the day of independence in 1962 to the military takeover in 1992. In this debate, Madani was quoted as saying, "You refer to the concept of sovereignty and argue [that] it is incorporated into the constitution. . . . I do not find it in the Qur'an and thus cannot accept it. In committing yourself to this concept, you are falling back behind the age of Islam; you are returning to the *jahiliyya*. . . ."[28]

The geopolitical concept of Algerian fundamentalists is *"al-Maghreb al-Islami al-kabir*/the Islamic greater Maghreb." The Maghreb is the geopolitical and cultural area of the Arab West comprising the Arab North African states, that is, Morocco, Algeria, Tunisia, and Libya—with the exception of Egypt, which belongs to the Mashreq/Arab East. The quoted concept strongly rejects the nation-state. It is clear that the Muslim state thus envisaged encompasses all of northern Africa, and whether this entity might even touch upon Europe (for example, in formerly Islamic Spain) was left to be pondered. Some of the FIS flyers that I saw in Algiers in January 1992 and again in 1993 did not fail to provide a reference to Islamic conquests in Southern Europe (for example, in Spain, Sicily, and the southern Balkans) as part of a geographically enhanced "Islamic greater Maghreb," while presenting the Mediterranean itself as the *bahr Islami*/Islamic sea.

Undergraduate students in the West learn early in their classes that the normative foundation of the nation-state is the idea of popular sovereignty.[29] This concept is a political expression of the humanity-centered view of the world as a crucial component of cultural modernity. For fundamentalists, government of the people by the people is heretical, inasmuch as it is an expression of *ta'til*. This term, which stems from the political thought of the orthodox Islamic jurist Ibn Taimiyya, invokes human measures that serve to suspend the rule of God.[30] In employing this medieval concept in a modern context, the conflict between Islamic fundamentalism and the system of nation-states assumes, ideologically, the character of a conflict between politicized theocentric universalism and secular national sovereignty. These are of course profoundly conflicting worldviews, and a state-centered analysis proves incapable of understanding that this conflict is what underlies the rise of Islamic fundamentalism.

To interpret the conflict in this manner is not to suggest that the existing nation-states in the Middle East are really secular, that is, governed by the principle of popular sovereignty: to be sure, this principle in Middle Eastern states prevails only on the surface, in that it is not an expression of a government of the people by the people. To varying degrees, all of the states in the Arab Middle East are governed by authoritarian and despotic regimes based on the political culture of "neo-patriarchy."[31] These states are nation-states only in a formal sense, because they lack the requisite structural and institutional underpinning; they are only nominally nation-states or, as Robert Jackson suggested for most "Third World" states, "quasi-states."[32] From modernity they adopted the *technology* of rule, but not the *democratic logic* of government. Rhetorically, they claim to have the legitimacy of governments by the people, and by the standards of international law all Middle Eastern states, in being organized ostensibly as sovereign nation-states, enjoy international legitimacy. Internally, however, these states lack—by all reasonable measures—the legitimacy they claim.[33] Under these conditions, the rise of Islamic fundamentalism contributes to de-legitimizing these states and thus to their political destabilization. Can religion in this role be the solution? To be sure, the rulers of the quasi-states in the World of Islam try to suppress fundamentalism not so much because it is inimical to *democracy* but out of their justified fear that they could be toppled and thrown out of work.

Are the undemocratic rulers of the World of Islam to be blamed for the failure of the nation-state? And why is this institution alien to Muslims? The nation-state presupposes the existence of a political community designed along the lines of the modern idea of a civil society[34] in which the people share basic norms and values as a general consensus that links them to one another on pluralistic grounds. Citizenship[35] in a civil society, politically disposed as a democratic nation-state, is the expression of the political identity and loyalty of the people constituting the body politic. But in the Middle Eastern nation-states, as elsewhere in contemporary Islamic civilization, there are imposed structures in which all of the aforementioned requirements are missing. Citizenship there has no substance and is only formally related to the issuing of identity cards and passports, not to any awareness of belonging to a genuine political community and to the related polity. In the Middle East, an awareness of being a member of a community connotes membership not in a civil society but in an ethnic or sectarian sub-community and its subordinate identity. In these subcommunities political loyalty grows not from consent to the political order, but from the force of coercion. The Middle Eastern state is thus a "Republic of Fear,"[36] as exemplified by Iraq under Saddam Hussein, and his *mukhabarat* (security apparatus) state is not a special case, as many in the West believe. Fundamentalist groups contrast religion with the failed nation-states they see around them and view their recourse to religion as a legitimate alternative to a corrupt nationalism. Religious salvation ideologies replace secular nationalism, and the result is neither democracy nor even pan-Arabism.

In looking beneath the conflict between nation-state and fundamentalism in the Middle East, we see, as well, the revival of particular solidarity groups, which I shall consistently address as ethnic groups, in terms of the concept of *ethnicity*. There are in the Middle East both ideal and real patterns of collective identity. The religious ideal of an all-subsuming Islamic *umma* / community underlies the supposition that there is a superordinate Islamic identity given to the faithful by an overarching Islamic civilization. Similarly, the belief that there is an Arab *umma* / nation derives from a superordinate, multinational pan-Arab identity. In Arabic, the term *umma* is employed indiscriminately for both meanings.[37]

Within these supranational and superordinate collective identities there are identities imposed by the existing nation-states. We might, for example, refer to the idea of "*al-Iraqiyya* / Iraqihood"[38] outlined and imposed in Iraq by the *mukhabarat* of the totalitarian regime. This constitutes a pattern of national superordinate identity, since the real identity patterns in Iraq are either ethnic (for example, the Kurds) or sectarian (for example, the Shi'ites) or both. These superordinate identities are ideal, not real; they are visions or ideological concepts, and they imply an expectation enforced among the people through coercion. The real identities in the Middle East are related to communal, ethnic, and/or sectarian subgroups, each within its own local culture. The real conflict is thus not a conflict between Islamic fundamentalism and pan-nationalist or local-nationalist regimes. In reality, fundamentalism is, despite its universalist rhetoric, imbued with ethnicity and sectarianism. Similarly, the crisis of the nation-state lies not in the threat of an Islamic system of government, but rather in the potential breakdown of existing nation-state regimes induced through mobilization on religious grounds. Put differently, the threat is rather *dis*order, not an emerging *new* order.

The term "Lebanization" has been employed in this context to denote a process of emerging domestic disorder by which ethnic and sectarian communities defy the existing state order while employing religious formulae to justify their rival legitimacies. A more recent term, "Afghanization," alludes to the continuing disorder in Afghanistan, where fundamentalist militias, having routed the invaders, have turned to fighting one another most bloodily. Needless to say, fragmentation along these lines is not what the Islamic fundamentalists have in mind. Rhetorically, they envisage *hakimiyyat Allah* / God's rule,[39] not an ethnic rule. The problem is that their challenge to the existing nation-states could expedite, rather, a Lebanization or Afghanization of these regimes. In Sudan, where fundamentalists have succeeded in seizing power (on June 30, 1989), their government has clearly been enforcing the ethnic and sectarian supremacy of the Arab and Islamic north against the non-Arab and non-Muslim ethnic groups of the south.[40] On a global level the superordinate identity is Islamic civilization, directed against the West; regionally and locally, the superordinate identity can be found in an existing state or in a state aspired to. But true subordinate identities based on experienced awareness in everyday life are always ethnic and/or sectarian. Owing to the divisiveness of these ethnic and sectarian forces, mobilization against the West at the level of Islamic civilization is undermined locally and domestically.

As Leslie Lipson, in his comparative study of civilizations, puts it,

> Neither Iran of the Shi'ites nor Saudi Arabia of the Sunnis looks like the wave of a promising future. In fact, of all the major civilizations, the Islamic appears the least likely to undergo a successful revival in the century ahead. There are two factors which draw me to that conclusion. One is the prevalence of acute divisions within Islamic societies [deriving from] tribalism and the ferocity of religious sectarianism. . . . This weakness is connected with another defect . . . intolerance. . . . As a consequence, . . . true believers will fight fanatically.[41]

The problem here is that these true believers are basically irregulars; they fight even against one another, as the cases of Algeria and Afghanistan clearly reveal. It would be misleading, however, to infer from this chronic inner-Islamic strife that Islamic fundamentalism is a challenge only "to the Muslim people themselves,"[42] as Halliday argues. Even though I agree with his assessment that the problem of internal violence and tension among fundamentalist groups "reduces their ability to play an effective international role" (ibid.), I believe (as I outlined in the first chapter while discussing Halliday's views) that the disorder they create is not limited to local and domestic confines. A disordered Middle East would mean a disordered Mediterranean region, adjacent to a potentially disordered Europe (think already of Bosnia). Now let us ask: why this inner-Islamic strife? The lack of a tolerant political culture of pluralism is one explanation. Ethnicity, I believe, is the other. The irresistible force meets the immovable object.

THE NATION-STATE: BETWEEN ETHNICITY AND FUNDAMENTALISM

Ethnicity, which has become a major source of conflict in the World of Islam and elsewhere, undermines the universalist claims of Islamic fundamentalism. Ethnicity is, nevertheless, related to religion, inasmuch as political groups are chiefly ethnoreligious in their composition, ideology, and outlooks. This new phenomenon can be observed throughout the World of Islam, but perhaps most clearly in Afghanistan, where three major ethnic groups—the Pashtun, Tadjik, and Uzbek—struggle for power, in the name of religion. In the multiethnic Afghan society, we see clearly that religion does not unite, but rather is mingled with, ethnicity as a divisive force. In Afghanistan and in Sudan, ethnic fragmentation undermines the capabilities of the Islamic fundamentalists, and in Sudan the fundamentalists are in power. In Algeria, fundamentalist banners carry the slogan *"al-Jaza'ir 'Arabiyya wa al-Islam dinuha* / Algeria is Arab and Islam is its religion." The Berbers, who are Muslims as well, but not Arabs, understand this slogan as a declaration of war on them. About one-third of Algeria's populace is Berber, and the Algerian-Muslim Berbers align themselves clearly against Sunni-Arab fundamentalism to protect their ethnicity. During my lectures in Algiers in winter 1992 and spring 1993 the Berbers present underlined their faith in Islam but made clear their opposition to the notion of *Jaza'ir 'Arabiyya* / Arab Algeria, the stance taken by the fundamentalists. Algerian-Muslim Berbers reject the equation of Islam with Arabism and, moreover, the idea of a political Islam.

In Sudan, which is governed by the fundamentalist Islamic National Front (see note 40), the Algerian Berbers see a clear precedent, a warning of what could happen to non-Arab ethnic groups that do not commit to a Sunni-*Arab* Islam. Simply for ethnic reasons, the two Algerian Berber parties, *Front des Forces Socialistes* (FFS) and *Ressemblement de la Culture et*

Démocratie (RCD), were decidedly anti-fundamentalist in their actions during the crisis of 1991–92 and later on, as well. That ethnicity can be a source of conflict also became clear in Iraq after the Gulf War, when the tensions between the ruling ethnic Sunni clientele of Takrit and the Kurds, on the one hand, and the Shi'ites, on the other hand, erupted.[43] The most dramatic example of ethnic tension is Sudan, where ethnic conflict amounted to a civil war, and the current conflict between the Sunni majority and the Alawites in Syria[44] could also lead to such an inner war.

Any serious analysis of ethnicity as a source of conflict within the Middle East must draw on several scholarly disciplines. In an earlier day, ethnicity was a major concern only for ethnosociologists and anthropologists.[45] No longer. Only recently, in particular following the ethnic fragmentation of the former Soviet Union (see note 2) and the crumbling of many of the nominal nation-states in Africa (for example, Somalia and Liberia), have professional international relations scholars begun to discover the pertinence of ethnicity for the study of world politics. Basically, it is ethnicity that underlies the rise of the various ethnonationalisms and ethnofundamentalisms that stand opposed to the liberal concept of Western nationalism and the nation-state. I distinguish between these ethnic nationalisms (for example, Kurdish nationalism) and the mix of ethnicity and religion resulting in an ethnofundamentalism (for example, the Serbian case).

In dealing with these issues I employ the subsystem approach. The peoples of Islam belong to one civilization, but it is a civilization that is subdifferentiated into many regional subsystems. The Arab-Islamic Middle Eastern nation-states, for example, constitute their own regional subsystem.[46] The other concept I draw on in these analyses is ethnicity.

The point of departure here is the insight that in the Middle East the nation-state did not arise from a domestic heritage, but was externally imposed. The fact that it is built upon the Ottoman and colonial legacies exacerbates the problem inherent in the process whereby a state pattern might take root in an alien environment. In the liberal nation-state model[47] of nationalism, it is shared symbols (flags, anthems, heroes, etc.), not ethnic bonds, that relate the citizens to one another in a communicative-discursive context.[48] This means that the norms and values that have been developed in a communicative discourse are then shared by the entire populace (for example, the American Constitution and the related view of Americanness). Ethnic bonds, on the contrary, suggest that a community shares a common descent. There can also be a *mixture* between ethnicity and national awareness, for example the local ethnic sentiments in a country like Morocco (people who are ethnic Fasis, that is, from Fez, but nationally Moroccans). Peter Weinrich argues, for instance, that the "vast majority of people in the typical nation-state will have one core social identity in common, namely that of a common ethnicity. . . . [If] those sharing it agree on its meaning and value, then it will dominate their behavior. The other social identities . . . would become subordinated."[49]

In the Middle East the existence of subnational and subethnic divisions within the confines of a given nation-state stands in the way of establishing and sustaining the new institution. Moreover, the claims of supranational (pan-Arab or pan-Islamic) entities generate conflicts among the subordinate ethnic communities. To complicate the matter further, in the entire Islamic civilization, superordinate formulae (Islamic fundamentalism) are intermingled with subordinate formulae (ethnicity). In this intermingling, Islamic fundamentalism defeats itself, for ethnicity is the major force undermining the universal claims of political Islam. But defeated or not, the fundamentalists continue to sow disorder.

In past years, "ethnicity" has assumed many diverse meanings in the published literature, and the term itself has replaced the notion of minorities employed earlier. Michael Hudson has suggested that there is a core of an overall Arab identity whose hallmarks are, "on the ethnic dimension, Arab language and culture and, on the religious dimension, Islam."[50] In the Middle East, by Islam is meant Sunni Islam, and within these confines, non-Arab Sunni Muslims, such as Kurds and Berbers, as well as non-Sunni Muslim Arabs, such as Alawites, Druzes, and several sectarian offshoots of Shi'i Islam, are referred to as minorities within the meaning of communal solidarity groups. To be sure, Hudson is aware of the fact that conflict between the minorities (as so defined) and the majority can assume an ethnic character.

Contemporary history has shown that it is very unlikely that superficial levels of modernization could trigger mobilization processes sufficient for the envisaged assimilation of minorities, in the fashion that had been possible in modern European and early American history. Ethnic and sectarian groups in the Middle East, as defined earlier in terms of minority and solidarity groups, cannot be integrated along the lines of the European model of the formation of the nation-state. To take this into account is to acknowledge that the "possibility for ethno-sectarian conflict remains a constant danger, should the conflict-precipitating circumstances arise."[51] Under the particular conditions of current history this ethnosectarian conflict is assuming a fundamentalist character, and the tensions between superordinate and subordinate identities do affect the witches' brew of fundamentalism and ethnicity.

Unlike the superordinate identity based on Islam, which serves both as a local cultural system and as a referent for the grouping around a civilization, the idea of an Arab nation is a superordinate identity that lacks the underpinning of firm social and political foundations. Islam has deep roots, but the idea of belonging to a "nation" is based on a transplant, that is, on a construct coming from the West.[52]

Compared to Africa, as Hudson puts it, the Arab Middle East "is fundamentally homogeneous in terms of its widely shared national and religious values"; but "in a political culture noted for affectivity and persisting salience of primordial identifications, Arabism must coexist or compete with certain other parochial identifications. . . . It would be much too simple . . . to assume that modernization is performing an assimilationist melting-pot function in this area."[53] This line of argument leads us far from the dichotomy of majority/minority, inasmuch as it takes into account the ethnic and sectarian subdivisions within Arabism.

In the Middle East, seen as a regional subsystem and the hub of the civilization of Islam, I see each component social group of the larger populations being bound together on ethnic grounds. The core of ethnicity resides in the socially produced and ever-changing quartet of common myths, memories, values, and symbols.[54] Thus, ethnicity cannot be properly defined in terms of static cultural elements, such as Arabness, or shared essential religious beliefs, such as Sunni Islam. Nor can we come to grips with ethnicity along the lines of the suggestion by Esman and Rabinovich that ethnicity can be defined as "collective identity and solidarity based on such ascriptive factors as imputed common descent, language, customs, belief systems and practices (religion), and in some cases race or color."[55] In preference to such static definitions, we draw rather on the concept of historically perceived forms of the common myths, memories, values, and symbols, which are constantly in flux. This concept can be applied equally to communal solidarity groups such as the Alawites or Druzes of Syria, the Dinka of the Sudan, or the Berbers of Morocco, as well as to overarching populations such as the Arabs, who are claimed to constitute a modern nation—if a Middle Eastern aggregation based on a Western transplant may be said to be a nation.

Every nation is supposed to have its ethnic origins. Nations are neither primordial nor perennial, but entities that have crystallized from ethnic origins in modern times.[56] Nations are thus a modern phenomenon, one that dates from the late eighteenth century onward. In each case, national ties underlying the new pattern of identity replaced the hitherto prevailing local communal identifications. Structurally generated processes of integration and cultural assimilation, supported by the new modes of communication made available by novel technology, made it "possible and necessary to 'imagine' communities, at once sovereign and limited, through which a sense of immortality can be evoked and with which otherwise anonymous individuals can identify."[57] The crisis of the nation-state in the World of Islam has been due to its inability to generate this complex of integration-assimilation-communication functions, which could have contributed to the formation of a national identity. The idea of the nation in this civilizational subsystem is a transplant imported from the West with no local soil to grow on. The nation-state thus constructed failed to supersede ethnicity, and the result has been religious fundamentalism, as if by default.

ETHNICITY, REGIONALISM, AND THE SEARCH FOR IDENTITY

Dealing with changes within collective units and sentiments requires an analysis of the differences and similarities between modern national units and sentiments and the collective cultural units and sentiments of previous eras, those that Anthony Smith terms "ethnie." The differences between the two reflect differences in identity-building and identity patterns. The relevance of Smith's analysis to the kind of inquiry I pursue here is not restricted to the uncovering of the particular ethnic origins of nations. Smith explores also the nature and durability of ethnic forms and contents and the transformation of these into national forms and contents—or their persistent defiance of such a transformation. This approach is of great value to our inquiry into ethnicity in the subsystemic context of the Middle East.

The preexisting, relatively strong cultural homogeneity among the Arab populations of the Middle East—as defined in static terms—is evidence for the supposition that there is a superordinate identity engendering community in the Middle East. The contributions to this issue by Arab writers such as Ali Dessouki, J. Matar, and Saad Eddin Ibrahim[58] rest on this assumption, the inference being that the subsystem at issue is basically an ethnic Arab subsystem. It follows that the region's identity is an Arab identity. And although the Middle East is not restricted to its Arab part, a focus on the Arab element, in examining the ethnic subdivisions within Arabness itself, is justified. In so doing, we are in a position to discern competing superordinate and subordinate ethnic identities and also to view the tensions among them as a source of conflict. In his work, Ghassan Salamé[59] analyzes the identity conflict in the Arab Middle East as a tension between the rhetorical claim of an overall unity in each of the existing nation-states and the actual diversity of the populations within these states. Ghassan Salamé's analysis strikes me as important for understanding the vulnerabilities in the claimed common identity of an Arab subsystem (see also note 17).

We are now in a position to differentiate between pre-national and national identities, that is, in the latter case, identities oriented to a community linked to a nation-state. Social identities are related to local cultures, but in this context culture is not referred to in static terms such as language, religion, or alleged primordial values. Rather, culture is based on the existing societal realities and necessities, that is, not necessarily on language and religion. The addressed realities and necessities underlie the production of meaning in the Geertzian sense of a symbolic dimension of social behavior in a given structural context.[60] Viewed in this manner, every culture is local, since the production of meaning is regularly related to a concrete sociocultural context. Thus there can be no all-embracing Islamic *culture*, but there *can* be a cross-cultural Islamic *civilization*. By defining culture in the static terms of Arab language, scriptural Sunni Islam, and imputed shared values, Arab nationalists speak of one culture, spread from the Persian Gulf to Morocco. In terms of sociocultural analysis, however, the production of meaning underlying the variety of concrete cultures in this broad realm differs significantly from one culture to the next. To put it bluntly, Muslim Arab Kuwaitis and Muslim Arab Moroccans are not of the same culture, and do not perceive themselves as such, even though they speak the same language and worship the same faith.

Regionalism or, in the pan-Arab political language, *iqlimiyya*, conveys the meaning of a local-nationalist sentiment hostile to pan-Arabism. Owing to their mutual enmity, secular pan-Arabists and Islamic fundamentalists fail to acknowledge the locality of cultures and of the ethnicities related to them. The idea of a sweeping superordinate Arab ethnicity is challenged by subordinate local ethnic realities that cannot simply be reduced to an ideological commitment to *iqlimiyya*. The decline of pan-Arabism, which has been fed by the crisis of the nation-state, has contributed to strengthening these local real identities. Paradoxically, that decline also gave rise to the competing superordinate identity of Islamism. I doubt, however, that Islamic fundamentalists can succeed where pan-Arab nationalists have failed. Sectarian and ethnic ties, when intermingled with one another, stand in the way of a united Islamic civilization. Not even in one country, like Afghanistan, are rival fundamentalist groups able to unite. Creating disorder is ostensibly the only common ability they share.

In seeking an overall political consciousness, the Islamic civilization, as any other entity, is most successful in uniting forces when responding to the perception of external threats, such as Western policies. The lack of appropriate Western policies and the related insensitivities of some Western politicians contribute to the perception of threat and unwittingly lead to strengthening Islamic fundamentalism. The Gulf War and the war in Bosnia, the latter seen by Islamic fundamentalists to be in continuity with the former, support this contention. In other words: adequate Western policies, when earnestly pursued, as for example the solution of the Israeli-Palestinian conflict, can contribute to dismantling conspiracy perceptions and to averting the clash of the Islamic and Western civilizations. The Islamic world, after all, has enough problems to solve within its own confines. It will be more beneficial for the Arab states to come to grips with pending issues than to engage themselves in external confrontations like the perpetual one with the West. Such confrontations not only distract Muslims from doing their homework, they also threaten regional peace and world stability.

The pan-Arab and Islamic superordinate identities are ideal types, not real sociocultural constructs. With respect to "ethnie," in Smith's sense of ethnic community as a population with shared (ancestry) myths, (historical) memories, and ever-changing common values and symbols, one can argue that both secular and religious superordinate identities can under certain conditions assume a genuinely ethnic character. Thus, the superordinate ethnicity of Arabness competes for favor with its various subordinate everyday ethnic—though Arab—communities. The political ideology of Islamism, being the Islamic variety of religious fundamentalism, is integral with a religion, and no religion, except in its scriptures, is viable in the rarefied atmosphere of abstract universal beliefs, for beliefs are always a part of the social production of meaning. Thus it is possible to see religion fusing with ethnicity and, above all, becoming politicized. Bosnia is a case in point, inasmuch as the Muslim Bosnians, the so-called Bosniaks, are both a distinct ethnic group and adherents of a common faith. The Bosniaks' common awareness of being Muslim is not a fundamentalism, but rather a response to Serbian ethnofundamentalism. Here, too, we speak not of Islamic universalism but, rather, concrete ethnicity.

Despite its claim of universalism, we find Islamic belief reinforcing local ethnic sentiments. The ideal of an Arab-Islamic ethnoreligious identity could draw on these local sentiments. W. Montgomery Watt tells us, for example, that the "federation of Arab tribes" in the Islamic city-state of Medina formed a "supertribe,"[61] depicted as *umma*. The distinction in early Islam between Arab Muslims and *mawali* / non-Arab Muslims produced a level of ethnic conflict that supports the contention that ethnicity cannot be superseded by religion. In the course of the spread of Islam beyond Arabia, Islam was no longer restricted to Arab ethnicity but nonetheless succeeded in fusing itself with other ethnicities. Only when outside powers, in this case the West, are involved do we find this referent of the *umma* succeeding. Islam itself can fuse with ethnicity on a local level, because ethnicity is always concrete, but without that focus on a hostile outside power, the Islamic fundamentalists will fail to override the ethnic and sectarian subordinate identities and subsume them within their superordinate identity.

The ethnically subdivided religious identity of Islam, as superordinate identity, is relevant for understanding several varieties of inter-state conflict (Iran–Iraq) and intra-state conflict (ethnic strife in Afghanistan, or the Alawites versus the Sunni Muslims in Syria). These religious subdivisions, when fused with ethnicity, assume an ethnoreligious character, and sectarianism is the vehicle of this process. As Anthony Smith argues, "the rise of religious sectarianism . . . provides a . . . fertile field for an ethno-religious community. . . . Sectarian, even heretical forms of . . . Islam became associated with remote provincial communities, whose earlier religious association gradually became ethnicized."[62] This analysis leads to the conclusion that competing superordinate and subordinate identities also underlie the crisis of the nation-state in the Middle East. In the course of the rise of Islamic fundamentalism, the recourse to politicized religion has been laden with these ethnicities. When at odds with ethnicity, fundamentalism is destabilizing the existing nation-states in the World of Islam.

Structural change can render traditional forms of ethnicity insignificant. Today, intra-state ethnic conflict is an expression of a competitive struggle over the policies of the state, in its role as the steward of the state's resources, and politicized religion serves as a vehicle for articulating the claims of the subordinate ethnic communities against the basically nominal nation-states.

Religion then becomes a shield against the imposed superordinate secular identity and loyalty patterns. The relating of these ethnic-subordinate determinants to the universalist referents of political Islam creates a great puzzle for the social scientist and the student of religion.

THE INSTITUTIONALLY FRAGILE NOMINAL NATION-STATE

With the exception of Egypt, and to a lesser extent Morocco, the statehood of the contemporary states of the Middle East and North Africa is of fairly recent vintage. The postcolonial state in the Middle East, once established as a nation-state, had to muddle through pan-state-related superordinate claims and identities (equally pan-Arab and Islamic) as well as local subordinate identities. (The Kurds are an exception insofar as they claim a Kurdish state, and other identities are not necessarily related to the claim of the state.) The superordinate formula is an ideal, whereas subordinate identities of local nationalisms and ethnicities are realities underpinned by both subjective and structural networks. In fact, the nation-state of the Middle East, like other non-Western states, is a "historically derived heterogeneous collectivity thrown together by the processes of colonialism."[63]

The existing pattern of the nation-state did not emerge from the area's historical experience with dynastic-territorial and imperial states. Sovereignty as the logical substance of the modern nation-state is alien to that experience, and the new state pattern has been externally imposed on an environment that lacks the needed institutional and cultural infrastructure for establishing it. Thus, the state is institutionally weak, for it not only lacks the framework for resolving conflicts arising from its accommodation of an ethnically heterogeneous population thrown together but also is expected to be the basis for a national community.

Today, intra-state conflicts lie mostly in the mingling of politicized ethnicities with religion within the framework of a struggle over the assets controlled by the state. Patron-client linkages[64] within ethnic communities that compete with each other over the control of these resources tend to shape the new patterns of conflict. The institutionally weak Middle Eastern nation-state lacks the procedural and substantive consent of its several constituencies to the rules of competition and the regulation of ethnic conflict. By default, then, state power rests on imported, technological means of coercion. It has been argued that the Middle Eastern state has never been as powerful politically as it is today, but although this statement is true, it does not contradict the description of the Middle Eastern state as a weak entity conspicuously infantile in the institutionalization of its foundations. The power it commands is the power of coercion, not of institution. Gabriel Ben-Dor argues with some justice that "the European colonial powers exported to the Middle East the most advanced governmental technology available in the form of state apparatus. This governmental technology has a logic of its own, which, however, is not easily exportable. . . . Thus the Arab world ended up with the powerful instrument of the state, but instead of tempering this instrument by its own logic, it was inflamed by the passion of nationalism."[65] Nation-states in the Middle East are unable to arbitrate ethnic conflict, nor can they cope with the ethnopolitics arising from the competition among real subordinate ethnic communities over access to state resources. If we are to understand these problems, it strikes me as imperative that we draw not only on the global background of the Middle Eastern nation-state, as a basic unit of the modern subsystem, but also on its Ottoman and colonial legacies.

The state patterns known to the history of the Middle East prior to the imposition of the nation-state in this century were, again, the imperial and the territorial states. And as Charles Tilly[66] and other distinguished historians have shown, the present international system of states can be traced back to the European system of states established in the seventeenth century. With Islamic civilization in mind, Bernard Lewis argues that since the nineteenth century the idea of the nation has been the major preoccupation of Western-educated intellectuals concerned with imposing Western patterns of organization on their own communities.[67] It was, however, not simply the influence of *ideas* that led to the present state of affairs, for an argument confined to the history of ideas would fail to explain the phenomenon at issue. Better, perhaps, that we look to the Ottoman imperial legacies.

What we find is that the Ottoman Empire, unlike the modern nation-state, did not demand a core social identity related to the state structure, namely the identity of a common ethnicity. As the leading Ottomanist Kemal Karpat puts it, in a remarkable paper on ethnicity in the Ottoman Empire,

> the establishment of religion as the chief identifying characteristic of both Muslims and non-Muslims . . . did not destroy the ethnic sense but in fact strengthened it as well as the religious identity. . . . While the Ottoman government took its legitimacy from Islam and enforced, to the extent possible, Islamic legislation,

it did not identify itself politically and ideologically with the Muslim community until the nineteenth century. . . . The Muslim community encompassed a great number of ethnic and linguistic groups [and] . . . the early Ottoman state recognized these as ethnic divisions.[68]

Compared to the period of globalization of the European economy and of its networks, the colonial penetration of the Ottoman Empire stretched across a vast span of time. Prior to its engaging in direct colonial conquests, the West's program of colonialism drew on contacts with ethnic groups in an effort to establish local support systems. And during the period of colonization, European powers made full use of the existing ethnic divisions, which had hitherto, under Ottoman rule, been fairly insignificant. The Moroccan example of playing ethnic communities against one another (Arabs versus Berbers) became the general tactic for which Syria later became another case in point. In Europe, the unfolding of the sovereign nation long preceded the establishing of the nation-state. In the Middle East, however, nation-states were established *without the prior existence of nations.* Moreover, these new nation-states were burdened with the expectation of "development" and defined as developing countries. The new nation-states failed to meet the task. Crisis was imminent, and gave rise to the resort to religion as a fount of new expectation, as a solvent. Religious fundamentalism replaced secular nationalism as an ideology for the nascent, still sickly nation-state.

Colonial rule had thus unwittingly contributed to the rise of anti-colonial movements based mostly in urban centers, as was the case in Syria. Philip Khoury informs us about the conflict among domestic forces in Syria over the issue of separatism and nationalism. "The birth of the nationalist movement within a relatively unified and integrated political culture" occurred in Syria's urban centers during the French colonial rule (1920–46), and it was carried out by the "cohesive Sunni upper class in four towns."[69] Opposed to this development was the ethnic culture of the Druzes and the Alawites, supported by the French colonial rule. This was a culture divided along tribal or clan lines, the basis of which Khoury interprets as "separatism." The national culture of the major towns was, however, not less ethnically distinct (in the meaning employed in this book) than were the separatist cultures of the Druzes and Alawites, even though it was avowedly supportive of the idea of the nation as the superordinate identity. As Khoury tells us, "the French promoted certain Alawite leaders" (ibid., p. 515) and used them against the national movement. A colonial legacy of this sort rests heavily on the postcolonial state, and when the ethnic Alawite elites succeeded in acquiring national political power, they established their own rule along ethnic and patron-client lines.[70] The ethnic clientele of the Alawite regime legitimized its ethnically exclusive power nationally, as had the urban elites of Damascus and Aleppo earlier.

Ghassan Salamé aptly comments on the rural base of the politically ruling elites, who have an ethnic *'asabiyya* in the Ibn Khaldunian sense, but legitimize themselves nationally. The concept of *'asabiyya* was developed by the famous fourteenth-century Arab-Islamic philosopher of history Ibn Khaldun in his masterly *Prolegomena*.[71] By *'asabiyya* he means the referent for group solidarity affecting the action and the political as well as social cohesiveness of tribes. In the view of Ibn Khaldun tribes thrive when their *'asabiyya* is strong, and their decay is inevitable when their *'asabiyya* begins to weaken. Ghassan Salamé is among the Arab social scientists who draw on this Ibn Khaldunian concept for understanding contemporary Middle Eastern history. He states, "These *'asabiyyas* hate to sign their political practices with their own real name. Instead, they present their state as if it were the exemplary instrument standing in the service of the entire society, a feature which characterizes modern Arab discourse. . . . The ruling Arab authorities are imprisoned in the ideology of [the] modern state, which compels them to obscure their ethnic origins."[72]

Uncovering this nationally disguised tribal ethnicity, which Salamé, in following Ibn Khaldun, refers to as *'asabiyya*, should not distract us from the ethnicity of the urban-national movement itself. Despite its national ideological, that is, pan-Arab, claims, the urban-national movement was ethnic in nature as well. In a recent monograph by a Palestinian-American writer on the origins of Palestinian nationalism, we learn of the insensitivity of the Syrian and Iraqi urban notables to the concerns of the Palestinians. These notables are Arabs, but they constitute a different ethnic community. The tensions spawned by this situation formed the background of the emergence of early Palestinian nationalism. "For all the pan-Arab fervor of dominant Syrians and Iraqis, the Palestinians were not at the top of their agenda," says Muhammad Y. Muslih.[73] This judgment spells out ethnic sentiments even in the pan-Arab nationalist movement.

In the period of decolonization, secular pan-nationalism as a formula for a superordinate identity legitimized the Arabs' struggle against the colonial powers. In the formative years of the Arab element of the Middle Eastern subsystem, the ruling royal national elites made use of this formula, and in moving beyond the confines of the nation-state, they found it useful for the articulation of their aspirations to regional postcolonial power. The year 1952 saw a shift from the royal pan-Arabism of the Arab kings to the populist-inclusivist secular pan-Arabism of the military led by the radical Egyptian officer Gamal Abdel Nasser following the toppling of the monarchy in Egypt. Nasserism was a forceful and honest effort to contain ethnicity under the umbrella of an Arab superordinate identity. The new claim was supported by proposing the model of development for Egypt as the model for the entire Arab world. It failed.[74] The internally and externally determined failure of the secular nation-state as a model of development led to the revival of ethnic subordinate identities, and to the resort to religion.

When pan-Arabism, in the form of Nasserism's nation-state model, subsided, ethnopolitics began once again to thrive, and it is today more than ever a major source of inter-state and intra-state conflict. The politicization of ethnicity and its incorporation into political Islam are intimately related to the crisis of the existing nation-states, and nowhere in the Islamic world is a genuine nation-state to be seen. Instead of the contended unity, one sees on all levels ethnic, national, and sectarian tensions and divisions. In reality we find clienteles, not the alleged sense of citizenship or the universal Islamic *umma*. What we see are "imagined communities" (see note 20) not upheld by corresponding realities.

CONCLUSIONS

The projection of the modern European idea of the nation into the Arab realms of Islamic civilization in the latter half of the nineteenth century served as a legitimating device for an entity nationally defined in terms of superordinate secular Arab ethnicity. Other collectivities living within this entity had previously been defined as minorities, but more recent research suggests that we must go beyond static definitions in identifying ethnicity. Ethnicity properly defined can be transformed into a nation only if two requirements can be met: first, a citizenship-backed internal sovereignty and a corresponding political culture; and second, an institutionally structured polity. In the Islamic world, nation-building took place as state-building, but without the corresponding institutions of political participation. Under these conditions a nation-state is doomed to a nominal status, or what Hedley Bull termed a "nation-state by courtesy."[75] The major source of ethnopolitical conflict in most of the 52 Islamic states is the lack of substance of the nation-state. This is an ethnopolitics in which ethnic, national, and religious commitments are intermingled.

The universal claims of Islamic fundamentalists, which suggest that the politicization of religion unites diverse peoples against the divisive forces of ethnicity, are nothing more than illusions. Religious and ethnic ties have proved to be stronger than ties to the nation-states. Similarly, the imagined universal Islamic community cannot stand, and the claim of Islamic fundamentalists to be establishing a holistic *nizam Islami*/Islamic order ends up creating only disorder.

A political community can sustain itself if the sense of membership in it is structurally upheld and is not simply an idea to be debated among intellectuals and ideologues. "The exigencies of industrialism . . . demand the diffusion of common modes of thought and belief to the state, which is the means of their coordination. . . . The disintegrative impact which is wrought upon preexisting traditional cultures by modern economic and political development creates a search for renewed forms of group symbolism, of which nationalism is the most potent."[76] Without this structural underpinning, citizenship cannot thrive in a political community simply as an awareness of a superordinate identity, and it cannot be "anchored psychologically in [the] distinctive features of modern societies. . . . The extension of communication cannot occur without the conceptual involvement of the *whole community as a knowledgeable citizenry.* A nation-state is a conceptual community in a way in which traditional states were not" (ibid., p. 219). In contrast to this model, the real community in the civilization of Islam is the subordinate ethnoreligious group, not the population of any territorially bordered nation-state. The other competing pattern, the ideal community of an Islamic *umma,* is an "imagined community" (see note 20). The monumental research of the leading German Orientalist Josef van Ess shows that "the notion of the umma, highly exaggerated in our times, [had] little meaning in early Islam."[77] In contemporary history the *umma*-awareness serves as a framework for a civilization-consciousness. In consequence, fundamentalism can function as a unifying force only under conditions of conflict, preferably conflict with an outside power. The challenge of fundamentalism becomes a challenge of turmoil and disorder.

—ɷ—

The Fundamentalist Ideology

Context and the Textual Sources

The Western public sees religious fundamentalism chiefly through the lens of news coverage related to acts of terrorism and other sensational events. Western perceptions of fundamentalism, preoccupied with the equating of it with extremism, are thus misperceptions. True, most of the published views of fundamentalists reflect rather more a new variety of totalitarianism than an effort to "Islamize democracy."[1] But it is deplorable to see some observers taking at face value the window dressing of eloquent Islamic fundamentalists living and acting in exile in the West. After all, no deeper understanding of Islamic fundamentalism is to be reached simply by pinpointing the anti-democratic direction of the movement. Being preoccupied with democracy is a characteristically Western way of looking at things, but in the ideology of Islamic fundamentalism—or, for that matter, in the minds of the Islamic peoples—democracy is not an important issue.

To understand the currents that *should* concern us, we need to study the ideology and major themes of Islamic fundamentalism, as it is propounded by operatives within Islam. The pivotal concept of its ideology is what the fundamentalists call *nizam*/order. Their goal is an Islamization of the political order, which is tantamount to toppling existing regimes, with the implication of de-Westernization. Thus each theme in their ideology is related to a set of dichotomies: divine order versus secular order, *nizam Islami*/Islamic system versus the secular nation-state, *shura*/consultation versus secular democracy, *shari'a*/Islamic law versus positive law

or human legislation, and, above all, *hakimiyyat Allah* / God's rule versus government of the people by the people. In this chapter and the next,
I will introduce the ideology of Islamic fundamentalism by drawing upon
its major Arabic sources and the phenomena I observed on the spot during numerous research visits, not restricted to the Arab parts of the World
of Islam, over the past decade. My focus, however, is on the Arabic sources.
This approach is justified by the fact that the Arab part of Islamic civilization is the religiopolitical center of Sunni Islam. In the West there have
been great exaggerations of the impact of the Islamic Revolution in Iran
on the rest of the World of Islam.[2] These exaggerations overlook the fact
that Sunni Muslims have a concept of order different from that of the
Shi'i Muslims in Iran.

Ideologies do not fall from heaven, and they do not stand in isolation.
They are always articulations of specific historical conditions. But in arguing thus, I do not mean to suggest that ideologies are simply reflections
of an objective situation. Ideologies that are based on religions as cultural
systems are shaped by the realities, and they in turn contribute to shaping the reality by giving it symbolic meaning. This was the Geertzian approach I employed in my earlier book *Islam and the Cultural Accommodation of Social Change,* and I have kept true to it here.[3] In studying the
social context of Islamic fundamentalism I do not reduce its ideology to
existing social and political structures. I am inclined rather to discover
the interplay between the ideological and structural components of
this context.

Islam is a religious belief, not an ideology. As a Muslim I believe in Islam as a faith and honor its precepts as a source of ethics for humans and of
orientation in their conduct. But this is not the way fundamentalists see Islam. Fundamentalisms, of whatever stripe, are not expressions of a renaissance of religion, but rather reflect political ideologies ostensibly drawn
from religions in an effort to remake the world, thus clearly for political
ends. The true fundamentalist is basically a political man with a political
outlook, and in some cases a political activist with little or no interest in religious ethics and divinities. It becomes obvious, then, that my concern here
is to study Islamic fundamentalism as a political ideology, not to inquire
into the religion of Islam itself. The distinction between Islam as a faith and
the political ideology of Islamism as a variety of religious fundamentalism
is most important to denying Islamists their claim that they are the true
representatives of Islam. They are not!

THE REPOLITICIZATION OF ISLAM
IN PURSUIT OF A NEW ORDER

The repoliticization of the Islamic cultural system occurring today in the shape of a political revival[4] has been the most salient feature of public life in countries belonging to Islamic civilization. In the age of Arab liberal thought and secular nationalism, Islam was maintained as a belief and a cultural identity but was, however, depoliticized in the decoupling of concepts of political order from religious faith. Traditional Islamic political thought is based on the religious universalism of Islamic revelation, and a political interpretation of this universalism runs, of course, counter to the modern institution of the nation-state. But although the current revival of political Islam is an expression of an Islamic revolt against the prevailing international order of nation-states and its local configurations, it is *not* a revival of traditional Islamic political thought. Islamic fundamentalists do not speak about the restoration of the traditional Islamic order of the caliphate, but rather of the *nizam Islami* / Islamic order, with clearly modern implications.

Western academic literature on the phenomenon of the repoliticization of Islam can be classified in three categories:

1.   Writing that deals with the phenomenon in terms of day-to-day events, its authors relying on the news coverage by the media and on other published secondary materials in Western languages, mainly English. (There are also some books and articles in French and German.) This category can be further subdivided into (a) survey articles and books, consisting largely of narratives of events, and (b) conceptually oriented works informed by social science theories. All of the literature in this category is hampered by its apparent failure to use primary sources.[5] Most of these authors do not watch the phenomenon at first hand, do not read Arabic or other Middle Eastern languages, and thus fail to encounter fundamentalism on the ground.

2.   Scholarly writing that deals with various movements related to political Islam, as well as writing that extends this scope to deal with the phenomenon empirically, within the framework of field work on a national level (case studies).[6] These studies, though at times suggestive, lack the conceptual overview that would have produced a better grasp of the phenomenon. Some of the authors who have encountered political Islam on the spot, such as the French writer Olivier Roy in Afghanistan, tend to generalize from their one-country experience while lacking an appropriate con-

ceptual framework. Any generalization from one case must be flawed, aside from the fact that the lack of an overarching concept leads to a sweeping impressionism.[7]

3. Scholarly writing that requires the ability to read materials in Arabic and other Middle Eastern languages and to find ways of gaining access to them, requirements that are often neglected. An analysis of the writings of the current revival promises major insights, and studying political literature in its native languages is an excellent way to seek an understanding of its ideology. Aside from a handful of scholarly works on political Islam, such as those of Emmanuel Sivan, Nazih Ayubi, and Youssef M. Choueiri,[8] we find not much of this category. Few of the authors of the large and continually growing body of writings on political Islam published in the West over the last two decades seem to make use of primary sources.

In the following I shall be focusing on Sunni Islam and thus dealing with the literature produced by the Sunni Arab fundamentalists published in Arabic. Shi'i material is published mostly in Farsi, the dominant language of Iran. The major topic of the literature of resurgent political Islam is the Islamic system of government, *al-nizam al-Islami*, which we shall deal with in the next chapter. In the view of the authors of these works, all existing political systems in the Middle East, except those of Iran and Sudan, and in some cases Saudi Arabia, are un-Islamic. It is time, they infer, to return to true Islam, to the divine order established in Medina by the Prophet Muhammad himself. In so doing, they are pursuing for their prospects a decidedly backward orientation. But the choice of the neo-Arabic term *nizam*[9] to denote the old order of the seventh century that so enthralls these authors reveals a typical confusion between the old and the new. It is therefore hardly surprising to discover in their effusions a great many projections of the present into the past. Understandably, most of the concerns of Islamic fundamentalists are related to the current crisis situation, but they articulate them in the traditional language of Islam. Still, a closer look at their belief in the authority of scripture discloses its embedding in the modern context. Moreover, even the language used (for example, the term *nizam*) often consists of modern additions to the classical Islamic lexicon.[10] The fundamentalists are thus not so much reviving classical Islamic concepts as they are introducing new ones that have grown out of the modern context. For fundamentalists, whatever they may claim, are not traditionalists: the much touted *nizam Islami* is something new that resembles more a religiously legitimated dictatorship or an otherwise totalitarian rule than it does the traditional caliphate.

Islamic political groups in the Arab states of the Middle East resort to Islam as a frame of reference (and a source of legitimacy and respectability) in their opposition to the nondemocratic orders of these states. They invoke the concept of *shura* / consultation, integrate it into their concept of an Islamic political system, and present it as an Islamic alternative to Western democracy. Again, we are confronted with the old religiopolitical symbols filled with new meaning, in the Geertzian sense (see note 3). As we shall see in the next chapter, there are just two very brief sentences in the Qur'an encouraging the Prophet Muhammad to have consultation (*shura*) with his companions, and the content of these two lines can scarcely be considered a "concept" unless radically reinterpreted—which is, in fact, what the advocates of the new political Islam do. Despite being anti-democratic by nature, the new concept of *nizam Islami* is adorned with the trappings of democracy through reference to the notion (lacking in the Qur'an) that counsel is *incumbent* on Muslim rulers. Thus our reading of the contemporary political writings of Islamic fundamentalists must focus on the related notions of the *nizam Islami* and *shura,* which fundamentalists consider central.

All Muslim fundamentalists set the implementation of the *shari'a* / Islamic law (*tatbiq al-shari'a*) as the primary condition for the realization of an Islamic system of government. Our examination of the *nizam Islami* must therefore be cognizant of the call for the implementation of *shari'a.* With its reappraisal of political Islam in the guise of current Islamic *usuliyya* / fundamentalism, contemporary Arab political thought has undergone a major change: a shift from secular to religiopolitical commitments. Even once-leading Arab Marxist authors such as the celebrated Anwar 'Abd al-Malek have suddenly discovered that the Qur'an had enjoined political practice long before Marx did: "Twelve centuries ahead of the praise of *praxis* in the Marxian 'Theses on Feuerbach' the Qur'an had urged the believers to commit themselves . . . to the practice [of politics]."[11] The ex-Marxist 'Abd al-Malek thus speaks with contempt of the authors of various secular writings, including 'Ali 'Abd al-Raziq (*al-Islam wa usul al-hukm* / *Islam and the Basis of Government,* Cairo, 1925) and Sadiq Jalal al-'Azm (*Naqd al-fikr ad-dini* / *Critique of Religious Thought,* Beirut, 1969). This shift to a religiopolitical commitment is compelling to the extent that a discussion of the major themes of the currently prevailing political writings published in Arabic will remain incomplete if the discussion fails to deal with this issue.

The publication dates of the politically salient contributions to the fundamentalist ideology in question lead us to conclude that the rise of political Islam clearly began in the Arab part of Islamic civilization; it did not take hold, as commonly believed, through the Iranian Revolution. The prominent contemporary ideologue of Islamic fundamentalism, Yusuf al-Qaradawi, published his call for *al-hall al-Islami*/the Islamic solution[12] in the early 1970s, at a time when Khomeini's name and the ideology of Khomeinism[13] were completely unknown in the Arab areas of the Middle East. The first printing of the major contemporary treatise on the alleged political system of Islam, written by Muhammad Salim al-'Awwa,[14] was published in 1975 in Cairo, without reference to Khomeini or to Iran. Only in the later editions (sixth printing, 1983) do we find such references. For this reason, it seems justifiable to exclude the Shi'i Iranian Revolution from the arguments of this chapter and to focus on Sunni Arab Islam, without denying (or exaggerating) the later interplay between the two (see note 2).

In their writings, the Islamic fundamentalists present themselves as true scripturalists, though they invoke the scriptures (wittingly or unwittingly) in a highly selective manner. In any event, I shall not restrict myself to a scriptural approach in studying the relevant writings. Instead I will offer a contextual understanding of their content, concentrating on the political structures within which Islamic fundamentalism operates. There exists no geographically isolated Islamic world, but rather a religioculturally diverse Islamic part of our current world, addressed here as an Islamic civilization. Ideologically, political Islam is based on the rejection of the global system of nation-states. Thus the spirit of rejection that we see set forth in the political writings of Islamic fundamentalists: even though political Islam claims a new alternative to the prevailing order, it is based rather on reviving old dreams and, hence, is primarily millenarian in character. Still, Islamic fundamentalists are not traditionalists; their ideal is the selectively perceived and arbitrarily purified state of seventh-century Islam. This primeval golden age is presented as a referent for solving the problems of the present crisis on a global basis, that is, as an alternative world order. The selectively scriptural recourse to the past is assumed to set the norms for the future of Islamic civilization. But this millenarian notion helps us little in understanding the real issues. In fact, Islamic fundamentalism addresses current issues with a new ideology. I shall spell out this contention.

THE REGIONAL AND GLOBAL CONTEXT OF
THE FUNDAMENTALIST WRITINGS

Our context here is a global one, our time is world time, and the history involved, as affected by modernity, is global history. As earlier outlined, the
Peace of Westphalia in 1648 marked the decay of the divine order and the
emergence of the modern international system of secular states. In the three
hundred years following the Peace of Westphalia, Europeans imposed this
system of states, each enjoying internal and external sovereignty, on the
rest of the world. In much of the World of Islam this sovereignty exists in
only nominal form, and I have therefore coined the term "nominal nation-
state." The decline of the Ottoman Empire[15] was not the result of a "Western conspiracy against Islam," but a part of unfolding global history; it
marked the end of the long historical epoch of divine orders that had reigned
virtually throughout the world.

After the abolition of the caliphate in 1924 the Arabs adopted the idea of
the nation as a concept for political action, but chose not to restrict it to any
one of the Arab nation-states that had come to exist in reality. The Arab
dream of a pan-Arab state embracing all individual Arab states remains
technically feasible, and is not incompatible with the framework of international order as a system of nation-states. This was the dream that gripped
the thinking of Arab nationalists and thus superseded and deferred the
dream of an Islamic universalism. As we have seen, the political option of
an Arab nation is consonant with a real structure, the modern, globally prevailing, international system of nation-states.

Arab nationalism, though irredentist in nature, has been imprisoned in
the idea of the nation-state for the simple reason that it has aspired to the
larger goal of an overarching Arab nation-state. Pan-Arab nationalism was
at odds with the notion of Islamic *umma* because, on the one hand, it excluded all non-Arab Muslims (for example, those in Indonesia, the largest
Islamic nation) from this entity and, on the other, because it included Arab
Christians (for example, those in Lebanon and Egypt) as citizens and no
longer as *dhimmi* / protected people, that is, minorities. The writings of Sati'
al-Husri are a literary manifestation of this period, which began in the early
1920s and lasted until the late 1960s.[16] The Arab defeat in the Six-Day War
of 1967 was a turning point, because the war's outcome contributed to the
de-legitimization of the secular Arab regimes involved in this crushing defeat. In an authoritative book published in French, Arabic, and English, the
preeminent Moroccan historian Abdallah Laroui views the historical period

triggered by the Six-Day War as a period of crisis,[17] and the crisis has not receded since, but rather has intensified. The Gulf War only complicated matters, by adding its own bitter legacy to the post-1967 Arab predicament.[18] In an article in Arabic published in Beirut in the literary/critical journal *Mawaqif,* edited by the preeminent Arab poet Adonis, I called the process of self-chastisement in the years 1967–70 "From Self-Glorification to Self-Criticism."[19]

Secular pan-Arab nationalism, as once reflected in the many writings of Sati' al-Husri (see note 16), had to step aside to make way for political Islam. The new political pamphleteering has superseded the voluminous, hitherto prevailing writings of pan-Arabism, and reflects more recent attitudes. In one of the politically pioneering works of this new genre, the previously mentioned Egyptian Muslim Brother Yusuf al-Qaradawi (see Chapter 5) declared *al-Hall al-Islami faridha wa darurah* / The Islamic Solution as an obligation. This option provides the "*ma'alim fi/ial-tarq* / signposts" (Sayyid Qutb) on the road to the future of Islamic civilization.

In the Arab part of the Middle East, the repoliticization of Islam began as a response to the repercussions of the Six-Day War.[20] Spillover effects soon spread far beyond the Arab core of the "abode of Islam" to its periphery. In the process, political Islam has become a global issue related, in varying degrees, to all of Islamic civilization.

Again, one could question this statement by observing that Islam has always been political, even after the abolition of the caliphate in 1924. The birth of the Muslim Brotherhood movement in Egypt in 1928, as well as the emergence of Wahhabi-inspired Saudi Arabia, could be advanced as further evidence against the argument of a retreat of political Islam since the 1920s. Furthermore, one could cite the involvement of Islamic symbols in the struggle against French colonial rule in Algeria,[21] as well as in Morocco.

In fact, secular ideologies, primarily pan-Arab nationalism, emerged in the post-World War I period as the dominant political discourse, while Islam as a political ideology, but not as a religious belief, seems to have receded ever since,[22] at least until the early 1970s. This assessment is not meant to so exaggerate the dynamics of the period that one might conclude that the political understanding of Islam had vanished altogether. Students of the contemporary history of the Middle East know that even Sherif Hussain of Mecca, the "leader" of the Arab Revolt of 1916 against the Islamic (essentially Turkish) order of the Ottoman Empire, coveted the thought of becoming the caliph of all Muslims himself. In fact, he made just such an attempt, in his abortive caliphate of 1924, shortly after the abolition of the Ottoman caliphate.[23] Nevertheless, and notwithstanding the fact that Hassan al-Banna, the founder of the Muslim Brotherhood movement, considered the i'adat al-khilafa al-mafqudah / restoration of the lost caliphate to be the chief political goal of his party,[24] political Islam had by then receded and was no longer the driving political force in the Arab part of the Middle East. In the global context of world time those political ideologies based on the idea of a secular nation uniting the Arabs replaced the then seemingly abandoned understanding of a universal umma that included all Muslims. Even a leading Syrian shari'a scholar, Muhammad al-Mubarak, at times dean of the faculty of shari'a at the University of Damascus, drew a clear distinction between al-umma al-'Arabiyya, the uniting of both Muslim and Christian Arabs as one nation, and al-umma al-Islamiyya, a very loose understanding of solidarity (al-ukhuwwa / brotherhood) among Muslims, lacking decisive political consequences.[25]

In Arabic there exists no particular term for the secular meaning of la nation, as defined in the historical context of the French Revolution. In classical Arabic and in the formative years of Islam there was a clear distinction between a qawm, that is, the particular tribe to which an Arab belonged, and the umma / community, which is the supreme frame of reference of identity for all Muslims. In modern times la nation has been translated into Arabic as the very term umma, thus confusing the religious meaning of the political community established by the Prophet Muhammad in the seventh century with the secular meaning that had unfolded in Europe in the course of the eighteenth century. "Nationalism" has been translated into Arabic as the neo-Arabic term al-qawmiyya, which is based on the classical Arabic term qawm meaning tribe, people. This translation opened the way for the polemical cry of Islamic fundamentalists that secular Arab nationalists are reverting to the pre-Islamic jahiliyya / age of heedlessness of tribes. Truly, the Islamic umma historically aimed at replacing the qawm / tribe in uniting all Arab tribes in one community.

In the secular literature of pan-Arab nationalism we confront chiefly projections of modern European meaning, such as that of la nation, into the classical Arab history and lexicon. Most of the authors of this literature trace the Arab nation back even into pre-Islamic times.[26] The ethnic conflict between Arabs and the mawali (non-Arab Muslims) is being translated into a national conflict between those who want to maintain the Arab purity of

Islam and those who want to welcome non-Arab elements into it. Enmity and confusion—between tribes, ethnosectarian communities, and the modern nation—have been at work among Islamists and secularists alike.

Political thought always reflects a worldview. In interpreting Islam as a cultural system along the lines of the anthropology of Clifford Geertz (see note 3), I want to advance the hypothesis that Islam has always been the underlying cultural basis of the particular worldview of Muslims, and even of pan-Arab secularists. In the Middle East there has never been a process of structural and cultural changes underlying an orderly shift of the worldview from a religious to a secular one, as happened in the historical process that once unfolded in Europe. In this sense, there has never been a real societal process of secularization underpinning secular ideologies in the Middle East, not even in secular Turkey. In Turkey the state claims to be secular, but the society is not; and it cannot be described as secular in the sociological meaning of the term. We can argue, in fact, that the continuity of the Islamic worldview, persisting even in the midst of social change, has facilitated the recent shift from secular ideologies to those of political Islam and to the worldview it reflects.[27] In examining Islam's function as a cultural system underlying a worldview, one cannot escape the fact that secular ideologies were never able to put down strong structural roots in Islam, or to affect the prevailing worldview. Thus, secularization as a separation of religion and politics has remained a surface function.

Long before the rise of Islamic fundamentalism a former sheikh of al-Azhar who received his academic education as well as his doctorate from a German university (Hamburg, 1936)[28] defined the worldview of Muslims as one based on a separation of the world into "the West" and the "abode of Islam." To him, the West has intruded upon the World of Islam, and in the process has provoked a deviation from Islam.[29] The concern of Muslims should ultimately be to return their people and their ideas and institutions to Islam. It follows, then, that the desire "to rebuild Islamic social life on the very principles of Islam"[30] has always been a salient feature of Muslim thinking.

Preoccupation with the glorious Islamic past characterizes the views of both the secularists and the fundamentalists in the Middle East. This preoccupation is a major obstacle to the unfolding of a worldview adjusted to the structure of the real, existing world of today. Muslim fundamentalists for the most part continue to be preoccupied with dichotomizing the world into an Islamic East and a Christian West, but our world can no longer be reduced to such a simplifying dualism. Although the war in Bosnia enforced this dualistic worldview, the realities of our modern world are characterized by far more complex structures, and the preoccupation with West/Islam dualities hampers the development of insights into these structures. If one agrees with Edward Said that the "East" is a creation of the "West,"[31] then one can hardly exclude modern Arab and Islamic writers from culpability for creating a "West" that is the enemy. The alleged holistic "West" does not exist; it is a creation of Islamic thought. It seems to me fruitless to continue such a debate.

Still, we do need to understand how Islamic fundamentalists deal with the issues of government, democracy, and the disruptive effects of rapid social change, for these are the dominant issues informing the present ambiance of crisis, and it is dismaying to see them debated within the framework of the "Orient/Occident" dichotomy. I have no inclination to engage in the polemics of the debate on orientalism, but it is nonetheless appropriate and fair to concede that orientalism is not an invention of Edward Said. The label describes a real attitude of some ethnocentric Western authors writing about the "Orient," not to mention the trappings of decades of Western cinematic melodramas. Said, however, stretches the argument too far. Those who, in his footsteps, adopt the concept simplify the issue and even reverse the idea of orientalism. A Damascene critic of Said, Sadiq Jalal al-'Azm, in a piece no less polemical than Said's *Orientalism* itself, has argued that Muslim authors *orientalize themselves* when they claim for themselves a frame of reference different from those of the rest of humanity. In al-'Azm's view, this is orientalism in reverse.[32] While giving Said his due, I cannot overlook the trap of romanticizing manichaeism he unwittingly falls into while dealing with the Orient/Occident dualism.[33]

Many Muslim writers argue that Islamic thought is distinct,[34] altogether different from the analytical tools of social science. Implicitly, then, they subscribe to the idea of *homo islamicus* originally put forward by Western orientalists themselves. The program of "Islamization of knowledge"[35] is one of the discouraging aspects of current political Islam. I argue that we Muslims, like peoples of any other civilization and their traditions, can engage in dispassionate reasoning. It is true that ostensibly neutral tools of analysis can have sensitive cultural connotations, since by necessity they originate in a specific cultural context. It is, however, wrong to infer from this acknowledgment of an existing cultural diversity the disputable generalization that there can *be* no general knowledge in these terms, owing to the lack of a universal civilization. Islamic fundamentalists insist that there is an Islamic knowledge that by its nature divorces them from the West, but surely political Islam can be understood and analyzed by thoughtful interpretation of its texts in the light of the concomitant historical context. The literary production of Muslim authors, like that of any group embedded in a given civilization, is generated from encounters with real issues and is based on human knowledge and experience. Studying and understanding these issues in their historical context is possible even for non-Muslims. To concede the distinctive character of a culture is not tantamount to contending that these specifics can be properly understood only by members of the culture itself.

All political thought reflects continuity. Topical issues relate to recent events, but their articulation often reveals far older concerns and, hence, a conspicuous historical continuity. Fundamentalist writers—like writers elsewhere—seldom embark upon truly new grounds. For the most part, they revive the discussion that arose in the aftermath of the abolition of the caliphate in 1924, though in a new language and with new concerns. Most of the new writers find time to refer to the aforementioned book by 'Ali 'Abd al-Raziq, *al-Islam wa usul al-hukm / Islam and the Basis of Government*, either to continue refuting and demonizing him or to set new precedents.[36] In discussing Islam and government[37] only a few of the adherents of political Islam insist on the restoration of the caliphate. The larger debate is on "the Islamic system of government" (see note 14). Most fundamentalist writers stress the political character of Islam, but no longer insist on maintaining the term "caliphate," as we shall see later. Fundamentalist thought is clearly embedded in a new context, one that differs markedly from that of classical Islam. In short, the issue of whether Islam is basically a religious belief or is, rather, a system of government manifested as an expression of a divine order—whether domestic or global in purview—situates the fault lines between secularists, liberal Muslims, and fundamentalists in the Islamic world.

CALIPHATE, THE *FETWA*, AND THE DISTORTION OF HISTORY AND SCRIPTURE

The ongoing debate on Islamic government may raise expectations that the fundamentalist approach is in fact dealing with the real problems emanating from the crisis of the nation-state. There is a need for finding an appropriate political system for the people of Islamic civilization, but in the course of reviewing the literature of Islamic fundamentalism, we find that the political thought expressed seldom goes beyond the self-congratulatory assertion that divine order in general is preferable to any secular one. In keeping with the classical tradition of Islamic thought, in which politics was inseparably linked with the *shari'a*, the political writings of Islamic fundamentalism are convictional in attitude and scriptural in method. One's first glimpse of this literature reveals that in addressing the current state of affairs it neither offers a political analysis nor shows a way out.

The notion of *al-nizam al-Islami,* to be dealt with in the next chapter, is set forth as a conviction lying beyond evidence and the need for firm grounds. Those who share it are viewed to be true Muslims; those who question it, whatever their sympathies, are scorned as deviants of the Islamic *umma,* or even "infidels." Since the symbol of Islamic order so easily projects different patterns of meaning, it is not surprising that it is an issue in contention even among its own adherents. Islamic fundamentalists of various currents insist on the righteousness of their own views, and deny righteousness to their fellow Muslims, other fundamentalists included. Scriptural argumentations[38] provide the logic of the debates, for only the scripture is conceded to uphold or to reject any given interpretation of the notion of an Islamic system of government. The lessons of history, the actuality of existing political structures, and the efficacy or inefficacy of institutions do not matter as a source or defense of argument, for if their reality does not accord with the precepts invoked, then they are merely refutable deviations from true Islam. A liberal Muslim thinker, Mohammad Arkoun, recently denounced this sort of anti-intellectualism and made the point that every religion, Islam not excluded, is subject to rethinking, that is, to the lessons and forces of history.[39] Needless to say, the response by the representatives of political Islam has been mostly hostile.

Again, there is considerable historical continuity in Islamic thought, as there is in the thought of cultures elsewhere. Most of the Arab-Islamic contributions to the debate on the *shari'a* draw upon two Islamic writings of the early twentieth century, works that are already acclaimed as classics. One is Rashid Rida's *al-Khilafah wa al-imamah al-'uzma / The Caliphate and the Great Imamate;*[40] the second is 'Ali 'Abd al-Raziq's *al-Islam wa usul al-hukm / Islam and the Basis of Government.* In the first we encounter the idea that Islam is *din wa dawla / unity of religion and state;* in the second we learn the opposite, that although such a unity has been imputed to Islam, the notion lacks any justification in the primary sources, that is, in the Qur'an and the *hadith.*

Those Muslims who side with Rida against 'Abd al-Raziq no longer insist that the caliphate is the only legitimate Islamic system of government. True, there was a protracted silence concerning the issue of Islamic government in the years preceding the reappraisal of political Islam. Anyone who follows the intellectual currents of Arabic publications is familiar with such books as Muhammad Yusuf Musa's *Nizam al-hukm fi al-Islam / The Political System of Islam,* Muhammad Dia'uddin al-Rayes's *al-Nazariyyat al-siyasiyya al-Islamiyya / Political Theories of Islam,* and 'Abdulhamid Mutawalli's *Mabadi' nizam al-hukm fi al-Islam / Principles of the System of Government in Islam,* none of them less than 30 years old.[41] (I will return to these works in Chapter 8.) This category of Islamic political writings was rare, however, before the 1970s or, at the least, was not the dominant genre in the political literature. Moreover, these writings were not generally as appealing upon publication as they have become since. But one cannot infer from their newfound following that Muslims had earlier done away with Islam, as most of the current fundamentalist writings suggest. Islam never ceased to be the major source of the Islamic worldview. It did recede, however, as a framework for the legitimation of a political order.

Prior to the rise of political Islam, the dominant understanding of Islam was to be found in the authoritative textbook on Islam, *al-Islam, 'aqidah wa shari'a / Islam, Doctrine and Law,* by the late sheikh of al-Azhar, Mahmud Shaltut.[42] This book, which saw ten printings, includes a chapter on *al-umma fi al-Islam /* the community in Islam. Shaltut argues that Islam does not restrict the meaning of *umma /* community to a specific *dawla /* state, because this would lead to a "delimitation and narrowing, contradicting the universalism of Islam."[43] Shaltut stresses the *ukhuwwa al-Islamiyya /* Islamic brotherhood. The fraternity of Muslims, which is the ethical value and the content of solidarity among Muslims, is the salient meaning of the Islamic *umma.* Fundamentalists refute this view by invoking the Islamic principle of *shura,* as a principle of Islamic government. Shaltut states unequivocally that "neither the Qur'an nor the Prophet set a specific system of *shura.*"[44] In other words, no less an authority than Mahmud Shaltut indirectly depoliticizes Islam while putting greater emphasis on the ethical content of *umma,* in the sense of moral fraternity, than on *dawla /* state, as an expression of a political system.

In denying that the primary sources of Islam provide a "specific system of *shura*," Shaltut clearly intends to reduce this Islamic precept to an ethical norm and virtually dismisses the notion of *hukumah Islamiyya* / Islamic government. This term, which has been used extensively by Khomeini, conveys the same meaning as the term *hakimiyyat Allah* / God's rule preferably used by Sunni Arab fundamentalists. To be sure, all fundamentalists subscribe to this concept of divine order. Shaltut's understanding of modern international relations, to which he adheres in this work, is also striking. In his view, Islam is primarily a mission of peace: "If non-Muslims maintain peace, so they must be in this case, from the point of view of Islam, considered brothers to the Muslims, comprising with them humanity. Each has his own religion. . . ." (ibid., p. 453, which makes no mention of sisters). In so stating, Shaltut formulates an Islamic alternative to fundamentalism. Although his book, along with the more recent two-volume handbook by al-Azhar, *Bayan li al-nas / Declaration to Humanity*,[45] is not a particularly enlightened contribution to an Islam quite capable of embracing the cultural accommodation of social change (see note 3), it is nevertheless a significant effort to adjust the Islamic worldview to the changed conditions of our age.

In reviewing the political writings of Islamic fundamentalism, we no longer encounter this notion of plurality in humanity ("each has his own religion"). Political Islam is of a completely different caliber. Those Muslims who regard their religion more as an ethical than a political context, as a source of conduct and not a system of government, are considered by fundamentalists to be "misguided Muslims," or even apostates. Thus the fundamentalists draw the conclusion that they are justified in slaying these Muslims they arbitrarily declare apostates. In a widely read popular book by two exponents of political Islam, *Asalib al-ghazu al-fikri li al-'alam al-Islami / Methods of the Intellectual Invasion of the Muslim World*, we encounter some of the new fundamentalist attitudes. The authors of this book, Jarisha and Zaibaq (professors teaching in Medina), do not exclude even 'Abduh, the foremost intellectual father of Islamic modernism, from their polemic. Muhammad 'Abduh (1849–1905) lived in Cairo and after the years of exile in Paris became Grand Mufti of Egypt in 1888. 'Abduh made an effort at a synthesis between Islam and cultural modernity. In the view of fundamentalists 'Abduh and all Islamic reformers are themselves products of the "intellectual invasion" by the West and are therefore indicted.[46] The edge of the polemic becomes even sharper when the authors turn to Rifa'a R. al-Tahtawi, who, in his well-known diary of his experiences as *imam*/religious and political leader to the contingent of Egyptian students in France in the 1820s, gives an enthusiastic account of Parisian life. Tahtawi viewed Europe as a model for Muslims.[47] The fundamentalists Jarisha and Zaibaq condemn Tahtawi. For them the only adequate understanding of "true Islam" is the one that first acknowledges that "the major task of the Qur'an is to govern [*an yahkuma*] . . . [and] the unity of state and religion is the crucial part of this understanding, not such that religion is a partial dimension of the state, but on the contrary, such that religion is the major element of the state [*qism lahu la qasim* / a part of it, not a partner to it]" (ibid., pp. 38–39).

As Jarisha and Zaibaq put it, there has been a colonial *mu'amarah*/conspiracy[48] directed against Islam, a conspiracy that resulted in the destruction of the caliphate. The authors apparently do not consider the fact that the concept of a caliphate cannot be found in the Qur'an. True, the verb *khalafa*/to succeed does occur in several of the Qur'anic *suras* (the Qur'an is subdivided into 114 *suras*) but in meanings quite different from "to succeed in office." A role in this alleged conspiracy is assigned to Arab nationalism, which is seen by Jarisha and Zaibaq as a product of "missionizing crusaders."[49] Moreover, "Arab nationalism was disseminated by the British spy Lawrence" (ibid., p. 41). Arab nationalists are mostly secularists, in the sense that they distinguish between a divine order and the secular nation-state. But in the view of Jarisha and Zaibaq, Arab nationalists are victims of the Jews, who are held to be the precursors in the conspiracy to separate religion from state in order "to destroy religion. . . . Islam, however, does not permit such a separation. The state is in the *fiqh*/Islamic jurisprudence of Islam an indivisible part of the religion, so that there can be no religion without the state and vice versa."[50] The fact that the political culture of our age is based on the nation-state denotes, for Jarisha and Zaibaq, a "return to the *jahiliyya*," that is, to the pre-Islamic age of heedlessness. The "return to Islam" promoted by the *sahwa al-Islamiyya*/Islamic awakening expresses an Islamic determination to overcome the setbacks suffered by Islam. The call for *al-nizam al-Islami*/the Islamic system of government is considered the major feature of this awakening, which in the view of these authors, as a return to the divine, focuses on three issues:

1.   Islamic legitimacy (*al-shar'iyya al-Islamiyya*);

2.   The Islamic *umma*, which supports the *shar'iyya*; and

3.   The political power necessary for upholding this concern, that is, the implementation of the *shari'a* (Jarisha and Zaibaq, p. 239).

Quite apart from their obsession with conspiracy it is striking to see Jarisha and Zaibaq drawing on a neo-Arabic term simply translated from modern Western languages: *al-shar'iyya*. Students of Islam are familiar with the traditional Islamic concept of *al-siyasa al-shar'iyya*, in which the adjective *shar'iyya* is derived from the noun *shari'a*. The traditional concept of the classical jurist Ibn Taimiyya[51] gives *siyasa* the meaning "the running of a state." This concept renders the state authority valid only if standing in conformity with the *shari'a*. In the language used by Jarisha and Zaibaq the adjective *shar'iyya* becomes a *noun* that in modern Arabic means "legitimacy."[52] In this equation the term *shar'iyya* covers the meanings both of "legitimacy" and "*shari'a*-based policy." This acrobatic wordplay results in the formula "*la shar'iyya bi ghair shari'a* / there can be no legitimacy without implementing the *shari'a*,"[53] which epitomizes the view that every political system of government is devoid of legitimacy if the commitment to the practice of Islamic *shari'a* is missing. This striking example reveals the fundamentalists' play of language in mixing old and new concepts, as well as introducing new meanings and simultaneously claiming both originality and authenticity.

The question arises now whether the caliphate is indeed the political system our authors acclaim in their formula of *al-shar'iyya al-Islamiyya*, supported by the Muslim *umma* and upheld by the true Muslim rulers. Jarisha and Zaibaq do not evade the question; they present their position as follows:

> If political rule, first, is based on the *shari'a* of God and, second, is accepted by the Muslims, then the form matters little. We may name it *caliphate, imamate,* or we may refer to whatever names so long as the aforementioned requirements are fulfilled. If, however, these requirements are missing, then no political authority can claim to have legitimacy. . . . This is the true understanding of the protection of religion and of . . . how to refer to it as guidance for worldly affairs. In fact, this is the definition of the *caliphate,* and properly the definition of any legitimate order.[54]

As this passage shows, the authors no longer insist in their *fetwa* on the restoration of the caliphate. Their goal is a political system based on the *shari'a* or, more properly, on their understanding of it, because, as outlined above, the *shari'a* is a post-Qur'anic construction. As most of the Islamic fundamentalists do, Jarisha and Zaibaq resort to the neo-Islamic and neo-Arabic term *al-nizam al-Islami*. They plead, too, for the absolute imposition of the Islamic *shari'a* as the incontestable framework or orientation for resolving all issues, to be applied in all times, in all places, and for all peoples. "If the *shari'a* is established in this sense and if the Islamic law is practiced under the aforementioned conditions [that is, unlimited, absolute validity], then it follows that there is an Islamic system (*nizam Islami*)" (ibid., p. 244). Any other option, and especially options based on secular views, are considered contrary to the tenets of Islam. For Jarisha and Zaibaq, "Secularization is an assault (*'udwan*) on Islam" (ibid., p. 249). The suspension (*ta'til*) of the *shari'a* is equated with the suspension of God's will and therefore considered to be the source of all evils.

As a liberal Muslim with a Middle Eastern background I agree wholeheartedly with Mark Juergensmeyer's plea that the West ought to overcome its arrogance and be more tolerant[55] toward non-Western cultures. This must not amount, however, to a consent to religious fundamentalism (or, as Juergensmeyer names it, religious nationalism). Indeed, I would not care to live in a divine order overseen by Islamic fundamentalists. When one learns of the *fetwa* / religious decree by the late Egyptian fundamentalist sheikh Muhammad al-Ghazali (died in 1996), renowned as an authority on the Islamic concept of human rights,[56] the limits of tolerance are reached. In his *fetwa* of June 1993 he declares that "every Muslim who pleads for the suspension of the *shari'a* is an apostate and can be killed. The killing of those apostates cannot be prosecuted under Islamic law because this killing is justified."[57] There is no justification in the Qur'an for such an entrée to the slaying of fellow Muslims. There is not one revelation in the Qur'an that sanctions the killing of *murtad* / apostates. The command to slay reasoning Muslims is un-Islamic, an invention of Islamic fundamentalists. The *shari'a*, after all, is a post-Qur'anic construction.[58]

The right to view religious belief as an ethics and to refuse to permit its politicization to be part and parcel of intellectual freedom ought not to be questioned. Freedom of belief is a basic human right,[59] and the Qur'an rigorously forbids the killing of Muslims (Qur'an-Surat *al-Nisa*, 4/92). It is thus frightening to realize that on the authority of this *fetwa* the killing of the Egyptian essayist Faraj Fuda (in June 1992) was justified. Algerian fundamentalists, who in 1993 alone slew twelve leading Algerian intellectuals,[60] also resort to this *fetwa* and legitimize their killing of Muslims as *shari'a*-decreed executions. Islam as a religious belief is thereby distorted, and the fundamentalists defile Islam not only by legitimizing the totalitarian rule they seek but also by silencing reasoning liberal Muslims. In the terms of scriptural fundamentalism, simply coining the formula "Rethinking Islam" (see note 39) puts the enlightened Algerian Muslim Mohammed Arkoun at grave risk, for fundamentalists view "rethinking" of this sort as heresy. Rethinking Islam can lead to one's being listed among those apostates to be executed. Arkoun is careful, but courageous enough to use this formula as the title of one of his important books. "Rethinking Islam" may suggest to some that *shari'a* and human rights are at odds (see note 59).

An unbiased reading of the political writings of current fundamentalists leads one to conclude that we are dealing with a brand of political propaganda. The style, language, and method of argumentation of these works all reveal propagandistic tactics, not a theology or an intellectual discourse. Reasoning is for these zealots a heresy.

The importance of books produced by Islamic fundamentalists lies, of course, in their great political impact. I have encountered the cited Jarisha and Zaibaq volume throughout the Islamic world. Other, more serious works are being published to meet the increasing demand among Muslims to learn more about the caliphate as the historical form of political rule in Islam. Among these current writings is a fairly scholarly work, based on historical sources, titled *al-Islam wa al-khilafah / Islam and the Caliphate*, by 'Ali Husni al-Khartabuli. Although he defends the Islamic caliphate, al-Khartabuli indicates clearly that there exists no single scripture, either in the Qur'an or in the *hadith*, supporting the idea that this is the true Islamic system of government. He nevertheless insists that "despite the fact that the caliphate was abolished in Turkey, it is still divine and respected by all Muslims. Ever since its abolition Muslims have never stopped asking for its restoration."[61] This is the only judgment related to the present that is included in this most comprehensive book, which covers the history of the caliphate from its inception after the death of the Prophet Muhammad until its abolition in 1924. Without so much as a blush, al-Khartabuli refers to events of the tenth century, during which Muslims had simultaneously *three* caliphs, one in Baghdad, the second in Cairo, and the third in Cordoba (now Spain), *each one* claiming to be the true Islamic successor of the Prophet. Al-Khartabuli merely describes this bizarre state of affairs and restricts himself to reporting that the rule of the caliph over the two holy shrines (in Mecca and Medina) was no longer a requirement for establishing the caliphate.

More outspoken is the liberal Muslim and jurist Muhammad Said al-Ashmawi in his courageous book on the Islamic caliphate, published in Cairo. Ashmawi bluntly states that neither in the Qur'an, as the Islamic revelation, nor in the sayings of the Prophet (*hadith*) does there exist a religious justification for the political order of the caliphate. "The caliphate has no Islamic grounds . . . it did disservice to Islam in confusing religious belief and politics."[62] Ashmawi is among the Muslim intellectuals in Cairo hunted for his rational arguments by fundamentalists.

CONCLUSIONS

Aside from these references to the debate on the caliphate we can conclude from the study of Islamic fundamentalist literature that the caliphate and its restoration are no longer pivotal issues in contemporary political Islam. The focus now is on another concept, the *nizam Islami*—the formula of the search for a divine Islamic order in the age of fundamentalism. Within Islam there is considerable dissent on the authenticity of the concept of *nizam* in Islamic sources. There are neo-Islamic advocates of an Islamic system of government based on implementing the *shari'a*. These are the fundamentalists. Then there are Muslims who believe that in Islam there exists no clear precept that might determine how a government should be assembled if it is to have an Islamic legitimacy. And there are also Muslims to whom Islam—in the tradition of Sufism/Islamic mysticism—is a source of ethics and a way of life, not a formal system of government. Islamic Sufi-mystics believe that religious faith is spiritual and based on "love of God," not on a rigorous implementation of *shari'a*/Islamic law. In the Middle East and North Africa, the warriors of political Islam have seized the lead from these tolerant Muslims.

Some bright liberal Muslim thinkers do not contest the political character of Islam. They do, however, refuse any dogmatic solution to the crisis of the nation-state in Islamic civilization, be it purely secular *or* fundamentalist. It is unfortunate that these Islamic thinkers[63] are such a small minority and that they are already exposed to the threat of being slain as *murtad*/apostates. It is not only Westerners who denounce this distressing intolerance in contemporary Islam. Muslim liberals do also. Must we who condemn intolerance then feel "guilty of intolerance of our own,"[64] as Juergensmeyer himself does for not having been perceptive enough to anticipate the anti-secular views of those who plead for a divine order?

The Idea of an Islamic State and the Call for the Implementation of the *Shari'a* / Divine Law

One of the salient features of fundamentalist ideology is the novelty of the views presented in the name of "*al-Islam al-siyasi* / political Islam."[1] In the political pronouncements of Islamic fundamentalists we encounter no call for the restoration of the caliphate, as the traditional order of Islam.[2] Rather, we face the new concept "*dawla Islamiyya* / Islamic state," presented basically in terms of a *nizam Islami* / Islamic system of government. For Islamic fundamentalists, their claims notwithstanding, faith is based more on a political conviction than on the tolerant and spiritual concept of "God's love" that informs Sufi Islam.[3] The Islamic state aspired to is clearly not an "Islamization of democracy," nor is it the "perfect state" once outlined in the political philosophy of medieval Islamic rationalists, Abu Nasr al-Farabi[4] foremost among them.

The model state presented by Islamic fundamentalism is basically a form of totalitarian rule, even though some writers perceive it as an Islamic pattern of democratic state-making. In this chapter we shall hear about some populist Islamic fundamentalists. Unlike totalitarian fundamentalists, Islamic populists accept with some restrictions the idea of popular sovereignty. But their efforts notwithstanding, mainstream fundamentalism is dominated by the views of the Pakistani Abu al-A'la al-Mawdudi, which can be described with both justice and charity as a "divine pattern" of totalitarianism.

This chapter focuses on the diverse views that attend the notion of "the Islamic state," populist and totalitarian alike. Two issues stand at the hub of this debate. The first is the implementation of *shari'a*/divine law; the second is the notion of *shura,* whether as an Islamic *substitute for* democracy or, what some allege, as a specifically Islamic *pattern of* democracy.

DIN WA DAWLA / UNITY OF RELIGION AND STATE:
BUT WHAT ELSE?

On the level of generalities there is no dispute among the writers who produce the ideology of political Islam, particularly with regard to the formula *din wa dawla*/unity of religion and state. What usually follows, by way of articulation, is nothing but vague statements on which the idea of an Islamic state is precariously based. In this regard, the Tunisian writer Mahmud 'Abdulmawla is representative: "Islam is a political system inasmuch as it is a religious one."[5] Aside from the familiar litany of polemics against the Islamic-reformist effort at depoliticizing Islam and determining it solely as a religious faith, as once articulated by the Islamic scholar 'Ali 'Abd al-Raziq,[6] Islamic fundamentalists have very little to tell us about the nature of the political system they aspire to. We need to ask, what specifically *is* an "Islamic state"?

The most comprehensive and most widely disseminated contribution of Islamic fundamentalism to the concept of an Islamic political system is an authoritative book by Muhammad Salim al-'Awwa, already reprinted and updated a number of times. Stretching his argument a bit, al-'Awwa claims that Islam provided the first authentic political and legal system of state in the history of mankind.[7] He supports this assertion with a reference to the binding character of *shari'a*/Islamic law, as the legal underpinning of the state. In the preceding chapter we had a taste of the linguistic wordplay perused by Jarisha and Zaibaq. These fundamentalist writers believe they can derive the neo-Arabic word *shar'iyya*/legitimacy from the classical Arabic term *shari'a*/divine law. Al-'Awwa published the first edition of his book (1975, sixth expanded edition 1983, seventh printing 1988) before Jarisha and Zaibaq's book, *al-Ghazu al-fikri,* was published.[8] He argues in a similar vein, though his writing is more serious in its use of language and more careful in its citations of the published literature and other sources. His belief that Islam provided the first legal political system rests on the argument that the system was the first to be based on legitimacy and not on coercion. Underlying this argument is the expectation that "Islamic government" subordinates both the process of governing and the political behavior of the ruler to the legal system of the *shari'a*.[9] The truth is that this is a projection of Max Weber's modern notion of "legal rule" into early Islam. Weber's well-known typology informs us about three patterns of political rule: the traditional, the charismatic, and, in modern times, the "legal" rule (*legale Herrschaft*).[10] Not surprisingly, Weber's name does not occur in al-'Awwa's bibliography, for he is of the firm belief that legal rule is the authentic achievement of the Islamic system of government, not a product of modern times. Al-'Awwa seems not to be aware of his projection of a modern system of government into Islam, nor is he, evidently, familiar with the classical history of Islam.

The fact is that rulers in Islamic history were either charismatic (the *"rashidun*/ rightly guided" caliphs Abu Bakr and Omar), autocratic (most of the Umayyad rulers), or traditional. Some of the rulers of the traditional type projected considerable charisma (Harun al-Rashid), but most caliphs were basically tyrants (most of the Abbasids), as Muhammad Said al-Ashmawi (see note 2) has shown. None of them was a legal ruler in the modern constitutional sense. It is true that religious doctrine obliged them to comply on the normative level with the *shari'a*, but there existed no institutional authority able to control their compliance with this obligation. In the authoritative history of Islamic civilization by Marshall G. S. Hodgson we learn that, at the height of Islamic history during the Abbasid period, the caliphate, as the traditional Islamic system of government, was an "absolute monarchy."[11] The caliph was addressed as *"zul Allah*/ the shadow of God." Moreover, as historical records show, "as a symbol of his power, there stood beside him the executioner ready to kill the most exalted personage at a word" (ibid., p. 283). This was the case even in the age of the revered caliph Harun al-Rashid, known as the "ideal great monarch."

It is true that in the Abbasid period an Islamic court system, based on the *shari'a*, was developed, but as Hodgson tells us, "to supplement the shari'ah, there was no generally recognized dynastic or monarchic body of law, based on the nature of the office as such, . . . [no] definition of the rights of an office as such, which would have a prior claim on men's consciences and allow them to brand al-Rashid's covenant as illegal, even apart from shar'i principles" (ibid., pp. 299–300). In my study of the Islamic-fundamentalist writings I fail to find awareness of these historical facts on absolute monarchy as an Islamic system of government. To my knowledge, no fundamentalist is familiar with the outstanding *Prolegomena* of the great Ibn Khaldun, the fourteenth-century Islamic philosopher, in which he shows how the caliphate shifted into monarchy.[12] Al-'Awwa, for example, dismisses these historical facts, as do other fundamentalists. To them all that matters is the scripture, not history itself: "The correct scientific method [al-'Awwa says] obliges us to agree upon the principle that we have to judge the people on the basis of their adherence to Islamic precepts and not the other way around: we should not judge Islam in terms of the behavior of Muslims, be they the rulers or the ruled."[13] Such an argument leaves no room for the study of history, and historical discourse is eliminated: Islam, as a pure principle expressed in the scripture, is immutable, regardless of history, time, culture, location, or whatever. Muslims may change, but Islam will not. Muslims have only themselves to blame for their deviation, for that is the source of all incongruities between scripture and reality. These deviations are in fact depicted in fundamentalist writings as the source of the current Islamic malaise. Any reference to the modern systems of government unfolded by man, as a pattern to emulate, is dismissed: "This would be a confusion between the understanding of Islamic principles and modern human political experiences, Western and Eastern alike" (ibid.). Al-'Awwa rejects any adoption of modernity on the level of government because "such a thing would generate more evil, far more than [the good that would result from] the expected advantage that some modernists may have illusions of" (ibid., p. 11).

After these preliminaries, the reader of al-'Awwa expects a clear description of the alleged Islamic system of government on which the new Islamic state is to be based. But what follows, in almost a hundred pages, is nothing but the fairly obligatory descriptive history of the formative years of Islam (ibid., pp. 35–128). The description, wrapped in modern terms, reveals conspicuously a great projection of modern legal rule into seventh-century Islam. And when at length we arrive at the conceptual outlining of the *nizam al-siyasi al-Islami* / Islamic political order, we witness again the excoriation of the scapegoat 'Ali 'Abd al-Raziq,[14] who allegedly forfeited his Islamic authority in stating that Islam is a religious faith and not a system of government. Following the publication of his book, 'Abd al-Raziq was dismissed from his office as al-Azhar professor and Islamic judge. He is still castigated today for having published this view in the aftermath of the abolition of the caliphate by "the dictator Kemal Ataturk and his Jewish adherents,"[15] as al-'Awwa states. In this fundamentalist perception, secularization in modern Islamic history is not simply a deviation from the scripture, but actually the product of a *mu'amarah* / conspiracy[16] directed against Islam.

The question of the character of the Islamic state, which al-'Awwa's reader expects to be answered, remains open at the end of this not very engaging 422-page book. Al-'Awwa tells us what this state system is not: "It is not an inherited monarchy" (it *was* during the Abbasid epoch, though al-'Awwa asks us to dismiss history and to rely on and accept only the principles); and "it is not an electoral system." It is also "not a theocratic order in which the clergy appoints the head of the state."[17] We may well ask, who were the *ulema*/legal scribes who acted as the *ahl al-hall wa al-'aqd*, literally "the people who loose and bind," that is, those who organized the ceremony of the *bay'a*/oath of allegiance. Behind this question lies the fact that this group had the function of a clergy. But again we are urged to refer not to history but to doctrine. The *ulema* are the Islamic scribes whose authority is based on their knowledge of the *shari'a*. As earlier indicated, the ruler is obliged to comply with the rules of the *shari'a*, and thus to follow the advice of the *ulema*. The *ulema*, and in particular among them the *fuqaha'* (plural from *faqih*/jurist of divine law), are the Islamic scholars who have the religious authority to "loose and bind," that is, to decide what is right and what is wrong. Certainly, this body of *shari'a* and *ulema*, that is, divine law and legal scribes, could justify the qualifying of Islamic rule as legal if the rulers were really bound by it. But as we know from the authoritative work of Joseph Schacht on Islamic law there existed no institutional authority in Islamic history for legally controlling the rulers. In fact, these rulers acted as autocrats, though they "maintained the fiction that their regulations served only to apply, to supplement, and to enforce the *shari'a*. . . . This fiction was maintained as much as possible, even in the face of contradictions with and encroachments on the sacred law. . . . The discretionary power of the sovereign . . . which had escaped the control of the *kadi* [judge] in early Abbasid times, was later called *siyasa*. This *siyasa* is the expression of the full judicial power which the sovereign had retained from the Umayyad period onwards and which he can exercise whenever he thinks fit."[18]

In Islamic doctrine there exists no clergy. Thus, Islamic order is not a theocracy. We may then ask, is this system a tribal one? Underlying this question is the ancient requirement that the Islamic ruler should be from the tribe of Quraish. Most Muslims fail to acknowledge the fact that the friction between the *ansar* (the people of Medina) and the *muhajirun* (the people of Quraish, who accompanied the Prophet in his *hijra* from Mecca to Medina) was a conflict over the supremacy of the tribe of Quraish and the claims of the other tribes. Exponents of political Islam dismiss this question, too.[19]

In repeatedly refuting 'Ali 'Abd al-Raziq, our influential mentor al-'Awwa makes the point that the "politics of the state is a part of the Islamic teachings, inasmuch as Islam is a religion as much as it is a legal system."[20] He indiscriminately revives all the old indictments of 'Abd al-Raziq, including the various *fetwas*/religious decrees issued by al-Azhar and religious leaders in Egypt and other Islamic countries. One of these, the *fetwa* of the Mufti of Tunis, Ben-Ashour, carries the obscure title *Naqd 'ilmi li kitab al-Islam wa usul al-hukm*/A scientific critique of the book *Islam and the Basis of Government*. The adjective *'ilmi*/scientific is also available in the linguistic repertoire of al-'Awwa. Here again we see the modernist bias in the argumentation of Islamic fundamentalists, who are quite content to invoke science as their authority in refuting the views of their adversaries. The reference to "science" here supports the interpretation that fundamentalists are not traditionalists; their worldview stands squarely in the context of modernity.[21] The conclusion of al-'Awwa's "scientific critique" of 'Abd al-Raziq is that the impact of the West has generated an "imitative attitude" that has misled some Muslims, including of course the renowned Muslim scholar 'Abd al-Raziq, to plead for the separation of religion and politics.

Our attentive reading notwithstanding, we still do not know what the distinct elements of the Islamic system of government might be. The only thing we do know at this point is that Islam is a *din wa dawla*/unity of religion and state, no more, no less.

When we turn to Part Two of al-'Awwa's allegedly authoritative political tract we encounter the same question: What is the substance of the Islamic system of government? We are then told that the "establishment of the religion" is the substance that distinguishes Islamic government from others.[22] This *"al-'unsur al-mumayiz*/distinctive element" is the conditio sine qua non of Islamic government. By way of analogy, one is tempted to quote the Arabic homily, *"wa fassara al-m'a ba'd juhdin bi al-ma'i*/this is like defining water by saying that it is water." It is nothing more than saying that Islamic government is based on the Islamic principles of government, as al-'Awwa repeatedly does in his tautological manner.

Al-'Awwa's definition of Islamic government is one primarily concerned with the *ghayat al-dawla al-Islamiyya*/goal of the Islamic state, which amounts to the *iqamat al-din*/establishment of religion. Here we face yet another tautology. Al-'Awwa is more specific when he moves from "political science" for defining the state to "constitutional law" for dealing with the political implications of the *shari'a*. He names five constitutional provisions of Islamic rule: *shura*/consultation, *al-'adl*/justice, *al-hurriya*/freedom, *al-musawah*/equality, and *musa'alat ra'is al-dawla*/accountability of the head of the state.[23] But it is distressing to find that the discussion of these five provisions does not afford us even a suggestion of certainty about the subject. Great vagueness paired with muddled projections of modern concerns into Islamic history confronts us on every page. I have not, however, selected this ideological work simply to ridicule its author, but rather to introduce a wholly representative work by a renowned fundamentalist authority. Al-'Awwa is a respected lawyer in Cairo and one of the most significant leaders of the movement of *al-Ikhwan al-Muslimun*/the Muslim Brethren.

Only in the six pages entitled "The Islamic State in the Modern Age"[24] does the author deal with the question of how Islam should be politically managed in our times. He offers the following judgment: "The call for an Islamic state in our age on the basis of a commitment to Islam is supported by millions of Muslims all over the world. This call simply means that the institutions of the government must be built up in accord with the political values of Islam. . . . As regards the details concerning the implementation of these values we must state that the *umma*/Islamic community has to decide upon this in each case."[25] The only condition al-'Awwa attaches to the free scope of action herewith accorded the Islamic *umma* is that legislation must be set along the lines of the *shari'a*, for human legislation is a heresy. With regard to establishing Islamic government on the basis of the interpretation of Islam along the lines of the formula *din wa dawla*, al-'Awwa believes that the late Iranian leader Khomeini has established closer links between Sunni and Shi'i Muslims. It is now simply the turn of the Sunni Muslims to understand Khomeini properly. "If those who call for the unity of the Islamic *umma* succeed in understanding Khomeini adequately, and if they are able to make use of his ideas, then the outcome will be that the sons [*abna'*] of the two great Islamic groups [*firqatayn*], the Sunna and the Shi'a, will come closer together."[26] All is not well here, however. Those Arab nationalists who, in the wake of Islamic fundamentalism, have shifted away from secular pan-Arabism to political Islam raise basic objections against this statement. True, they capitulate on the idea of a secular Arabism, but they do not on the claim that an Arab should lead the Islamic community. Arab fundamentalists deny the Iranian Revolution the legitimacy to lead all Muslims. Secondary to the question what are Islamic government and order, then, is the question who leads. The Arab challenge to the Iranian claim to lead[27] brings us to an intra-Islamic conflict.

With al-'Awwa's vague views on the Islamic state representing the mainstream of political Islam, the debate on how to interpret the political character of Islam goes on. The most concrete content of his contribution to the matter is the idea that this system derives its *shar'iyya*/legitimacy from *shari'a*/Islamic law. Leaving aside the wordplay involved, this pronouncement focuses on the call for implementing the Islamic *shari'a*, as the substance of Islamic government. In fact, *shari'a* is a post-Qur'anic construction, initiated basically to regulate, as a kind of civil law dealing with affairs of inheritance, marriage, and the like. In Islamic history the *shari'a* was never a constitution of the traditional Islamic caliphate, which was in fact an "absolute monarchy" (see notes 11 and 18). Today, fundamentalists invent the tradition of *shari'a*, as an Islamic constitution of the state. This is the interpretation of *din wa dawla*/unity of religion and state, which is a fundamentalist "invention of tradition," as Eric Hobsbawm puts it.[28]

IS THE *SHARI'A* AN ISLAMIC CONSTITUTION FOR AN ISLAMIC STATE?

One of the critics of the "Islamic state," Husain Fawzi al-Najjar, argues in a well-known book that there is no single authentic text in the primary classical sources of Islamic *shari'a* that supports the formula of *din wa dawla*: "We do not believe that Muhammad came to establish a kingdom or a state. He was simply a Prophet and messenger to all mankind. . . . Islam does not oblige the people to submit to this mission. . . . The Qur'an clearly says, 'There shall be no compulsion in religion' (sura *al-Baqarah*, verse 256)."[29] Al-Najjar, after elaborating on this argument, concedes that early Islam was involved in politics, but insists that "this fact does not mean that Islam as a religion is bound to the state. There is nothing in the Islamic *shari'a* that compels one to bind religion to any state setting. The *shari'a* does not deal with any specific system of government."[30] On these grounds al-Najjar concludes that Islamic revelation is not based on a unity between the religion of Islam and an existing state structure or even one yet to be achieved. In other words, the contention of a *din wa dawla* in Islam is nothing but a recent addition, an Islamist variety of an "invented tradition." Islam addresses all humanity, whereas a state is always restricted to a limited and specific group of people. Nevertheless, al-Najjar does not infer from this argument that Islam is apolitical. On the contrary, to him Islam is unquestionably a political religion, although not in the sense of providing a concept for a specifically "Islamic state," but in clearly outlining a political ethic for governing a polity. This is an enlightened Islamic position standing against the fundamentalist notion of order. Al-Najjar deploys the classical notion of *umma* against the newly introduced notion of *dawla* / the state and repeatedly argues that it is not the business of Islam to furnish a system of government. In this sense he rehabilitates the book *al-Islam wa usul al-hukm* and its author, 'Abd al-Raziq, who did nothing more than show with Islamic arguments that the primary sources of the religion of Islam do not include prescriptions for a political system.

Like 'Abd al-Raziq, our enlightened though thoroughly political author al-Najjar argues that historical circumstances imposed on the Prophet the need to act politically and to assume political functions in a hitherto stateless society. The correspondence between religious and political functions in early Islam is, in the view of al-Najjar, a historical coincidence rather than a constitutive part of Islamic religious beliefs. The caliphate has always been a worldly office and not a religious calling.[31] This was exactly the argument of 'Abd al-Raziq that led to his dismissal and his firing from al-Azhar. Al-Najjar particularly criticizes ascribing to the caliphate a divine character during the Abbasid period. That decision led to the stagnation of political discourse in Islam, since politics had become a domain of divine issues, and since dealing with politics was restricted to justifying the political actions of the rulers after the fact.[32] Against those who contest this interpretation of Islam and politics, al-Najjar asks, "If Islam was meant to be a political order, then why does the Qur'an leave this issue without further clarification?"[33] This question ought to be embarrassing to the adherents of the *nizam Islami,* for one particular reason: in the conviction of the Islamic fundamentalists, the Qur'an, as the ultimate revelation, is a comprehensive compendium of knowledge, on every issue. To al-Najjar, who also believes in this characterization of the Qur'an, the question is not embarrassing, because he is of the view that "Islam is a religion and not a state order. It is a religion which aims at organizing the entire human entity in establishing the ethical and social principles for the most refined civilization on earth" (ibid., p. 74). Thus, Islam is political only in the sense of providing the ethics for governing but not the technical instructions for establishing a government in an "Islamic state." An Islamic ruler can claim only to protect the *shari'a*, for Islam forbids him to be a part of it. In the view of al-Najjar only the Prophet Muhammad and the first two righteous caliphs Abu Bakr and Omar (but not Uthman and 'Ali) governed in the spirit of Islam as an ethic. Only in an historical manner can the *bay'a* / oath of allegiance given by Muslims to the first two caliphs be compared with the rules of a modern election.

Here again we are confronted, if in a more productive way, with modern projections into Islamic history. The true spirit of Islam is based, in the view of al-Najjar, on the *iradah al-ammah*. In fact this is a modern Arabic translation of Rousseau's *volonté générale* (general will). Reading this concept into Islam leads to the conclusion that the Muslim *umma* is "the source of sovereignty [*siyadah*] and the origin of political rule [*sulta*]. This understanding is ultimately in contradiction with theocracy and with any idea of divine order, since Islam does not recognize any divine state and does not restrict religious knowledge to any class of people" (al-Najjar, ibid., p. 16). Al-Najjar supports this view by referring to the two Qur'anic verses on *shura* / consultation (which we shall discuss later). In this sense the *umma*, in the understanding of "the people," is the source of all powers, but the contention that this idea has guided political thought in Islamic history cannot be supported by any study of Islamic history of ideas, for it is, rather, a recent addition.

Though al-Najjar's study, published in Cairo, is a very sympathetic interpretation of Islam, it nonetheless remains as vague as al-'Awwa's plea for an Islamic system of government is fierce. Al-'Awwa puts the emphasis on the state as the alleged incorporation of Islam, if it fulfills the requirement that its legitimacy (*shar'iyya*) be derived from Islamic law (*shari'a*). Unlike al-'Awwa's view, the focus of al-Najjar is not the state (*dawla*) but society (*mujtama'*), as a component of the *umma*, for *umma*, and not the state, is the place for the realization of the *shari'a*. Al-Najjar, again: "The Prophet Muhammad had aimed at achieving the societal unity [*al-wihda al-ijtima'iyya*] of Muslims rather than their political unity [*wihda siyasiyya*]. He did not want to establish a state so much as he wanted to melt the diverse races that had submitted to Islam in one societal pot, by means of Islamic brotherhood" (ibid., p. 131). This is the modest view of an Islamic liberal. The fundamentalist al-'Awwa, by contrast, argues in totalitarian fashion in stating that the *nizam siyasi* / political system of Islam encompasses the totality of all realms of life, and in alleging that it provides all of these realms with precepts that are to be guarded by the state.[34] Al-Najjar, for his part, views the interplay between Islam and *siyasa* (politics) in ethical terms. In this interpretation the Islamic commitment to the *shari'a* is a realm of belief rather than a provision for a police state that the fundamentalist concept of an "Islamic state" approximates. Despite these great differences, both of these Islamic authors are extremely vague about the nature of the "state" and the "society" they are talking about. Al-'Awwa is unable to tell us precisely how the *shari'a* can be imposed or instituted as the legal system of the state, and al-Najjar, though persuasive and sympathetic, cannot enlighten us about the ethically inspired Islamic society defined by the virtue of brotherhood. In both cases, be it understood, women are excluded, a clear indication of a neo-patriarchal culture.[35]

The interpretation of the *shari'a* has become the fault line dividing Muslims in contemporary Islamic civilization. Should you call the *shari'a* the holy constitution of the state, then you are a fundamentalist (like al-'Awwa), and if you view it as an ethics, then you are a liberal reformist (like al-Najjar). Legal scholars studying Islam are aware of the fact that there exists no homogeneous, defined, and delimited legal body that we can call *shari'a*.[36] Most of the political activists of Islamic fundamentalism know little about Islamic *shari'a* and are unaware that, should they seize power, they will not find a coherent legal system at hand that they may apply to situations, conditions, and events overnight—as events will demand. This of course opens the way to arbitrary totalitarian politics and governance, in the name of Islamic *shari'a*. The introduction of the *shari'a* in Sudan, first under the military dictatorship of Ja'far al-Numairi (September 1983) and, since June 1989, under the fundamentalist government of the Islamic National Front, is a case in point.[37] In short, any application of the *shari'a* on a state level is vulnerable to the arbitrary practices of the ruler. Totalitarian Islamic fundamentalists like al-'Awwa, however, do not busy themselves with the abuse of the *shari'a* for political ends, and repeat in most tedious fashion the mantra that Islam should be judged in terms of principles, not in terms of the behavior of Muslims. More scrupulous Islamic thinkers like al-Najjar believe they can avoid such abuse in shifting the realm of the *shari'a* from the state to society, but are unable to explain persuasively how this should be brought about.

The idea of an "Islamic state," then, is a vague concept based on politicizing and reviving various arbitrarily selected components of Islamic doctrine while unwittingly projecting modern concerns into classical Islamic history and thought. Most arguments seldom extend beyond rearward-oriented millenarian references inspired by a yearning for the "Golden Age of

Islam." In short, the notion of Islam as *din wa dawla* and the contention that *shari'a* is the constitution of an Islamic state are invented traditions with little content and no real background in classical Islamic history or the authoritative sources of the scripture.

Most important, these concepts serve as grounds for de-legitimizing the existing political orders, which are condemned for their secularity and soon toppled. The "Islamic state" aspired to is a confused and angry response to a crisis situation, a response ultimately imprisoned in romantic protest. If manifested in a successful revolt, it could lead to disorder and turmoil, as in Algeria or Afghanistan, if not to an oppressive totalitarian state, as in Sudan or Iran.

ISLAMIC CRITICS AND THE ISLAMIC STATE: IS IT TRUE THAT THE *SHARI'A* RULES?

When asked for a clarification of the notion of *nizam Islami,* or for a further elaboration of it, Islamic fundamentalists regularly resort to the concept of *shari'a,* and hasten to add that the implementation of Islamic law is the basic criterion for the realization of an Islamic system of government. In their books, Jarisha and Zaibaq, as well as al-Qaradawi and al-'Awwa, all of them representative of the new political movement, speak clearly and authoritatively on this issue. Students of Islamic law may contest this ideological claim on scholarly grounds, and they can support their doubts by citing the classic works of Schacht and Coulson.[38] They may, further, argue that in Islamic tradition there exists no consistent and coherent legal system, whether the *shari'a* or otherwise. *Shari'a* is rather a *legal methodology,* and, I would add, an ethics, not a law in itself.[39] Not surprisingly, Islamic fundamentalists single out the commitment of a Muslim to an implementation of the *shari'a* as the foremost criterion for determining his belief in Islam. Though there is not, and never was, a coherent legal body for this kind of law, *shari'a* becomes the yardstick for whether one is a Muslim or not. In this context, an influential fundamentalist sheikh, the late Muhammad al-Ghazali, has ruled (as alluded to earlier) in a notorious *fetwa* that every Muslim who pleads for the separation of religion and politics, that is, for the suspension of the *shari'a,* is to be branded a *murtad*/apostate. In al-Ghazali's *fetwa* "there is no punishment in Islam for those Muslims who kill these apostates."[40] The killing of intellectuals in Egypt, in Algeria, and even in "secular" Turkey is the consequence of this ruling.

Characteristic of the revival of the political version of an Islamic *shari'a* are the constitutional amendments seen in recent years in the states of the Middle East. Egypt is a representative example. In order to mollify the demands of the fundamentalists, the Egyptian state under the reign of Anwar al-Sadat introduced into the new constitution of 1971 an Article Two that carries the provision that "the principles of the *shari'a* are a major source of legislation." Later on, in 1980, again under Sadat, the indefinite article *a* became the definite article *the,* thus transforming the constitutional reference to Islamic *shari'a* from "*a* major source" to "*the* major source" of legislation. The assertion did not, however, satisfy the Islamic fundamentalists and could not prevent Sadat's assassination by a fundamentalist zealot in October 1981.[41] In Egypt, the fundamentalist opposition has two wings: a legal one acting publicly and a second one that operates underground. For the Islamic militants among the fundamentalists in Egypt "the holy book and the sword"[42] are the basis of their religiopolitical action. They were not willing to settle for a verbal reference in an altered constitution. Those Islamic fundamentalists acting legally in the institutions are willing to put through the *shari'a* as the legal system of the "Islamic state" in infiltrating the system. (In the Preface I alluded to the *shari'a* law of *hisbah* having been legislated by the Egyptian parliament on January 29, 1996. On these grounds Professor Nasr Hamid Abu-Zaid was declared apostate and was unwillingly divorced from his wife. See my report from Cairo in *Frankfurter Allgemeine Zeitung* of July 3, 1996.)

In examining the argument of Islamic fundamentalists, one should return to the scripture, to the Qur'an itself, for proper answers. We will be surprised to learn that the term *shari'a* occurs there *only once.* In sura 45, *al-Jathiya* (kneeling), verse 18, we read, "And now we have set you on the 'right path' (*shari'a*). Follow it."[43] There are two other passages in the Qur'an that employ a verb related to this noun. In sura *al-Shura* we read, "He has ordained for men [*shar'a lakum*] the faith He has revealed to you" (verse 13), and in sura *al-Ma'idah* we read, "We have ordained a law and assigned a path [*shar'an wa minhajan*] for each of you" (verse 48). There are no passages in the Qur'an enjoining legal stipulations, whether using the verb *shara'a* or the noun *shari'a*. Clearly, these scant references are no legal system, and were not thought to be.

According to the Muslim reformist al-Ashmawi, the Qur'an stipulates *shari'a* as ethical orientation and does not provide an underpinning for any sort of state whatsoever.[44] This Muslim legal scholar is a prominent critic of fundamentalism in Egypt. He is also a retired senior judge who has participated in the ongoing Islamic debate on the *shari'a*. In his most interesting book (cited here), published simultaneously in Cairo and Beirut, he discusses the Qur'anic content with regard to the *shari'a*. Al-Ashmawi argues that the term *shari'a*, in linguistic terms, originally meant "source of water" or "the mouth of [it]," meaning the methodology of (*minhaj*), or the way to (*tariq*) [something]. In fact, this is the Qur'anic meaning of *shari'a*. "Neither in terms of language usage nor in terms of the meaning of the Qur'an does *shari'a* mean legislation or law."[45] Al-Ashmawi draws our attention to the fact that in the history of early Islam the term *shari'a* "became a term that covers all Islamic precepts, the religious and the legal alike" (ibid., p. 34). One striking aspect of Islamic history, in the view of al-Ashmawi, is the way Muslims have consistently confused religion (as the revelation of God) with religious thought, that is, the human understanding of religion as expressed in a wide variety of interpretations. He points out,

> It is unfortunate that the distinction between religion and religious thought is not always clear to the majority of Muslims; hence the confusion between the two still occurs. The call for the implementation of the *shari'a* does not refer to the Qur'an itself. It relies mostly on the acquired meaning of the term in traditional religious thought. . . . Ultimately, the implementation of the *shari'a*, in this sense, is the implementation of a body of Islamic political thought." (ibid.)

Al-Ashmawi's closer reading of the Qur'an (dealing, for example, with the gradual prohibition of wine drinking) reveals that the Qur'anic precepts now interpreted as a legal system named *shari'a* were always related to specific historical situations.

> In this sense, the *shari'a* neither was revealed at once nor has existed as an abstract issue. It was always related to existing realities . . . ; it drew on prevailing traditions and customs and derived its own rules from them. It also adjusted itself to further developments of those traditions and customs in keeping up with the change. . . . Without taking into consideration these reality-related origins of the *shari'a* while [nonetheless] pleading that it be implemented, we will be dealing with theoretical and logical concerns contradictory to the spirit of Islam. (ibid., p. 89)

In an age of desperation and the subsequent rise of salvation ideologies based on the repoliticization of the cultural system of Islam, al-Ashmawi's inquiry into the origins of the *shari'a* (*usul al-shari'a*) is a beacon of hope on the horizon. Al-Ashmawi demands acceptance of the view that Islam's concern is "man and society, not the states or empires as such, because establishing a state or an empire is not the business of religion" (ibid., p. 94). He reminds us that the Prophet "restricted his message [when in Mecca for thirteen years] to the call of God's oneness in the cosmos" (ibid., p. 56). He acknowledges the fact that Islam has a political character, and he refuses to classify himself as a secularist, as he insisted in an interview with me in Cairo in June 1993 and again in January 1996. Although al-Ashmawi does not seek to emulate professor 'Abd al-Raziq of al-Azhar or Nasr Hamid Abu-Zaid[46] in depoliticizing Islam, he nonetheless draws an important distinction between two patterns of government: (1) *hukumat Allah*/the government of God, and (2) *hukumat al-nas*/the government of the people. In his view, the first pattern existed only once in history, that is, during the time of prophecy; the Prophet Muhammad was the messenger of God, and hence an arbitrator but not a governor. Only under such conditions, al-Ashmawi argues, can a government of God be established, because such a government would be a *tahkim*/arbitration and not a *hukm*/political rule. Al-Ashmawi asks contemporary Muslims to accept and understand the difference between God's religion and the human understanding of it, as well as the distinction between a "government of God" and a "government of the people." In so doing, Muslims would come to understand the *shari'a* properly, that is, in the Qur'anic meaning of path/method (*tariq*/*manhaj*), not in the imputed meaning of "legal system" in an "Islamic state." A historicized understanding of Islam is possible, and it can be drawn upon in combating the anti-intellectual and selective use of the scriptures by fundamentalists.

In a civilization determined by Islam there is nothing wrong with basing the ethics of government on Islamic morality, *except that shari'a as an ethics provides guidelines, not the system itself*. In this sense al-Ashmawi accepts the call for an Islamic system of government. He states that "the true Islamic system of government would be the order that emanates from the realities of the society and originates in the will of its members. Each Muslim would participate in sharing the responsibilities, casting the legislation, and devising the social controls. Such a true Islamic system of government will be able to adjust to international progress and to adopt the noble principles of freedom, justice, and equality" (al-Ashmawi, *Usul al-shari'a*, p. 153).

Another enlightened Muslim, Hussain Ahmad Amin, the son of the well-known Egyptian historian Ahmad Amin, makes a similar argument. In a book dealing with the vague call for "*tatbiq al-shari'a*/implementation of

Islamic law" he is harsh with those who lack knowledge of Islamic law and incorrectly assume that there is a comprehensive as well as consistent body of legal rules constituting the alleged Islamic legal system. Amin argues, "[t]he majority of those people do not read the history of Islam, nor are they familiar with the basic books on *fiqh* and *shari'a*. They mostly rely on storytelling and preaching, as well as on poor and stupid pamphlets touching on all kinds of issues."[47]

As do most writers on the issue, Hussain Ahmad Amin returns to 'Ali 'Abd al-Raziq's book *al-Islam wa usul al-hukm*. He does not refute it anew, however, but discusses it in a new light. Amin shows clearly that 'Abd al-Raziq, to support his argument that Islam is a nonpolitical religion, relies heavily on the Meccan Messages of the Qur'an and overlooks the Medinese ones. Amin does not seek to discredit 'Abd al-Raziq, but rather to further the argument that Muslim thinkers did not, and still do not, desire to expose themselves to the idea of *al-tatawur*/evolution. Supporting this argument is the fact that the Qur'anic suras are not historically ordered or organized. "We find the same sura consisting of Meccan and Medinese verses. . . . We read the call to excuse unbelievers followed by the call to fight them and kill them. This is an issue that has greatly contributed to keeping the evolutionary character of the Prophetic call away from the awareness of Muslims."[48] During the contemporary period of the ever-intensifying revival of political Islam, it is courageous for scholars to publish such statements—in this case in Cairo in a book already in its second printing.

One contemporary Muslim, the Sudanese reformer Sheikh Taha, was at pains to revive the Mecca model of Islam (spiritual belief) against the Medina model of an Islamic state (political Islam). For his troubles, Sheikh Taha[49] paid dearly with his life. He was executed without trial in 1985 in Khartoum.

IS *SHURA* AN ISLAMIC SUBSTITUTE FOR DEMOCRACY?

The preoccupation of Islamic fundamentalists with the conviction that the Qur'an provides them a consistent legal system is politically related to the view that the legal principle of the *shura*[50] is part and parcel of this system. *Shura* means counsel, and the verb related to it, "*shawara*," means "to consult [it]." In their plea for an Islamic system of government, the fundamentalists scorn Western secular democracy, arguing that Islam was the first democracy set on earth. There are fundamentalists, like the Algerian Ali Benhaj, who disdain democracy as *kufr*/heresy. Those among them who admit democracy maintain that the Qur'an contains the first theory of democratic government ever known to humanity. This contention is based on two very short verses of the Qur'an, stipulating the practice of *shura*/consultation. The first honors "[those] who avoid gross sins and indecencies and, when angered, are willing to forgive, [those] who obey their Lord, attend to their prayers, and 'conduct their affairs by mutual consent' [*wa amruhum shura baynahum*]" (Qur'an: Surat *al-Shura*, 42/37–38). The second passage is in the sura of *'Imran:* "Take counsel with them in the conduct of affairs [*wa shawiruhum fi al-amr*]" (Qur'an: *'Imran*, 3/159). Historically, this precept conjures the pre-Islamic system of intertribal consultation among the leaders of ethnic groups. In following the Qur'anic commandment and in keeping with this tradition the Prophet Muhammad consulted with his close contemporaries and followers, foremost among whom were Abu Bakr and Omar. The four righteous caliphs of early Islam maintained this tradition, the caliph Omar increasing the number of counselors to six. None of the Umayyad or Abbasid caliphs practiced the *shura*.

In the course of studying the bulk of the ideology of Islamic fundamentalism, we are consistently confronted with a poor awareness of historical records and with the lack of any vision of history, despite the fundamentalists' aim at remaking and reordering the world. In one of the major writings of populist fundamentalism, about *Fan al-hukm fi al-Islam/The Art of Government in Islam,* by Mustafa Abu-Zaid-Fahmi, we find a lengthy chapter on *shura* based exclusively on the two aforementioned Qur'anic verses. The significance of the chapter, then, derives not from the value of its statements, but from its exemplary projection of modernity into Islam in the debate on the Islamic state.[51]

In one of his works, the populist fundamentalist Mustafa Abu-Zaid-Fahmi begins courageously with the statement that, in Islam, "the people have the final say"—thus arguing that Islam had achieved popular sovereignty long before the European formulation of the concepts of natural law (Hobbes, Locke) and social contracts (the *Contrat Social* of Rousseau): "Most significant is the operative value of the *shura* as a major principle of government. The *shura* sets the will of the people at the forefront and obliges the rulers to honor this will in the conduct of public affairs. . . . Would anyone dare say that the modern constitutional approach is more progressive in this regard than Islamic thought had always been? . . . If anyone makes such an allegation it cannot, by any means, be accepted as being true" (ibid., p. 200). Islam, being the final divine revelation, "is by defini-

tion par excellence the intellectual progress itself in all realms, in the devotion to God, the conduct of public affairs, and in politics alike. . . . [In] any
realm of life no human thought can emulate Islam. Thus, regardless of times
in all epochs, the correct interpretation of the Qur'an guarantees the ultimate freedom, the ultimate dignity, and the ultimate security" (ibid.). Abu-
Zaid-Fahmi, the author of this poetry, further states that "if political democracy means simply that political rule should be based on the government of
the people by the people, and that the people are the source of sovereignty
of the state and of all its powers, . . . then Islam must be the first democracy
set on earth. . . . I wonder why scholars have hitherto ceased to . . . demonstrate how Islam protects the individual from tyranny no less than any of
the most developed modern constructions" (ibid., p. 201). True, Islamic
ethics is clearly against tyranny. At issue is, however, the real Islamic history, not the model for it.

Our great astonishment notwithstanding, we should be fair to our historically blind author, who seemingly lacks knowledge of the personalization of power expressed in the system of "absolute monarchy" (see notes 11
and 18) in Islamic history. Moreover, he deals not merely with values, but
also with practical aspects of transforming values into institutional realities, as he raises the question how one can institute this system. His prescription is that "the answer is very simple and clear. Islam knows only one
system of government, which is the system of *shura*. If we want to know
how to implement the *shura*, then we have to refer to the *shura* itself" (ibid.,
p. 204). This is typical of the circular argumentation that erupts within the
political thought of Islamic fundamentalists.

Aside from the almost apologetic quality of Abu-Zaid-Fahmi's book, and
its low intellectual profile, which is deemed representative by most authors
of this genre, it is noteworthy that the book introduces new dimensions into
fundamentalist political thought—the perorations of its author notwithstanding. In referring to Islamic authorities, Fahmi quotes them with great
devotion and subservience while nonetheless refuting their views on the
shura. Islamic fundamentalists like their precursor Abu al-A'la al-
Mawdudi, for instance, usually argue that God is the only sovereign. Accordingly, the sovereignty of a state must be based on the will of God, for
anything else is heresy. It follows, then, that the absolutism of the rulers is
divine, for their will is equated with the will of God. Resistance to unjust
rulers assumes the character of heresy. Here lies a crucial contradiction in
fundamentalist thought: on the one hand it preaches "revolt" against

existing order; on the other it sanctifies state rule. Religious faith is thus being used and abused, both by Islamic rulers and their fundamentalist foes. As Michael Hudson once put it, "Islam, as we are now discovering, can be quite as effective in legitimizing an opposition movement, as it has been historically in legitimizing incumbent regimes."[52]

In traditional Islam, only those Muslims with an intimate knowledge of Islamic sources, that is, the *ulema* and the *faqih*, are the appropriate class for interpreting the will of God, the one and only legislator. Some populist fundamentalists do not share this view, however. In referring to the Qur'anic verse *"wa amruhum shura baynahum/*they conduct their affairs by mutual consent"(Qur'an; Surat *al-Shura*, 42/37–38), these populists— Abu-Zaid-Fahmi, for example—castigate these Muslim authorities for *al-khalt/*the confusing of a *fetwa* with a *tashri'/*legislation (see Abu-Zaid-Fahmi, pp. 206–9). A *fetwa* is ordered on the basis of Islamic law, about which these authorities are said to be knowledgeable. In his interpretation of popular sovereignty, quoted above, Fahmi states that legislation must be enacted in accordance with the principle of the *shura*:

> The *shari'a* has admitted the *shura* as a major pillar in this [system of government], which means that legislative power must be set in accordance with the *shura* provision. The people can practice the *shura* as they want: either directly, if their number is small to the extent that a direct democracy in the sense of modern constitutional theory is feasible, or indirectly, through elected deputies, as in parliamentary democracy. . . . In the revelations, Islam has instituted the *shura* as a major principle of government: Muslims 'conduct their public affairs in mutual consent.' Thus, legislative power has to be organized along the lines of the *shura*. No minority is eligible to govern, not even if this minority were to be composed of legal scholars and muftis of Islam." (ibid., p. 212)

In this understanding, an Islamic constitution is a human product of legislation based on the practice of *shura,* and thus, virtually, no longer a result of a divine act. It is set by the people and approved by them, as Abu-Zaid-Fahmi argues again, with reference to the pair of verses quoted from the Qur'an. In his view, "Islamic *shura*-democracy" is the only true democracy in the world: "The Islamic system of government is the most advanced pattern humanity has ever known. Islam established democracy and instituted *shura* as its major element. . . . In this act Islam's achievement is unprecedented in the history of mankind" (ibid., p. 248).

I believe that Islam and democracy can be reconciled, and elsewhere I have pursued an effort in this direction.[53] I continue to believe, however, that a fundamentalist-democratic regime is a contradiction in terms.

Religious fundamentalism and Islam are (or should be) two different issues. Nevertheless, it is important that we distinguish between this variety of populist fundamentalism and the totalitarian fundamentalism that Mawdudi and Qutb helped to shape. Mawdudi himself openly pronounced that his visions of Islam and democracy are utterly at odds.[54]

If we ask why—contrary to the historical achievements alleged by Abu-Zaid-Fahmi—Muslims have been subjected to tyrannies throughout their history, and why most of the rulers were hateful despots, we are again given the familiar schematic answer: it is not Islam, but Muslims, that are to be blamed. Long before contemporary Muslim fundamentalists began once again to invoke the literal understanding of the scriptures, the early Muslim modernist Shakib Arslan had raised the question: "Why are Muslims backward while others have advanced?"[55] His answer was simple: Muslims did not live in accordance with Islam, as the Qur'an prescribes. Current fundamentalists continue this line of belief and commit themselves firmly to the authority of the text (*sola scriptura*)—to which they, however, conspicuously refer only on selective grounds, and clearly without honoring the tolerance inherent in the Qur'anic spirit.

CONCLUSIONS

In the political thought of Islamic fundamentalism, the references to the *shari'a* (and to the *shura* as its political component) are supposed to be the underpinning for the call for an "Islamic state." These references do not, however, make the call any clearer with respect to the concrete political demands. Clearly, Islamic fundamentalists are not traditionalists; rather, their reading modernity into Islam sometimes bears interesting fruit. But vagueness cannot be overcome by projections from present conditions into the distant past. Interpreting Islam in accord with the idea of popular sovereignty, which populist fundamentalists are wont to do, is clearly a challenge to the traditional views on Islamic order. But the mainstream fundamentalists continue to believe that God alone is the sovereign and, hence, the only legislator. To me as a Muslim this is a heresy, because this view willy-nilly presents the will of human rulers as the will of God. That interpretation supports the totalitarian view of political Islam that human understanding of God's divine law, the *shari'a*, provides us with binding precepts, according to which Muslims must organize their lives, in grateful subservience to the rulers.

The Islamic views analyzed here give us little hope that the approach of historicizing one's own history, that is, recognizing the pertinence of historical development, not simply repeating the allegations of the absolute, will find its way into Islamic thought in the foreseeable future. This, then, is fruitful ground for fundamentalist ideology, for as King Hassan II of Morocco reminds us, fundamentalism cannot be combated with armies and military force; the challenge of fundamentalism is related not to power and instrumental capabilities, but rather to creating disorder. To counter-challenge the fundamentalists, we must appeal to other means. What are needed first of all, obviously, are enlightenment in the Islamic world and a better life, if the fundamentalist appeal to desperate young Muslims is to be blunted. Toward these goals the Muslim reformer Mohammed Arkoun made a worthy contribution in his *Rethinking Islam;*[56] and another enlightened Muslim thinker, Abdullahi A. An-Na'im, continued Arkoun's reasoning in calling for an "Islamic Reformation,"[57] by which he means a *shari'a* reform.[58] If these proposals—along with the adoption of historicity, as proposed by the Moroccan Abdallah Laroui[59]—were to become public preferences in Islamic civilization, they would present a most effective stand against the fundamentalist challenge. Remaking the world is what fundamentalism promises; disorder is what it delivers.

NINE

—ᗣ—

Democracy and Democratization in Islam

An Alternative to Fundamentalism

The politicization of religion, as articulated in religious fundamentalism, is a response to profound crisis, a crisis occurring both on the nation-state level and in global structures and dynamics. Thus, fundamentalism is not simply an ideology to be scorned, ignored, or ridiculed, but part of the extant political, cultural, and social realities. The political articulation of non-Western fundamentalisms is peculiar in that it assumes the shape of a revolt against the West. But unlike the anti-colonial revolt early this century, this new pattern of revolt is not simply a political upheaval, for it is directed against Western norms and values, as well. It is nothing short of an effort to de-center the West; it mobilizes anti-Western attitudes and prejudices while developing alternative worldviews.

From the point of view of non-Western cultures and civilizations, contesting Western hegemony is a reasonable stance, for world peace between rival civilizations can be established only on grounds of equality and mutual respect and acceptance. It is distressing, however, that the ongoing "revolt against the West" gathers forces that also stand against the values and norms of cultural modernity, to which we owe the principles of democracy and human rights. Though embarking on a program of modernity, religious fundamentalisms paradoxically become a variety of parochialism.

In pondering strategies that might prove effective in thwarting numerous varieties of religious fundamentalisms and other divisive forces (for example, intolerant ethnic groups) in world politics, I dismiss the dominant Western

attitude of the day, which is to respond to the phenomenon by the deploy-
ment of military force and the instituting of economic sanctions. Continued policies of armament to defend the West against fundamentalism are
an inappropriate response to the pending challenge. Fundamentalists are
not a unified power, even less a military force, but rather a challenge to world
order that foments local and international disorder. What is needed is an
earnest search—beyond the limited capacities of Western supremacy—for
new mechanisms and sentiments for uniting humanity. The quest for
democracy and human rights, it seems to me, offers the most promise.

Considering that the worldwide growth of civilization-consciousness no
longer favors solutions based on this or that universalism, I foresee an ur-
gent need to shape new outlooks on cross-cultural grounds. Continuing to
impose the Western view of democracy and human rights on Islamic or any
other non-Western civilization affords little promise. We need to ask, how
can peoples of different cultures and civilizations speak a common language
of human rights and democracy *in their own tongues?* The question reveals
the essence of "cross-cultural grounds": before a roster of values and norms
can be shared internationally, its elements must be established, one by one,
with reference to local cultures and regional civilizations. I am of course
aware of the great obstacles to realizing such a concept of international
morality, one that is equally accepted and shared by the major civilizations
of the world, but I believe that this outlook is our only promising avenue
toward peace and fellowship beyond the turn of the century.

DEMOCRACY AND INTERNATIONAL MORALITY

The idea of democracy has its roots in ancient Greece. Democracies as social realities, however, are a modern phenomenon,[1] integrally related to the
unfolding of modernity in the West. For this reason, Western democracies
have been the model to emulate for non-Western cultures and civilizations,
and the processes of modernization and democratization in premodern societies have long been linked to one another. During the years of decolonization in this century most social scientists in the West believed that modernization and democratization would go hand in hand, around the globe,
along a steady path of progress. But in pointing out that democracy and human rights find their expression in individual freedom and individual rights,
some prominent modernization theorists, such as David Apter, have conceded that there are difficulties: "The norms of the sacred collectivity are

the antithesis of political democracy,"[2] as Apter then rightly argued. He believed, however, that modernization would take hold in these collectivities, without jeopardy to religious faith, and supplant the related political cultures. Well, we know now that it did not; rather, it produced the contemporary phenomenon of religious fundamentalism, and efforts to modernize and democratize in much of the postcolonial period seem to have failed. The institutional framework envisaged as the vehicle for achieving these goals, the secular nation-state, is in crisis in much of the world (see Chapter 6), and the values underlying the anticipated ends have in recent decades been sharply questioned. The Islamic world is the most prominent case in point.

The focus on the Cold War in recent decades contributed to adding another item to the list of obstacles to democratization. Whereas modernization theorists saw premodern traditions as the major obstacle to establishing democracies in non-Western settings, Cold War theorists believed that the "communist threat" was the greatest obstacle. The end of the Cold War thus encouraged great hopes for a new wave of democratization. It had been argued that the crisis of authoritarian regimes—including the communist regimes—combined with energetic programs of modernization and economic growth would soon lead to global democratization. Samuel Huntington, for one, prematurely announced a "Third Wave,"[3] in the course of which global democratization would come about. In discussing my paper on the potential of democratization after the Gulf War at the Harvard–M. I. T. Joint Seminar on Political Development with Professor Huntington and Myron Weiner, I argued that crises may lead not to democratization[4] but to a new kind of authoritarianism. In my view, fundamentalism, borne out of the crisis of the nation-state, is this new brand of authoritarianism, and indeed we are witnessing its rise on a global scale. Religious fundamentalism, in other words, is the antithesis of democracy.[5] Two years after that debate, Huntington published his most celebrated article, that on the "Clash of Civilizations," in which he rightly pointed to differences in the worldviews of people belonging to different cultures and civilizations, but most unfortunately overlooked the crucial distinction between Islam, as a religion, and Islamic fundamentalism, as an ideology.

In acknowledging that "democracy" is a Western achievement, thus often found suspect in the non-Western world, while observing the rise of religious fundamentalisms as an ideological expression of a "revolt against the West," we might well ask: How, then, can democracy be seen as a viable alternative to fundamentalism? My argument is based on the need to look beyond universal worldviews for means of establishing democracy on cross-cultural grounds.

In pondering Islam as the religion of a major worldwide civilization basing its unity on the concept of the *umma*, that is, a "sacred collectivity" (Apter's phrase), we need to pose the question, how can democracy take root there, in the bedrock of the fundamentalist program? Is the culture of collectivity not the antithesis of democracy? And if this is true, then will fundamentalism not prove to be more authentic in Islamic civilization than would any democratic movement? I will argue, against this view, that enlightenment vis-à-vis fundamentalism *need not be restricted to Western civilization,* but can be established on Islamic grounds. I believe that the philosophical rationalism of Islamic Hellenism in medieval Islam is an early tradition of Islamic enlightenment. I have supported this thesis with evidence elsewhere.[6]

In pursuing our analysis, we need to recall that the World of Islam comprises a great variety of local cultures united by ethical standards related to similar norms and values, as well as by a corresponding worldview. This pattern of unity in diversity can be addressed as an Islamic civilization.[7] We need, then, to introduce into our inquiry a greater differentiation of constructs and specifics, as well as a historical approach that traces the elements of Islam's religious doctrine and the intellectual thought of its enlightenment back into the Islamic legacy.

It is true that there are fault lines separating the world's civilizations, in particular between those of the West and the World of Islam, that is, between civilizations that clash for the simple reason that each claims universality for its particular views.[8] Given, however, that people who belong to divergent civilizations nonetheless share the essence of a single humanity, there must be some common core of ethical values that can unite us for the sake of peace and a better life. Our post-Cold War world is characterized by the rise of ethnic nationalisms and religious fundamentalisms that regrettably choose to emphasize a combination of figurative and geographic lines of separation as borderlines within humanity, not to be transgressed. The vision of civilizations living together in peace and dignity embraces the idea that human rights and democracy can be made the common core that I address, on cross-cultural grounds, as international morality.[9] World peace among civilizations requires this ethical convergence, which is not itself tantamount to yet another sweeping universalism, let alone an imposed one. To question universalism and thus to honor cultural pluralism does not equate to endorsing the current waves of cultural relativism and postmodern politics, which provoke division through emphasizing heterogeneity and incommensurability. In the pursuit of a united humanity sharing an international morality, it is essential that a basic program of human rights and democracy be asserted and honored by all of the world's civilizations, for all of them need to participate in the global process of democratization. Instead of a culturally insensitive universalism, what we need is a cross-cultural underpinning of democracy in non-Western societies. Unlike the fundamentalists, we must seek commonalities, not borderlines. Here lies the basic difference between my approach and Huntington's. What Huntington calls "fault lines of *conflict*" between civilizations is no more than a perception we must scrutinize, not a reality. Only in this sense is fundamentalism to be viewed as the ideology of the "clash of civilizations." In contrast, democracy is the platform for peace between them. Where is the place of Islam in this context?

ISLAMIC CIVILIZATION, THE WEST, AND DEMOCRACY

Viewed from, say, India, the hub of Islamic civilization is located in West Asia, that is, the region that Westerners ethnocentrically place as the Near and Middle East in their own geopolitics. Islam is also a major religion in Africa and in Central, South, and Southeast Asia. The secular nation-state of India has hitherto made an effort to accommodate Muslims, Sikhs, and Hindus, among others. If these people, of such widely divergent cultures, can share the citizenship of a single democracy while living peacefully within the territory of their respective states, then democracy would seem to be the right umbrella for the peace of civilizations. India can serve in this regard both as a model wherein people belonging to diverse civilizations can make democracy the referent of their common identity and, conversely, as a model for the "coming anarchy"[10] recently heralded by Kaplan. The future of Kaplan's model is pertinent for world politics, for Hindu fundamentalists are already threatening the democracy and inner peace of India. In the 1996 parliamentary elections in India the fundamentalist Hindu party, the *Bharatiya Janata Party* (BJP) succeeded in winning 195 of the 545 seats in the Indian parliament. In May 1996 the BJP fundamentalists, led by Atal Bihari Vajpayee, were able to govern India for thirteen days, until a coalition of all secular parties compelled Prime Minister Vajpayee to resign.[11] What may transpire next, however, is anyone's guess.

Indonesia is another Asian case where an enlightened and tolerant Islam currently seems to embrace democracy, gradually but steadily. In so saying, I credit Indonesian civil society and its Islamic traditions, but clearly not the government of President Suharto and his extended family. Given that Indonesia, with a population of 193 million, is not only the largest Islamic nation but the fourth largest nation in the world, the question to be asked is whether the conditions that encourage secularity and democratization there can serve as a model throughout Islamic civilization. An expert on Indonesia, Fred van der Mehden, who has subjected the interaction between Southeast Asia and the Middle East to close scrutiny, offers these telling facts: "Middle Eastern religious ideas still dominate the exchange between the two regions. There is relatively little influence by Southeast Asian Muslim intellectuals on the rest of the Muslim world. . . . [But] religious education in the Middle East, and in Cairo in particular, remains a major source of Muslim thought in Southeast Asia, especially in Indonesia."[12] This observation supports the assumption of the cultural centrality of the Sunni Middle East in Islamic civilization. Regrettably, the tolerant and pluralistic Indonesian model is unlikely to determine the future of democracy in Islamic civilization. But we may hope that the economic success of Islamic Southeast Asia, combined with its efforts at democratization, could at least *affect* policies in the economically and politically desperate Middle East.

Muslims have encountered democracy, a concept utterly new to them, only recently, in the context of globalization and through the exposure of their own civilization to cultural modernity (see Chapter 4). Early Muslim liberals were at pains to embrace democracy and to reconcile it with Islam. The first Muslim student sent to Europe, Rifa'a Rafi' al-Tahtawi, expressed deep admiration for the democratic culture of France. He was to witness the July Revolution in Paris in 1830, and was impressed to see the representatives of the toppled regime being treated well and granted human rights. For Tahtawi, this was evidence (as he states) "for how civilized the French are and how their state is bound to justice."[13] Early Muslim modernists, who had been critical of Europe, owing to its long colonial penetration, nevertheless continued their efforts to reconcile Islamic civilization with the cultural modernity of the West. In the Islamic liberalism[14] of the early twentieth century, democracy was at the top of the agenda of Muslim thinkers like 'Abbas Mahmud al-'Aqqad.[15]

In principle, Muslims have been able to draw upon their own civilization for a historical record of learning from other civilizations. In the Abbasid period, for example, Muslims adopted Greek philosophy and, from other civilizations, Persian-Sassanian administration (see Hodgson, note 7). The Islamic rationalism of the medieval period, here addressed as an early Islamic enlightenment, was in fact a synthesis of the Greek legacy and Islamic thought.[16] Islamic rationalism was the major stimulus for the European Renaissance that soon became one of the pillars of cultural modernity in Europe. And the primary source of modern democracy lay in cultural modernity. As I have previously quoted the Berkeley scholar Leslie Lipson, "Aristotle crept back into Europe by the side door. His return was due to the Arabs, who had become acquainted with Greek thinkers. . . . The main source of Europe's inspiration shifted from Christianity back to Greece, from Jerusalem to Athens."[17] Medieval Muslim philosophers had shifted earlier, on their own terms, from the "world of muftis" to the "world of reason."[18]

It is sad commentary that the Greek legacy transmitted to Europe by Muslim philosophers should have vanished in the World of Islam itself, where Islamic orthodoxy, gathered around the *fiqh* (Islamic sacred jurisprudence), took control and superseded Islamic rationalism, the *falsafa*.[19]

In modern times the early Muslim liberals were at pains to resume the Islamic enlightenment by coming to terms with democracy and adopting its norms and values in an Islamic context. As the late Muslim Oxford scholar of Iranian descent, Hamid Enayat, put it, the failure of these Muslim liberals has been caused not so much "by conceptual incoherence as by the absence of specific social and economic formations." Internally, "educational backwardness, widespread illiteracy, and the prevalence of servile habits of thinking and blind submission to authority" were the major obstacles. There were also, however (as Enayat continues), various external obstacles related to "the reluctance of the United States and some West European powers to adjust themselves to the realities of the postcolonial era."[20] There are many examples of this deficiency, and the American political scientist Richard J. Payne has discussed at length the insensitivity of U.S. foreign policy to non-Western cultures.[21] No prudent scholar studying these issues can escape acknowledging that the West, despite all its lip service, has not been favorable to the democratization process in the World of Islam. For instance, although Saudi Arabia is one of the most undemocratic of all Islamic states, it is nevertheless one of the closest allies of the United States in the Middle East. Instead of promoting democracy, Western states prefer to pursue their economic and political interests.

Many Islamic countries can point to a record of democratization in the early postcolonial period, when democracy was still on the agenda in the Middle East. The period between the 1930s and the early 1950s is considered to be the "liberal age" in Middle Eastern politics, and it was the rise of one-party authoritarian regimes and the populist ideology of pan-Arab nationalism[22] that marked the end of these efforts to democratize. In Egypt, for instance, the "Free Officers" under Nasser took over in 1952. Ever since, the levers of power have resided in the hands of lifetime presidents and other tyrants of all shapes and forms.[23] These regimes were formally secular, but their subsequent de-legitimization, in particular since the shattering defeat in the Six-Day War,[24] has given rise not to a new program of democratization but rather to political Islam as an alternative. Concurrently, there were signs of electoral democratization in Algeria, Jordan, Egypt, and Morocco, but the outcomes have not been promising.

In discussing Islam and democracy, John Esposito refers to the Islamization of democracy, and interprets this process as a democratization in itself.[25] Of course democracy in Islam need not be identical with Western democracy, and I share Esposito's resentment regarding the West's hijacking of democracy (i.e., asserting a monopoly over democracy and its standards). His problem, however, is the confusion of Islam with fundamentalism, and accordingly I fail to see that his contention of the compatibility of Islamism and democracy is supported by evidence in any of the actions or pronouncements of Islamic fundamentalists. I agree with the findings of the "Democratic Movements in the Middle East" project—to wit, that the Islamists are "committed to using the fragile reemergence of democratic processes to destroy any decisive move [toward] liberal democracy itself."[26] My own observations in Algiers, during the Algerian democratization process in 1991–92 and again in 1993, led me to similar conclusions.[27] Military rule in post-FLN Algeria after December 1991 is quite authoritarian, and I can scarcely imagine an Algeria taking a different path of development under the rule of the fundamentalist Front Islamique du Salut (FIS). The fundamentalist takeover in Sudan after the coup d'état of June 1989 is another case in point.

Before we take the opening steps of a substantive synthesis of Islam and democracy, in the tradition of Enlightenment, I want to quote the views of three leading authorities of the current religious fundamentalism movement in Islamic civilization. Next to the Egyptian Sayyid Qutb, who had been executed in 1966, the late Pakistani Abu al-A'la al-Mawdudi (1903–79)

is considered to have been the major ideological authority and source of political Islam.

In his book *Islam and Modern Civilization*, Mawdudi puts it bluntly: "I
tell you, my fellow Muslims, frankly: . . . democracy stands in contradiction with your belief. . . . The Islam in which you believe . . . is utterly different from this dreadful system. . . . There can be no reconciliation between Islam and democracy, not even in minor issues, because they
contradict one another in all particulars. Where this system (of democracy)
exists we consider Islam to be absent. When Islam comes to power there is
no place for this system."[28]

Qutb seems to have been the precursor, on the Islamic front, of the Huntington approach of a "clash of civilizations." But unlike Mawdudi he views
the conflict on a global scale: "After the decay of democracy, to the extent of
bankruptcy, the West has nothing to give to humanity. . . . The leadership
of Western man has vanished. . . . It is time for Islam to take over and lead."[29]

One of the most influential contemporary Islamic writers is the Egyptian fundamentalist Yusuf al-Qaradawi, who invented the formula *"al-hall
al-Islami* / the Islamic solution" versus *"al-hulul al-mustawrada* / imported
solutions." Atop the list of "imported solutions" he places what he calls "democratic liberalism." Al-Qaradawi tells his readers, "Democracy is a Greek
term that means the government of the people" and then continues that
"democratic liberalism came into the life of Muslims through the impact of
colonialism. It has been the most dangerous [influence] in the colonial
legacy."[30]

All three of these pivotal, old and new, fundamentalist thinkers reject
democracy on the grounds of its incompatibility with the religious teachings of Islam. To reiterate, Islam and democracy *are* compatible (see note
25), but democracy and popular sovereignty are inseparable, and Islamic
fundamentalists believe that only God can exercise sovereignty. The model
they present as an alternative to democracy is *hakimiyyat Allah* / God's rule
as the legitimization of an "Islamic state."[31] Are these really authentic Islamic
political views? Is it true that Islam and democracy "contradict one another
in all particulars," as Mawdudi contends? The problem is not that there *are*
such inherent contradictions, but rather that these fundamentalist thinkers
expound their *quite human* views, accord them a divine status, and dismiss
their critics as fools and heretics. As the liberal Muslim Muhammad Said
al-Ashmawi has shown, these Islamists confuse *shari'a* and *fiqh*.[32] *Shari'a*
is an ethics, set forth in the Qur'an, what is right, and therefore allowed

(*halal*), and what is wrong, and therefore forbidden (*haram*). Yet this is an ethics, not a legal body. With the death of the Prophet in 632 the revelation ended, and it was only in the eighth century, long after the death of the Prophet, that the four Sunni legal schools (*madhahib*) were established and the *shari'a* was constructed as a coherent legal body. It is for this reason that I argue *shari'a*, in the sense of a legal system, is a post-Qur'anic construction. In contrast, *fiqh*/Islamic jurisprudence is a human interpretation of *shari'a* rules. The confusion of *shari'a* and *fiqh* results in attributing a divine character to human thought and thus allows characterizing the liberal Muslims as unbelievers.

THE ACCOMMODATION OF DEMOCRACY WITHOUT A RETHINKING OF ISLAM

To be sure, in both historical and doctrinal terms there are—despite the compatibility I have emphasized—basic differences between Islam and democracy, and it would be dishonest to deny them. On an ethical level, however, there are strong affinities between Islam and democracy. It seems to me possible to identify significant commonalities between Islamic civilization and the West, where the pursuit of an international morality is concerned. I share the view of Hamid Enayat that it is "neither . . . inordinately difficult nor illegitimate to derive a list of democratic rights and liberties" from respected Islamic sources, "given a fair degree of exegetical talent."[33] Thus the contention of the Islamic fundamentalists that Islam and democracy are inherently at odds does not hold. The notion of *hakimiyyat Allah*, for example, does not occur in the Qur'an, nor can one find it in the *hadith*, the sayings of the Prophet, the only two authoritative sources in the Islamic faith. In fact, this concept of "God's rule" is a human—in this case fundamentalist—invention based on a correspondingly arbitrary reading of the present politicization of Islam into past Islamic history. In short, *hakimiyyat Allah* is a "neo-*fiqh* doctrine" (see note 32), and is not divine!

Aside from the philology of the scripture there are historical facts that run counter to the contemporary fundamentalist ideology of an "Islamic state" presented as an alternative to the democratic state. Islamic fundamentalists propagate the *tatbiq al-shari'a*/implementation of Islamic law as the single decisive criterion for determining the *dawla Islamiyya*/Islamic state. Those who are familiar with Islamic law[34] know well that the *shari'a* has been erected but never codified, because to codify it would run counter to its nature as an interpretive law based on the interpretation of divine revelation. There are four Sunni Islamic legal schools involved in the post-Qur'anic construction of the *shari'a*, each of which has its own tradition of lawmaking. Thus Islamic law has been a law of the Hanafi, Shafi'i, Hanbali, and Maliki, religious communities, no one of which was ever attached to the state. As Hamid Enayat puts it, the *shari'a* "was never implemented as an integral system, and the bulk of its provisions remained as legal fictions."[35] In other words, the *tatbiq al-shari'a* aspired to by Islamic fundamentalists is *also* a fiction.

Again, in fairness to the Islamic fundamentalists, one must—while again stressing the compatibility argument—acknowledge real tensions between Islamic thought and democracy, if the truth and not political expediency is to inform our analysis. Here again, I agree with Enayat: "If Islam comes into conflict with certain postulates of democracy it is because of its general character as a religion. . . . An intrinsic concomitant of democracy . . . involves a challenge to many a sacred axiom."[36]

In their effort to accommodate democracy in Islamic civilization, the early Islamic modernists and liberals deliberately avoided hot-button issues that could have called their plea for democracy into question. A successful adaptation of religious doctrine to changed realities requires what the contemporary Algerian Muslim thinker Mohammed Arkoun courageously heralded as "Rethinking Islam,"[37] a promise that he himself—the title of his book notwithstanding—does not fully deliver. This sort of evasion can be observed in most of the Islamic writings on democracy published prior to the rise of religious fundamentalism. In my book *Islam and the Cultural Accommodation of Social Change*[38] I argue that a conformity to changed conditions— undertaken pragmatically, without a concurrent rethinking of the relevant religious doctrine—cannot be equated with an adaptation or accommodation. The Islamic-Iranian scholar Hamid Enayat makes this same point: "What is blatantly missing . . . is an adaptation of either the ethical and legal precepts of Islam, or the attitudes and institutions of traditional society, to democracy. This is obviously a much more complex and challenging task than the mere reformulation of democratic principles in Islamic idioms. It is because of this neglect that the hopes of evolving a coherent theory of democracy appropriate to an Islamic context have remained largely unfulfilled."[39]

Islamic fundamentalists invoke these unavoidable shortcomings of Islamic liberals and modernists as grounds for denouncing them for allegedly deviating from the true religious doctrine. To introduce democracy into Islamic civilization unequivocally means that "efforts to synthesize Islam and democracy are bound to founder on the bedrock of that body of eternal and unchangeable doctrines which form the quintessence of every religion. Those Muslim thinkers who face this issue boldly, and free of any compulsion to keep their faith abreast of ephemeral political fashions, normally come up with the open admission that Islam and democracy are irreconcilable."[40] I agree with Enayat about the limits of a morality based on religion. In other words, references to the religious underpinning of democracy in Islamic civilization, as well as in other religion-based civilizations, must be both selective and limited in addressing the issues. This level of caution is necessary if conflict between Islam and democracy is to be avoided and compatibility is to be promoted. Even though I argue fervently for the incorporation of democracy into Islamic civilization on cross-cultural, not universalistic, grounds, I am aware of the limits of this approach. These limits make necessary a religious reform that enables us to accommodate social change culturally and permits us to go beyond the existing scriptural and doctrinal confines. In this sense, I am convinced that, unless there is a rethinking of Islamic doctrines, no Islamic contribution to an international cross-cultural morality can be offered. Even a scholar blessed with an extraordinary exegetical talent will stumble at the limits of a reinterpretation of doctrine pursued on scriptural grounds. Rethinking needs to be reason-based, not philology- and scripture-based.

THE REQUIREMENTS FOR DEMOCRACY: POLITICAL CULTURE AND DEMOCRATIC INSTITUTIONS

Having exceeded the normative need for establishing an international morality on cross-cultural grounds, I shall move now to an empirical analysis of the recent state of affairs in the Middle East, with a focus on developments since the Gulf War. The questions that I shall ask are inspired by the insight that democracy is not a fond dream but a necessity, one that can be pursued only on realistic grounds. In building democracies there are not only ethical but also structural requirements.

Democracy is a political culture that cannot flourish in a system lacking an appropriate foundation. Hence, to speak of democratization in Islamic civilization in general and in the Middle East in particular is to speak about change in two major areas. First, changing a political culture requires the development of favorable pluralist attitudes toward democracy as a politi-

cal culture of its own. This requirement runs counter to the political culture of *umma* collectivism. Second, political development in the sense of in-
stitution-building must take place in Arab and other Islamic societies now
characterized more or less by low levels of institutionalization and a high
degree of personalization of power.[41] With a few exceptions, both of the requirements for successfully promoting democratization are virtually absent
in Islamic civilization. (So as to provide a concrete analysis, my focus will
be on the Middle East.)

The Gulf War has made democratization a topical issue in the Middle
East. This is not to say that the issue had not been addressed previously. In
November 1983, a group of seventy Arab scholars, journalists, and
former politicians, myself included, addressed this issue as *azmat al-
demoqratiyya* / crisis of democracy in the Arab world. The assemblage met
in Limassol, Cyprus, after being denied permission to meet in any Arab
city, including Cairo (Saudi Arabia, it seems, pressured the Egyptian
government to deny the permission). The proceedings were published in
Arabic in Beirut in a 927-page volume. The general thrust of the volume
was how to deal with the obstacles to democratization, and the volume has
enjoyed wide dissemination in the Arab world, both legally and through
underground means.[42]

Most experts cite democratization as a crucial component of any post-
Gulf War regional order in the Middle East. Both of the local belligerents
in the Gulf War, Saddam Hussein's Iraq and the anti-Saddam Arab coalition (composed of dictators like Assad and medieval Saudi and Kuwaiti oil
princes), lack all elements of democracy in their home states. It is frequently
argued that the world would have been spared the Gulf War if the relevant
political systems had been of a democratic character. In Kantian ethics, genuine democracies do not wage war against one another, and in fact they
never have. Iraq might not have resorted to violent means to impose its economic and territorial claims, and Kuwait might have drawn upon the procedures of diplomacy and negotiation, long established in international relations, to deal with the Iraqi claims, instead of playing the intransigent
bedouin and provoking Iraqi aggression. The Kuwaitis are bedouin in ele-
gant modern cars, enjoying the commodities of modernity.

Some observers argue that a Western strategy for the Middle East needs
to emphasize democratization. After the Gulf War, William Safire charged
in one of his editorials in *The New York Times* (April 1, 1991, p. A17) that
the United States was too timid to impose democracy in the Middle East,

and he found this fact to be deplorable. For the sake of irony I agree with Safire's charge of "timidity"; I disagree, however, with his notion of imposition. Democracy cannot be imposed, and it cannot thrive, if the local foundation is lacking. To take this position is not to contradict my plea that the promotion of democratization be made part and parcel of Western Middle East policies, for to promote democratization is not to impose it, although in some cases—such allies of the West as Kuwait and Saudi Arabia come to mind—a certain amount of pressure is justified. The rulers of both these states believe they can dispense with democratization and nonetheless continue to rely on Western support—which they in fact receive. I shall show in some detail that the Saudi and Kuwaiti rulers are most reluctant to admit the need for democratic measures. The Kuwaiti and Saudi sheikhs are traditional rulers, but not fundamentalists. But like the latter, they are imprisoned in the illusion that Islam and democracy are at odds. For them, this view is a questionable and disingenuous defense of their legitimacy.

Most of the existing states in the Middle East are only nominally nation-states,[43] in the sense that they lack the basic institutions required for establishing a democratically designed political community. Among these institutions are a multi-party political system, parliamentarian institutions, and, foremost, an independent legal system. That these institutions have made no headway is because they are not wanted by the rulers. In Iraq, clearly, power holders and their opposition alike are divided along ethnic and sectarian lines related to the emergence of an artificially configured Iraqi state in 1921. Iraq consists of three ethnic and religious communities and their corresponding territories. First, the former Ottoman province of Mosul, inhabited by Kurds, in the northeast. (The Iraqi Kurds are, like those of Iran and Turkey, mostly Sunni Muslims, but neither Arabs nor Turks nor Iranians; they are a distinct ethnic group with their own identity, but have no state of their own. In Iraq, they occupy the north.) Second, the vast Sunni Baghdad province. And third, the Shi'ite province of Basra, in the south. The ruling Ba'th Party is well-known as a modern secular and totalitarian organization that has been trying—as violently as may be needed—to recast the entire country along the lines of its uniting pan-Arab ideology. One cannot help noting, however, that the ruling political elite in Iraq, despite its secular language and claims to modernity, is traditionally Sunni and Arab in character. Political communities in Iraq are formed on the basis of sectarian religion and ethnicity. The chief obstacle to true democratization in a country like Iraq is the fact that communities are not defined substantively, along political lines, but rather along ethnoreligious lines. Moreover, these communities view themselves as collective entities (the individual is subordinated to the group), and view their rivals similarly (see Chapter 6). Considering the ethnic and sectarian subdivisions within this entity—comparable subdivisions rend most other Islamic states—we must conclude that the idea of a holistic Islamic civilization is considerably more relative than absolute.

The weak institutional basis of the existing nominal nation-states in the Middle East, in conjunction with the prevailing neopatriarchal political culture,[44] creates great obstacles to democratization. Revisions in the Western understanding of democratization are needed for a proper accommodation of this concept in an alien civilization. In my view, a change in the prevailing patterns of political culture in the Middle East—toward the acceptance of cross-cultural democratic values, which is among the needed requirements for democratization—is imperative. I see no conflict between my commitment to individual human rights and my belief that consideration must also be given to collective freedoms for religious and ethnic minorities at the local and regional levels. Ethnopolitical power-sharing, as a component of democracy, is needed in the Middle East, not simply among mobile political interest groups, but rather among enduring religious and ethnic groups. Thus, Arabs need first to learn how to view human beings as free individuals, and not as obliged members of collective entities, which today are virtually the functional equivalent of the old Arab tribes (see note 43). Arabs also need to learn how to respect the ethnic and religious minorities living among them, and how to share political power with them. It is not only the Arab secular tyrant of Baghdad but also, for example, the fundamentalists in Sudan, who suppress minorities. Knowing that in Egypt and Algeria the fundamentalist opposition already violates the human rights of minorities, we may well ask: What would the fundamentalists do if they were in power there?!

THE CASES OF KUWAIT AND SAUDI ARABIA

Just as the legitimacy crisis ensuing after the Arab defeat in the Six-Day War of 1967 shattered pan-Arabism as a structure for ideological legitimacy, so the Gulf War and its repercussions have meant the end of pan-Arabism and paved the way for its funeral. Insofar as pan-Arabism, though secular, had predominantly Sunni-Arab foundations, its legitimacy was particularly doubtful in the multiethnic Arab states like Iraq, Algeria, Sudan, and many of the Gulf states. Kuwait is a special case, since the ruling Sunni Arabs there are themselves a minority ruling over a multiethnic and religious majority deprived of virtually all rights. Most of this majority is even denied legal citizenship, despite residing locally for generations. Let me, then, start my overview with Kuwait.

In Kuwait, real power lies exclusively with the al-Sabah family, which consists of about 1,500 princes and princesses. This family has governed Kuwait dynastically since 1756. Kuwait claims a formal democratic record encompassing four parliaments, the most recent of which was elected in 1992. Legally, 70 percent of the Kuwaiti population is composed of foreigners, that is, people born in Kuwait but denied legal citizenship. During the 1985 election only 10 percent of the Kuwaitis (60,000 males) had the right to vote, but not all of them are eligible to be elected. In Kuwait there are no political parties, and during the elections of the 1970s and 1980s, candidates for the National Assembly had to run their campaigns on behalf of their traditional families or tribal communities. No institutionalized participation in decision making exists, and Kuwait's only functional, premodern equivalent of political parties is the *diwaniyya*. The *diwaniyya* is a reception room where Kuwaiti men meet to talk about political issues while having tea and coffee. It resembles the European coffee houses of nineteenth-century Vienna, but lacks the public character, mobility in membership, and female attendance of the coffee houses. The ruling al-Sabah family has its own *diwaniyya*, currently overseen by the Crown Prince Saad al-Sabah, who receives his family members to discuss with them—and only them—the central social and political issues of the Emirate's life. The Emir of Kuwait himself is said to be devoted to weeklong marriages rather than politics. The merchants,[45] who are divided along tribal and family lines like all Kuwaitis, have in each case their own *diwaniyya*.

Kuwait is formally a democratic state, but the National Assembly has never really had an impact on the governance of the state. According to the leading expert on Kuwait, the Swiss writer Liesl Graz, one of the reasons for the dissolution of the parliament in 1986 was that too many assembly members had forgotten that Kuwait is governed by the al-Sabah family, not by parliament.[46] After the Gulf War, in response to Kuwaiti calls for democratization, the Crown Prince Saad al-Sabah alleged that democracy would divide the Kuwaiti people, who form one family.[47] This reflects the Islamic understanding of the polity as an indivisible collective entity ruled by a patriarchal authority—in a decidedly undemocratic manner. Moreover, those who disagree with this notion of the collective entity risk their lives. The reader may recall David Apter's words, quoted in the introductory remarks to this chapter: the norms of a collectivity are the antithesis of political democracy.

This culture of tribal collectivity confronts us again in Saudi Arabia, considered to be the foremost Islamic state in the Middle East. Even though most of the Islamic fundamentalist movements outside of the monarchy enjoy generous Saudi financial support, the Saudi state is not the model of the "Islamic state" these fundamentalists aspire to. In fact, the fundamentalists themselves are off limits in Saudi Arabia. The political structure in Saudi Arabia is quite different from that in Kuwait, and the chances for democratization here are even poorer than they are in Kuwait. As in Kuwait, the Saudi democratic opposition is composed of wealthy liberal merchants. But unlike their Kuwaiti counterparts, they do not go so far as to ask for elections, let alone a constitution. No record of elections or of any constitutional reform is to be found in Saudi Arabia, and the Qur'an is considered the only valid constitution, not only for Saudi Arabia, but for all of humanity. The repeated message to the opposition in Saudi Arabia is that democratization is not desirable, and the opposition dares ask only for the establishment of consultative *shura* councils and a curb on the fanatic surveillance of the people by the religious police, the so-called *mutawin*. In August 1993, the Saudi state did introduce a *shura* council, though its existence is in no way to be taken as a step toward democratization.[48]

It is significant that Western politicians never address the human rights violations in Saudi Arabia as they usually do in their comments on Iraq. Business as usual! It seems not to disturb the West that in Saudi Arabia there are no foreseeable prospects for democratization whatsoever. The urban liberal merchants urge the very ill King Fahd to combine economic modernization with political change, but they, unlike the Kuwaiti opposition, have no means by which to exert pressure on the King in the pursuit of these ends. Crown Prince Abdulla is even tougher in the rejection of democracy than his brother. Thanks to the effects of the oil economy, the Saudi state had undergone tremendous economic modernization prior to the Gulf War, but the current economic hardships are greatly retarding this process. Some analysts have believed that modernization would lead automatically to social and political change, and although I dispute the idea that economic modernization may lead *automatically* to political development, one concedes that Islam has no miraculous power to block social change, and in this respect Saudi Arabia is no exception. The Saudis must find a way to make democratization compatible with their Islamic legitimacy, and I believe this to be possible. There are—admittedly only a few—Muslim reformers keen on establishing an Islamic theory that renders democracy and Islam compatible. Meanwhile, however, the newly instituted practice of *shura* in Saudi Arabia is not much of a step in this direction.

CONCLUSIONS

In the Middle Eastern Arab core of Islamic civilization, the prospects for progressive change are seldom promising. Rapid economic (but not political) modernization, under way particularly since the 1970s, has led to a social crisis triggering a new pattern of political opposition: Islamic fundamentalism. Fundamentalists are not traditionalists; despite their anti-Western rhetoric, they draw instrumentally on modern achievements.[49] But its modernist drive notwithstanding, Islamic fundamentalism is the antithesis of democratization (see notes 5 and 25). Fundamentalists are not willing to introduce the changes that might make Islamic civilization compatible with the political culture of democracy, nor are there any signs that their formula of *al-nizam al-Islami/* the Islamic system of government promises to promote the institutionalization of the Middle Eastern political systems, as a prerequisite for democracy. The envisaged state promises, rather, a desperate mix of disorder and totalitarianism (see note 31).

Even in Jordan, the only Middle Eastern Islamic state with some record of democratic achievement, Islamic fundamentalism figures as the current mainstream opposition. Jordan holds real elections and enjoys a true parliament. But even though weaker than they were in the preceding parliament, the fundamentalists are a considerable faction in the current Jordanian parliament, and they oppose the peace process with Israel. The strategy of King Hussein is based more on keeping the fundamentalists in check than on the belief that their free political participation is a contribution to true democracy.

Egypt remains important to the future of Islam, in part because it is the home of the al-Azhar University, the most authoritative intellectual institution of Sunni Islam. The sheikh of al-Azhar can issue a *fetwa* that is binding for all Sunni Muslims. In Egypt the fundamentalists are active both legally (in professional associations, under the impact of the Muslim Brethren) and in the underground. Those in the underground are responsible for the slaying and the endemic violence, often approaching the character of a civil war, and for the spread of terrorism in Egyptian cities. Can the Egyptian fundamentalists—as in Jordan—be contained through an electoral-ballot politics? Given that fundamentalism currently represents mainstream *public choices* in that region, will genuine democratization lead—ironically—to the empowerment of Islamic fundamentalists?

To raise this question is not tantamount to raising doubts about the need for democratization itself. Democratization was in fact discussed in Syria before the Gulf War, when the breakdown of communism in Eastern Europe, and in particular the fall of the Ceausescu regime in Romania, evoked talk in the larger cities of the potential fall of various "Arab Ceausescus." One could not fail to understand the inference that one of the local Ceausescus might be Assad or Saddam Hussein. The Syrian government announced a verbal commitment to democratization and it did allow some formal, but by no means substantive, power-sharing. No more was necessary, for the context of resurgent Islamic fundamentalism allows the Syrian government to constrain its efforts to confines that in all decency should not be accorded the term "democratization." The same, sadly, applies to the status of governments in most other Islamic countries.

Thus, we ought not overlook the great appeal of a political Islam to the bulk of the peoples in the Middle East. While conducting interviews with fundamentalists during the late 1980s, as a member of the Fundamentalism Project of the American Academy of Arts and Sciences, I was in a position to observe the power of this appeal in Tunisia, Egypt, and Sudan. Among my findings is the fact that fundamentalism was the public choice *before* the Gulf War, and the war simply reinforced this tendency. I base this statement not on a poll, but on personal observation. (Alas, interviewing fundamentalists in the 1990s became an impossible endeavor.)

Western observers, even Middle East experts, have great difficulty in understanding the appeal and tactics of Islamic fundamentalism. The fact that fundamentalist demagogues can manipulate an audience as well as anyone else contributes to the difficulties that observers face, in particular those who lack knowledge of the local languages and thus can easily be deceived.

There can be no stable regional political order in Islamic civilization without some measure of democratization. The path, however, is not only thorny; it implies high risks. Any serious program of democratization must be matched by improvements in the living conditions of the people in these states, so that they might be made less susceptible to the salvational wiles of fundamentalism. An enlightened interpretation of Islam would free Muslims from the grinding despair and daily dangers of ghettoization and totalitarianism. Only in this manner can democratization be attempted if it is not to run the risk of playing into the hands of Muslim fundamentalists and bringing them to power. Despite the odds, democracy and democratization remain the only alternative to Islamic fundamentalism in that part of the world.[50]

—⚬—

TEN

Human Rights in Islam and the West

Cross-Cultural Foundations of Shared Values

Why does a book on fundamentalism conclude with a chapter on human rights? As the preceding chapter has made clear, democracy is part and parcel of any cross-cultural consensus on establishing an international morality as the underpinning of world peace. And inherent in the idea of democracy is some notion of human rights. Fundamentalism, by contrast, is a divisive force that subordinates individual freedom, ignites conflict, and threatens peace. Fundamentalisms are the antithesis of human rights.

Still, fundamentalism, human rights, and democracy are all intricately interlinked with modernity. We have seen (in chapters 2 and 4) that modernity has two principal dimensions, one cultural and the other institutional. Fundamentalists are usually highly affected by both dimensions of modernity—even while they contest it—but in particular by its cultural aspects. In dealing with this odd kinship between fundamentalism and modernity, in particular with fundamentalism vis-à-vis human rights, we face two ambiguities. The first lies in the extensive use of instrumental modernity by fundamentalists—from working the Internet to exploiting the mass media for their cause—while at the same time condemning modernity's intrusion into the World of Islam. The second ambiguity is seen in the fundamentalists' demanding human rights for themselves from the authoritarian, even despotic rulers of the World of Islam while denying these same rights to their foes. It is no exaggeration to state that the slaying of Muslim intellectuals who disagree with the visions and solutions presented by the fundamentalists—in, for example, Algeria, Egypt, and Turkey—is the foremost violation of human rights in contemporary Islamic societies.

I maintain that democracy and human rights are the primary guarantors of human dignity, and that Islamic fundamentalism is the most recent variety of totalitarianism, following in the wake of fascism and communism. The promotion of human rights on international, that is, cross-cultural, grounds is an effort to unfold an alternative to fundamentalism, on a global basis. Religion, in the meaning of religious ethics and faith, can be a part of the ethical grounds for establishing a program of human rights, whereas fundamentalism is a political abuse of religion and cannot contribute to such a program. Fundamentalism, of whatever sort, accords an ideological character to the faith, and mobilizes people against the perceptual enemy, the unbelievers.[1] In this case, the fundamentalism is Islamic, and the enemy is the West. There is of course some historical basis for the contention that Islam and the West are rivals,[2] and the two do have different worldviews. But the Islamic and Western civilizations are under pressure to come to terms with one another, to find ways for establishing patterns of peaceful coexistence. All the while, fundamentalism deepens the existing entrenchments.

ISLAM AND THE WEST: FROM DISSENT TO INTERNATIONAL MORALITY

Cultural differences are as old as humanity itself. The story of humanity is equally a history of clashes and a history of exchanges, between diverse cultures and distinct civilizations. One cannot find, in the whole history of mankind, a civilization that managed to persist in isolation, trusting strictly to its own devices, all the while taking no note of other civilizations and borrowing nothing from them, whether culturally or linguistically.[3] This is as true for Islam as it is for the West. Like the West, the civilization of Islam also embraces a great number of local cultures, and it should be viewed in terms of its cultural diversity as well as its civilizational unity.

The pertinence of the dialogue between Islam and the West in the years since the Cold War focuses on one basic issue. With the demise of the artificial umbrella that had been imposed on world politics, the true fault lines separating these sectors of humanity have been exposed. The "clash of civilizations" as a clash of *Weltanschauungen* is not an invention of Harvard's Professor Samuel Huntington, but results from the politicization of incompatible civilizational worldviews. Accordingly, all who study this clash should assiduously seek out mechanisms, models, and frameworks that might lead to the peaceful coexistence of these rival civilizations. An international morality of human rights that is based on cross-cultural foundations, not on an imposed universalism, promises to be the most fruitful vehicle for this endeavor.

We live in an age of ever-growing and almost overwhelming structural globalization. The international system of nation-states, the interdigitated world economy, and the shrinking of the world through global communication and transportation systems are the engines of globalization. Some would argue that the modern popular culture of consumption does function as a "world culture." But cheeseburgers are not the proudest export of the West, and Islamic fundamentalism is not simply a "Jihad versus Mac-World,"[4] or an indication that a worldwide culture is in the offing. Such arguments are grossly simplistic characterizations of a very complex phenomenon. Videos, fast food, jeans, and other items of the consumptive culture, when shared, do not bring people with different worldviews and outlooks appreciably closer. To bridge the gaps between both local cultures and regional civilizations, people need to pursue earnest dialogue, find commonalties, and address issues of dissent. Peoples in the non-Western world may drink Coca-Cola and enjoy American television's soap operas, but continue to be America's ardent foes. These things are of small consequence. Culture, as I have tried to make clear, does not lie in the particulars of popular consumption but is an expression of the social production of meaning by a specific human grouping. Thus culture is always local; there can be no world culture.

Like Islam, Western civilization unites a panoply of local cultures. What distinguishes the West from Islam is that Western civilization has undergone processes of secularization, and in the process has instituted a separation of religion and politics in society.[5] Sociologists of religion address this phenomenon as "the functional differentiation of society" (see note 5). In secular societies, religion has a social function but no longer determines the entire character of the social system. Yet, this is not the place to discuss whether this social process can take root in Islam as well; despite a century of efforts toward that end, it has not. In approaching the concept of human rights as the substance of an international morality to be shared by Islam and the West, I want to extend my deliberations to the divisive as well as the uniting elements in the two civilizations. My intention and point of departure is cross-cultural bridging. The major issues and the pivotal questions are these:

1.   Among the leading civilizations in our current world, only Islam and the West have universal outlooks, and the two therefore tend to clash with one another. That they have always been geographically and historically adjacent has encouraged, in equal measure, cultural borrowing and mutual distrust. The question that arises is this: How can we limit or blend the universalisms of the two sufficiently that both civilizations might live together peacefully on grounds of cross-cultural understanding?

2.   In the medieval period Islamic civilization accommodated cultural patterns that later became one of the wellsprings of Western civilization. The philosophical and scientific accomplishments of the ancient Greeks adopted by Islam became one segment of the Islamic legacy.[6] Moreover, it was the Islamic civilization itself that passed Hellenism to Europe at the eve of the Renaissance, and thus made it possible for Europe to shift its orientation from Rome to Athens, that is, from the authority of the pope to the authority of human reason as taught by Aristotle.[7] It is true that neither in Islam nor in the West does the man in the street know anything about this heritage. It has nonetheless affected the outlooks of both civilizations. By these encounters and cultural borrowings, Muslims and Europeans had come to share an enthusiasm for the primacy of 'aql / reason and the beauty of Aristotelian rationalism. Can this joint legacy—sustained wholeheartedly by the West but only minimally by Islam—serve as a model for a new and more friendly encounter between the two? I believe that the idea of human rights can be made the opening wedge for this fresh new encounter. (Accordingly, I will conclude my inquiry into the phenomenon of fundamentalism with a chapter on the cross-cultural foundations of human rights.)

3.   For a fruitful dialogue between the two civilizations it is also imperative that their emissaries and spokespersons determine frankly and honestly those issue areas that tend to divide and those that may unite. The politicization of religion, which spawns fundamentalism among Muslims, on the one side, and the cultural arrogance and political hegemony that the West so takes for granted, on the other, create insuperable obstacles to intercivilizational harmony. Cultural borrowing and dialogue, on the basis of rationality and international morality, could go far toward removing these obstacles.

4. The most pivotal issue in this respect is the idea of an international morality based on an irreducible cross-cultural consensus shared by all civilizations. In my view, the idea of human rights and the ethics attendant upon it lie at the hub of this morality.

An international morality that promotes human rights and is accepted by all civilizations must be founded on secularity, not necessarily in the complex meaning of a "functional differentiation of society," but simply and precisely in the meaning of a separation between religion and politics. To be sure, religion is here defined as an ethical belief, and politics as a pragmatic endeavor. To make my point unambiguously clear, I draw a clear distinction between secularism and secularization.[8] Whereas the former is a *construct* that can be stretched to embrace even an anti-religious ideology (Kemalism is a secularism, though there is little secularization in Turkish society), the latter is a social *process* based on the "functional differentiation of society." In other words, unlike the *ism* of secularism or any other political ideology, secularization implies a real process in society. As an avowed Muslim who, however, is critical of the unreformed *shari'a*,[9] thus committed to the separation of religion and politics, I long ago adopted a secular position vis-à-vis the fundamentalist challenge. I have a secular orientation, but I am not a secularist. This is no contradiction.

The Muslim community I belong to is only one element of a vast humanity. In thus acknowledging, I refuse the imposition of an unreformed *shari'a*, be it on Muslims or non-Muslims. To establish common grounds for bridging the gaps dividing humanity, we need an international, cross-cultural, and cross-religious morality—a morality, I believe, based on human rights. I argue further, in agreement with my reformist Muslim colleague Abdullahi A. An-Na'im,[10] that the traditional understanding of the *shari'a* conflicts with the idea of individual human rights.[11] There are in fact Muslims who contend that there are specifically Islamic human rights. In response, one might well ask: Are Muslims and non-Muslims not equally human beings? Can a roster of human rights reasonably be restricted to a single religious community? Are there, for instance, Hindu, Jewish, Christian, and other human rights distinct from Islamic human rights? As Muslims we have our distinct religion, but as humans we are like all others, and human rights are thus necessarily secular in nature and (ought to be) in application. All religious communities should therefore consent to an extended colloquium on cross-religious morality and develop a consensus on secular human rights. As a first step, the link between Islam and human rights would need to be restricted to developing a distinctively Islamic underpinning for an indigenization of these rights in Islamic societies.

For the sake of a clear inquiry it strikes me as imperative that we outline—at the outset of our discussions—the meaning and historical significance of the terms employed. On this basis, we may then proceed to ask in what way we might determine a modern concept of human rights as a universally acclaimed component of a shared international morality in a culturally plural world.

WHAT ARE "HUMAN RIGHTS"?
WHY DO THEY MATTER FOR MUSLIMS?

Most scholars writing on human rights are in agreement that, as used in the West, the term refers to an utterly modern concept of individual rights, insofar as these are seen to be entitlements accorded the individual by law. Thus human rights are understood to be the individual's claims vis-à-vis both state and society, not the individual's obligations *to* state and society. This concept is based on the central idea of European Enlightenment, that each man or woman is an "autonomous subject" (Habermas; see note 19) and thus the master of his or her fate. More specifically, the concept is the foundation of the *Declaration of the Rights of Man and of the Citizens* adopted by the French National Assembly on August 26, 1789, at the outset of the French Revolution and almost simultaneously adopted (in essence) in the *Bill of Rights* in the United States Constitution. In these declarations human rights are defined as *natural* rights. Understood in this way, these rights were not to be restricted to the French and American people, inasmuch as the cited declaration is universal and addresses all of humanity.[12] We must take note, however, that the concept of individual human rights, as a product of cultural modernity, did not exist in prior periods of history, anywhere. Thus the universalization of this concept would constitute a recent addition to the heritage of *all* religions and civilizations, and it needs to be culturally accommodated to make culturally different people speak the language of human rights in their own tongues.

An analysis of Islam's theocentric view of the world leads to the conclusion that this worldview is fundamentally in conflict with the basically secular concept of human rights understood elsewhere.[13] In Islam, God's right (*haq Allah*) stands far above the rights of humans (*haq adami*). Those

Muslims who read the modern notion of human rights into the Islamic heritage and tradition conceive these rights *within* the framework of God's rights. Thus these Islamic writers fail to see that "the premodern shari'a rules deviate sharply from modern human rights norms. . . . Islamic human rights schemes . . . lack any clear theory of what rights should mean in an Islamic context,"[14] as the renowned expert on this subject, Ann Elizabeth Mayer, states. She rightly argues, further, that Muslim proponents of Islamic human rights schemes do not look beyond the Islamic case to the wider case of cross-religious humanity. Instead of acknowledging the problems attendant upon making Islamic doctrines compatible with human rights, they "have been inclined to try to preserve traditional, anti-individualistic, communitarian values and priorities while paradoxically trying to insert human rights provisions [into this] unsuitable matrix."[15]

These concerns give rise to the question: Does the modern concept of human rights *matter* to Muslims? If the answer is "yes," how, then, can we truly introduce this tradition to Islamic civilization? Because the Universal Declaration of Human Rights is based on the secular concept of human rights as natural rights, we may also ask whether an understanding of the natural rights of man is compatible with Islam. Given that the two *do* conflict, any attempt simply to *impose* the foreign human rights concept on Islam would not be promising. But committed as I am to the *idea* of individual human rights, I, as a liberal Muslim, ask that we seek, instead, ways for us Muslims to speak the language of human rights *in our own tongues*. I am of course aware that in the World of Islam the introduction of a practice based on a secular concept is no easy task; a doctrine of human rights in all of its Western trappings ought not be the vehicle presented to Islamic civilization for these deliberations. But we need to share with the rest of humanity *some comparable formulation*. Is this a contradiction in terms? Whereas Islamic fundamentalists answer with an unequivocal "yes," I answer with a confident "no." There is no inherent reason—beyond sheer latter-day dogma—why such an outcome cannot be envisioned. Human rights emanate from a Western tradition, *but do not belong to the West*.

Aside from focusing on the cultural aspects of the issue, I want to make clear that human rights are not a religious issue; they are basically a political and institutional construct, not simply a normative, let alone an exclusively religious, concern. True, we need somehow to inject the cultural underpinning of human rights into Islamic thought and civilization, but an instrument with such powerful implications cannot be restricted to its cultural aspects, which are based on local norms and values, thus confining the instrument to whatever *Weltanschauung* that culture sees the world from. Again, human rights are a *practice*, not in essence a religious tenet; they require institutional enforcement as a basic element of their existence. Without this institutional framework, human rights may continue to exist, as an interesting abstraction from the mind of humanity. But there can be no material honoring of human rights as a practice in a society that denies the exercising of these rights. Despite all emphasis on the political and social character of human rights, we need also to see them in cultural terms. The same norms and values that justify these rights in one specific cultural context contribute to establishing them in societies where the norms are alien, seem strange, and have no cultural underpinning.

In considering the need for dealing with human rights in cultural terms, the point of departure is the traditional understanding of Islam of the *umma*/community as a collectivity. The *umma* takes precedence over the individual; the individual is bound to the *umma* within the framework of the doctrine of *al-fara'id*/religious obligations. In the Islamic cultural heritage, then, there is no tradition comparable to the modern Western theory of natural rights in the sense of individual entitlements vis-à-vis the community, or of their institutional enforcement. Though it is true that in historical terms the modern concept of human rights originated in Europe, its very *name* implies its universality. The universality of human rights is the universality of humanity. The proponents of this argument believe, on philosophical grounds, that they are not involving themselves in a universal reading of European history into other realms. This mode of thought is rather a contribution to placing Islam in the context of the people—all of the people—of a culturally and religiously plural world. Still, a way must be found to establish human rights in Islam on different grounds. It makes no sense to attempt to persuade Muslims of the universality of Western values or, to the contrary, that a human rights program designed in the West does not somehow favor the West.

Political Islam and all other varieties of fundamentalism—including those in the West—stand in the way of establishing cross-religious values and, similarly, impede a cross-cultural foundation of human rights. Fundamentalism and exclusivity are two sides of the same coin, and insisting on them places much of Islamic civilization in a ghetto within "global society." The embracing of secular human rights would facilitate placing Muslims in their proper place: humanity. It is important for us Muslims to underline the inherent open-mindedness of Islamic civilization and to draw a clear line between broadly tolerant Islam and single-mindedly intolerant fundamentalism. It has been suggested that we draw upon Sir Karl Popper's formula "The Open Society and Its Enemies" for speaking about "Open Islam and Its Enemies" while dealing with the Islamic rationalism of Ibn Rushd/Averroës and the Islamic fundamentalism as two opposite worldviews.[16] Islamic fundamentalists battle what they see as Western universalism with their own brand of universalism. But in contrast to the fundamentalists, Islamic rationalists, in the tradition of Ibn Rushd/Averroës, do not draw civilizational boundaries for rationality.

Establishing a tradition of individual human rights where there was none before requires a cross-cultural acknowledgment of the values involved and an institutional mechanism that guarantees the legal enforcement of these rights. To achieve these ends we need to explore avenues for establishing a synthesis between Islam, as an open-minded ethics, and individual human rights, as a secular concept that need not be seen as impinging on religious faith. Early Muslim secularists did wrong in wanting to put Islam aside; to no one's surprise, they failed in the attempt. It is dismaying that contemporary Muslim fundamentalists move to the other extreme in refusing secularity for its nonreligious nature and no longer translate the concept as 'ilmaniyya/secularism, but as ladiniyya/antireligious attitude. The lesson learned from the past is that secularity cannot be imposed on Muslims; it has, rather, to be introduced on cross-cultural grounds, allowing it to take account of Islam. Human rights need to be made compatible with Islamic ethics, and compatibility here cannot be made a code word for imposition. The goal is, rather, how to get us Muslims to speak the language of secular human rights in our own tongues, to reiterate the idiom used above.

A NEED FOR "RETHINKING ISLAM": THE CULTURAL ACCOMMODATION OF HUMAN RIGHTS

Thinking critically about Islam and "rethinking Islam"[17] are not heretical undertakings, but rather efforts to embrace rationalism within Islamic thought. These efforts have a long-standing tradition in Islamic history. But what is Islam? Methodologically, it can be analyzed in one of two ways, either with scriptural methods, as Western orientalists and orthodox Muslims alike proceed, or with social-scientific methods. Muslim scholars may emulate the social scientists who study Islam, as they do any other religion, in the scholarly tradition of the French sociologist of religion, Emile Durkheim, in analyzing Islam as a *fait social,* or social fact. Thus, they might focus on how Muslims act, how they practice their faith in everyday life, and how they place contemporary social actions into existing social structures. This method is more promising than the procedure of the scripturalists, who focus on religious texts and address the question whether or not Muslims act in accordance with Islamic precepts. In fact, scripturalism is a form of essentialism, and as such is questionable. The problem is that religious scripturalists believe that the revealed text is ahistorical, that is, valid for all times and places. The study of the text overlooks the context. Muslim scripturalism seldom addresses the issue of meaning, that is, what believers within a certain historical context derive from the text they read. Western scholars who, in the frayed tradition of Orientalism, study Islam as a scripture, not as a reality, are little better able to proceed than are the Muslim scripturalists themselves, despite differing from them so substantially in other ways. Those social scientists who go beyond the mere empirical-descriptive study of religion and hence deal with the problem of meaning realize that believers in different times and circumstances derive different meanings but impute to them all the same symbols—those symbols implied in their respective religious texts. For me, as a Muslim social scientist, this approach has informed my effort at rethinking Islam.

Human rights—as a new understanding of man or woman as an individual living in "world time"[18]—are a product of cultural modernity.[19] Prior to modern times these rights did not exist as a cultural understanding in any religion or civilization. It is unfortunate, then, that apologist Islamic writers nonetheless argue, in very unspecific fashion, that human rights have always existed in Islam.[20] Scriptural references to Qur'an and to the *hadith* / sayings of the Prophet are offered as the basics for the evidence presented. Perforce, however, the Islamic sources are read and referred to in the light of our age; the old symbols are filled with new meanings. There is nothing wrong with this approach if the efforts undertaken on its behalf are linked to a judicious rethinking of Islam.

The choice between a scriptural understanding of Islam and a social science analysis is not an indifferent one in a rethinking of the legacy of *shari'a* / Islamic law and its compatibility with human rights. Thus, the discussion of human rights in Islam necessarily encompasses a reinterpretation of the Islamic cultural values concerned, as well as a new reading of Islamic legal tradition.

For their enforcement—and thus, for all practical purposes, their existence—human rights require an institutional underpinning. As regards that prospect, the German sociologist Max Weber saw three types of rule: traditional, charismatic, and legal. The third is based on an institutional system of law that ensures basic rights. Without acknowledging this modern analysis some Muslim authors interpret Islamic *shari'a* as the underlying legal structure of political rule, and thus project a modern understanding of law into traditional Islamic law (see Chapter 8). This is obviously a thoughtless and pointless reading of modernity into Islam. In a similar vein, these authors trot out the *shura* concept, which occurs in just two passages of the Qur'an, and reinterpret it as a legal concept calling for broad political participation in a putative Islamic system of government.

It is my conviction that an Islamic understanding of human rights not exclusive for either Muslims *or* the West is urgently needed. Such an embracing of a cross-cultural concept ought not lapse into concerns serving the self-congratulatory claims that "we Muslims had everything, including a human rights tradition, before the Europeans did." The need to establish human rights as the substance of international morality is not consonant with any culturally exclusive or proprietary attitudes.

Individual human rights are, after all, secular, in the sense that they are not restricted to particular religious communities, but rather have been crafted for all of humanity. To argue that religious criteria separate blocs of humanity from one another is not to place oneself in an anti-religious stance, but rather to offer an insight into the need for establishing tolerance and individual rights among civilizations on shared ethical, that is, cross-religious grounds. The notion of "Islamic human rights" is thus impracticable and unacceptable; it completely misses the point. International human rights standards—established by general consensus of the world's civilizations—must be consistently accepted as the yardstick when a reference to cultural specifics is made. In fact, references to specific understandings of human rights by individual civilizations (e.g., Hindu or Islamic human rights) may contribute tacitly to legitimating human rights violations. Cultural specifics can thus be honored only if they do not conflict with these standards.

LOCAL CULTURES, REGIONAL CIVILIZATIONS, AND THEIR EXPOSURE TO GLOBALIZATION

Prior to the age of globalization, the processes of intercivilizational interaction were for the most part restricted to local or regional settings. A few notable exceptions, however, demonstrate that a civilization can generate dissemination processes far beyond its own boundaries. The Islamization processes (for example, the spread of Islam in Southeast Asia and West Africa through trade) engendered by Islamic civilization over the centuries are one of these rare exceptions. But as widely disseminated as it is, Islam has not constituted a global framework, for the simple reason that the globalization we see today is a contemporary issue related not to empire or religion but to cultural modernity. Islam's international system was a relatively regional one.[21] In the course of the expansion of the international system of states, the Islamic brand of universalism has had to compete with globalization. The response of the Islamic fundamentalists has been to reclaim the primacy of Islam in the world order. They argue that the globalization of modernity not only has been achieved at the expense of Islam, but has been morally debilitating to the West *and* Islam.

Despite my being a Muslim, my understanding of human rights is inexorably linked to the basic rights promulgated by the French and American revolutions and earlier articulated in the concepts of the European philosophy of Enlightenment. It would be dishonest to ignore the fact that the values of human rights as secular rights originated in this very European tradition of Western civilization and are deeply informed by it. But these rights are no longer confined to the West. The tradition has become a part of the general human heritage, as the term "human rights" suggests. For their own ends, non-Western governments may scorn the tradition, but the *people*, once they have come to understand the concept, perhaps will not.

At issue is not simply a commitment to the universal validity of human rights but rather an effort to base them on sufficiently cross-cultural grounds that we may pursue an international morality compatible with the norms and values of non-Western *and* Western civilizations. Given that the notion of human rights belongs to the heritage of liberalism, the critique of this liberal tradition can be stretched even to human rights. The response would be to accept the criticism that abstract individualism—mere political rights devoid of either social justice or responsibility in formal participatory politics—is a flaw of liberal Western theory. This flaw has been discussed by many scholars in an effort to reassess liberalism in our age. In arguing that our modern understanding of human rights is affected by the secular concept of democracy and has its foundations in the liberal values of this tradition, I do not simply subscribe to a liberal Western approach for understanding the modern world, nor do I read liberalism into non-Western history. My concern is rather how to establish a cross-cultural international morality shared, among others, by the individuals of Muslim and Western civilizations.

Human rights is a program deeply opposed to fundamentalism, but we do well to acknowledge that the process of globalization generated by the European expansion has not contributed to the global dissemination of the heritage of the French and American revolutions or the political culture of the Enlightenment. The structural globalization of European society, in short, was not matched by a universalization of cultural modernity. The expansion was, rather, directed at constituting an international framework for Western hegemony. This fact makes clear the understandable unwillingness of the bulk of Muslims, in their "revolt against the West," to embrace any foreign standards of behavior or ethics or to suffer the imposition of these standards on them. The exposure of non-Western cultures to the processes of globalization gives rise to defensive cultural attitudes.

But despite the anti-Western attitudes of most Muslims, provoked by their exposure to globalization and the prior insults of colonialism, it is conspicuous that non-Western intellectuals seldom escape a reading of their own cultural heritage in the light of the effects of the "world time" produced by European expansion. Thus, despite all their anti-Western rhetoric, they read new meanings into the inherited indigenous norms and values that have been so greatly affected by Western civilization. To be sure, European colonialists did not conquer Asia, Africa, and Latin America simply, or even primarily, to disseminate their humanistic heritage, nor did they do so to establish a worldwide tradition of human rights. They were looking for raw materials and markets—and even slaves—rather than opportunities for universalizing the values of human dignity. Notwithstanding, a by-product of their conquests was, to put it in the Hegelian sense, *List der Vernunft* (cunning of reason), the dissemination of the European cultural heritage, in which human rights are a crucial element. With some exceptions (for example, Khomeini), no prudent Muslim would dismiss human rights simply because they were conceived in European civilization. What is of concern should not be whether to accept or to refuse human rights but how to understand and express their essence when talking about them and pondering their validity.

The late eminent Oxford scholar of international relations Hedley Bull correctly observed that the shrinking of the world into an international system, by means of communication and a greater density and speed of

transportation, has been accompanied by conspicuous cultural fragmentation. Although the shrinking of the globe has brought societies to a far
greater degree of mutual awareness and interaction, "this globalization does
not in itself create a unity of outlook and has not in fact done so."[22] The result is that humanity becomes simultaneously more structurally unified
and more culturally fragmented. Sadly, the domain of human rights is affected more by the latter than by the former.

In the tradition of the age of Enlightenment, and thus equipped with an
awareness of some of its global effects, scholars ought to endorse cultural
pluralism and not infer cultural relativism from the predicament of cultural
fragmentation. The understandable lack of a global unity of outlook should
not deter the search for a cross-cultural foundation of human rights on
the basis of an international morality acceptable to all civilizations. Non-
Western civilizations need an authentic cultural underpinning of human
rights, one that speaks intimately to their several cultures, as well as an institutional framework for their enforcement. Human rights as a deterrent
against the destructive intolerance of fundamentalism could become a common interest of the Islamic and Western civilizations.

CONCLUSIONS

The exposure of Islamic civilization to the modern, increasingly Westernized world—with its political, economic, and cultural impacts, positive and
negative alike—has generated different responses in different quarters. In
the Middle East and North Africa, fundamentalism has been the outward
expression of the contemporary call for a return to the primordial Islam.
But there is nothing primordial in the ideology of fundamentalism. The belief and the reality are not consonant.

Underlying the fundamentalist call is a repoliticization of Islam, an en-
terprise that has superseded the earlier efforts at adjustment and reconciliation. The Universal Islamic Declaration of Human Rights of December
1981 seeks to establish specifically Islamic human rights and thus, unwittingly, divorces Islamic civilization from the rest of humanity. (Other
writers, such as Ann E. Mayer, have shown the inconsistency of these Islamic schemes with the international standards of human rights, and I need
not do so here.)

In my view, the worldwide phenomenon of fundamentalism is the evidence for my contention that the simultaneity of structural globalization

and cultural fragmentation has meant the loss of consensus on valid norms in international politics. In the belief that we *need* a cross-cultural consensus on values, I urge the promotion of cultural pluralism and the rejection of cultural relativism. The latter is a nihilism of values and cannot help us deal with fundamentalist absolutisms. The revival of norms and values believed to be authentically primeval leads to according them an absolute validity. Whereas cultural modernity means agreeing that every thought is revisable, neo-absolutism means permitting no revision of sanctioned thought.[23] Moreover, fundamentalism is *not* simply the voice of another culture. For those who are concerned with human rights as universal rights, the idea of cultural pluralism (honoring legitimate differences) must not become tantamount to a self-defeating cultural relativism, which permits itself to excuse even abhorrent differences. Thus, the acceptance or even sanctioning of practices constituting violations of human rights (for instance torture, as the suppression of freedom of expression, or the genital mutilation of women) as being simply expressions of a different culture cannot be tolerated by an enlightened world.

The pluralism of cultures presupposes a variety of means to an end, but not a variety of the ends themselves. In particular, there can be no compromise so far as human rights are concerned. In this sense we may speak of the cross-cultural validity of a program of human rights, a program that is coexistent and consonant with cultural varieties of how to create these rights on local but cross-cultural foundations. Further, we may argue that cultural pluralism in the realm of human rights cannot be allowed to mean more than a cultural indigenization of basic individual human rights in local cultures.

In Islam, the emphasis on the exclusively and authentically Islamic character of human rights, that is, the denial of their secular origin by those Muslims favoring these rights, is regrettable, but perhaps tolerable if the *substance* of human rights is honored. Thus, we may want to stretch the norm of cultural pluralism as grounds for creating different foundations of the same values. The most recent Islamic debate on *shari'a* / Islamic law provides, however, no guarantee for the protection of human rights, and the proponents of Islamism as a political interpretation of Islam can give us no clue in this regard. Their call for the implementation of *shari'a* takes no account of the historical record. The late Muslim Oxford scholar Hamid Enayat found that in Islamic history "the shari'a was never implemented as an integral system, and the bulk of its provisions remained as legal fictions."[24]

Moreover, the traditional understanding of Islamic law rested not with the state—there *was* no state as a legal institution in the modern sense—but rather with religious societal communities, the so-called *madhahib* (the four legal schools in Sunni Islam). The binding nature of selectively and arbitrarily fixed religious rules, presented today as law, leads me to fear a new variety of religious intolerance. The documented records of the fundamentalist states in Sudan and Iran make abundantly clear that substantive individual human rights can be guaranteed only by a secular state, not by a religious cabal. And fundamentalists in the illegal underground opposition are no more to be respected in these matters than those in power are; the slaying of intellectuals in Algeria[25] is an example of human rights violations by people who themselves are persecuted. In the course of combating fundamentalism, there will always be a place for true Islamic ethics in an international morality based on a cross-cultural foundation. Such a morality, if allowed to develop, promises to close the normative gap between the Western and Islamic civilizations, and to offer the best prescription against the militant Islamic fundamentalisms that are heating up the "clash of civilizations."

Notes

1. THE CONTEXT: GLOBALIZATION, FRAGMENTATION, AND DISORDER

1. Martin Marty and Scott Appleby, eds., *Fundamentalisms Observed* (Chicago: University of Chicago Press, 1991). See also note 8.

2. Hedley Bull, The Revolt against the West, in: Hedley Bull and Adam Watson, eds., *The Expansion of International Society* (Oxford: Oxford University Press, 1984), pp. 217–28.

3. Samuel P. Huntington, The Clash of Civilizations?, in: *Foreign Affairs*, vol. 72, 3 (summer 1993), pp. 22–49.

4. For more details, see Bassam Tibi, *Krieg der Zivilisationen* (Hamburg: Hoffman & Campe, 1995).

5. John L. Esposito, *The Islamic Threat: Myth or Reality?* (New York: Oxford University Press, 1992).

6. Mathew Horsman and Andrew Marshall, *After the Nation-State: Citizens, Tribalism and the New World Disorder* (London: Harper-Collins, 1994), p. 255.

7. The interview was conducted by Youssef M. Ibrahim and published as: Hassan's Fear for the Mideast, in: *The New York Times*. Here quoted from: *International Herald Tribune*, March 14, 1995, p. 7. See also *al-Hayat* (a London-based, Saudi-funded, highly distributed Arabic newspaper), March 14, 1995, p. 4.

8. See the principal work of the Fundamentalism Project (see note 1). The other four volumes are: *Fundamentalisms and Society* (Chicago: University of Chicago Press, 1993), *Fundamentalisms and the State* (Chicago: University of Chicago Press, 1993), *Accounting for Fundamentalisms* (Chicago: University of Chicago Press, 1994), and *Fundamentalisms Comprehended* (Chicago: University of Chicago Press, 1995). All four volumes are edited by Martin Marty and Scott Appleby. For a reference to my contribution to this project, see note 43.

9. T. K. Oommen, Religious Nationalism and Democratic Polity: The Indian Case, in: *Sociology of Religion*, vol. 55, 4 (1994), pp. 455–72.

10. See Norman Daniel, *Islam and the West: The Making of an Image*, new edition (Oxford: Oneworld, 1993).

11. Clifford Geertz, *The Interpretation of Cultures* (New York: Basic Books, 1973).

12. Hedley Bull, *The Anarchical Society: A Study of Order in World Politics* (New York: Columbia University Press, 1977), p. 273.

13. Anthony Giddens, *The Nation-State and Violence* (Berkeley: University of California Press, 1987), p. 255.

14. Ibid.

15. On this issue, see Bassam Tibi, *The Crisis of Modern Islam: A Preindustrial Culture in the Scientific-Technological Age* (Salt Lake City: Utah University Press, 1988), chapter 7, pp. 95–112.

16. Giddens, *The Nation-State*, p. 256.

17. Bassam Tibi, The Simultaneity of the Unsimultaneous: Old Tribes and Imposed Nation-States in the Modern Middle East, in: Philip Khoury and Joseph Kostiner, eds., *Tribes and State Formation in the Middle East* (Berkeley: University of California Press, 1990), pp. 127–52.

18. Giddens, *The Nation-State*, p. 258.

19. On legitimacy in Arab politics, see Michael Hudson, *Arab Politics: The Search for Legitimacy* (New Haven: Yale University Press, 1977), pp. 1–30.

20. Robert H. Jackson, *Quasi-States: Sovereignty, International Relations and the Third World*, second edition (Cambridge: Cambridge University Press, 1990).

21. Bassam Tibi, *Die Verschwörung: Das Trauma arabischer Politik* (Hamburg: Hoffmann & Campe, 1993), part two.

22. See Munir Muhammad Najib, *al-Harakat al-qawmiyya al-haditha fi mizan al-Islam* (Modern Nationalist Movements in the Balance of Islam), second edition (al-Zarqa, Jordan: Maktabat al-Manar, 1983).

23. Muhammad Salim al-'Awwa, *Fi al-nizam al-siyasi li al-dawla al-Islamiyya* (On the Political System of the Islamic State), sixth edition (Cairo: Maktabat al-Misri, 1983).

24. Lynn H. Miller, *Global Order: Values and Power in International Politics*, second edition (Boulder, Colo.: Westview Press, 1990).

25. Horsman and Marshall, *After the Nation-State* (see note 6), p. 74.

26. See, for instance, Samuel Wells, Jr., and Mark Bruzonsky, eds., *Security in the Middle East: Regional Change and Great Power Strategies* (Boulder, Colo.: Westview Press, 1987). See also Tibi, note 27.

27. Bassam Tibi, *Conflict and War in the Middle East, 1967–1991: Regional Dynamic and the Superpowers* (London: Macmillan, 1993), published in association with the Center for International Affairs, Harvard University.

28. See Stephen Philip Cohen, *The Security of South Asia: American and Asian Perspectives* (Urbana and Chicago: University of Illinois Press, 1987).

29. See Bassam Tibi, Die islamische Dimension des Balkan-Krieges, in: *Europa-Archiv*, vol. 48, 22 (1993), pp. 635–44; and Johann Georg Reissmüller, *Die bosnische Tragödie* (Stuttgart: Deutsche Verlagsanstalt/DVA, 1993).

30. Horsman and Marshall, *After the Nation-State* (see note 6), p. 75.

31. See, for example, James D. Davidson and William Rees-Mogg, *The Great Reckoning,* second edition (London: Sidgewick & Jackson, 1993), in particular chapter 7: Muhammad Replaces Marx, pp. 213–44.

32. Horsman and Marshall, *After the Nation-State,* p. 150.

33. Ibid., p. 266.

34. Fred Halliday, The Politics of Islamic Fundamentalism, in: Akbar S. Ahmed and Hastings Donnan, eds., *Islam, Globalization and Postmodernity* (London: Routledge, 1994), p. 92.

35. David Beetham, *The Legitimation of Power* (Basingstoke and London: Macmillan, 1991), pp. 191–204.

36. Halliday, The Politics, p. 92.

37. Ibid., p. 110.

38. Ali Benhaj quoted by Ahmida Ayashi, *al-Islamiyyun al-jaza'iriyyun bain al-sulta wa al-rasas* (Algerian Islamists between State Authority and Bullets) (Algiers: Dar al-Hikma, 1991), p. 57.

39. See the article by Hassan al-Turabi (in Arabic) in: *al-Mustaqbal al-'Arabi,* vol. 8, 75 (May 1985), in particular p. 13. See also Haidar I. Ali, *Azmat al-Islam al-siyasi: al-Jahba al-Islamiyya al-qawmiyya fi al-Sudan namuzajan* (Crisis of Political Islam: The Case of the National Islamic Front in Sudan) (Casablanca, Morocco: Markaz al-Dirasat al-Sudaniyya-Dar Qurtubah, 1991), in particular pp. 194–95 and 197.

40. Mark Juergensmeyer, *The New Cold War? Religious Nationalism Confronts the Secular State* (Berkeley: University of California Press, 1993), p. 1.

41. Ibid., pp. 1–2.

42. Ibid., pp. 4–6.

43. See notes 1 and 8 and Bassam Tibi, The Worldview of Sunni Arab Fundamentalists: Attitudes toward Modern Science and Technology, in: *Fundamentalisms and Society* (see note 8), pp. 73–102.

44. See the excellent contributions on each of the world religions in Arvind Sharma, ed., *Our Religions* (San Francisco: Harper/Collins, 1993).

45. Marty and Appleby, *Fundamentalisms Observed* (see note 1), p. 815.

46. See Bassam Tibi, War and Peace in Islam, in: Terry Nardin, ed., *The Ethics of War and Peace: Religious and Secular Perspectives* (Princeton, N.J.: Princeton University Press, 1996), pp. 128–45.

47. Horsman and Marshall, *After the Nation-State,* p. 267.

48. Robert Kaplan, The Coming Anarchy, in: *The Atlantic Monthly,* 2 (February 1994), pp. 44–67.

49. Anthony Arnold, *The Fateful Pebble: Afghanistan's Role in the Fall of the Soviet Empire* (Novato, Calif.: Presidio Press, 1993). See also Kurt Lohbeck, *Holy War, Unholy Victory: Eyewitness to the CIA's Secret War in Afghanistan* (Washington, D.C.: Regnery Gateway, 1993).

50. See the chapter on *jihad* in Kenneth L. Vaux, *Ethics and the Gulf War: Religion, Rhetoric, and Righteousness* (Boulder, Colo.: Westview Press, 1992), pp. 63–86.

51. On the theology of Serb Orthodox Christianity providing the basis of Serbian ethnofundamentalism, see Thomas Bremer, *Ekklesiale Struktur und*

Ekklesiologie in der serbisch-orthodoxen Kirche im 19. und 20. Jahrhundert (Würzburg: Augustinus Press, 1992), in particular part two, pp. 107ff.

52. On the Organization of the Islamic Conference, see the articles by Galam Choudhury and J. P. Bannerman, in: *The Oxford Encyclopedia of the Modern Islamic World*, 4 volumes, here vol. 3 (New York: Oxford University Press, 1995), pp. 260–66.

53. John Kelsay, *Islam and War: The Gulf War and Beyond* (Louisville: John Knox Press, 1993), p. 118.

54. On Islam in Europe, see Bassam Tibi, *Im Schatten Allahs: Der Islam und die Menschenrechte* (Munich: Piper Press, 1994), part four.

55. Jean François Revel, *Democracy against Itself* (New York: The Free Press, 1993), in particular chapter 12 on Islamic fundamentalism.

56. Bassam Tibi, Fundamentalismus und Totalitarismus, in: Richard Saage, ed., *Das Scheitern diktatorischer Legitimationsmuster und die Zukunftsfähigkeit der Demokratie* (Berlin: Duncker & Humblot, 1995), pp. 305–18.

2. THE STUDY OF ISLAMIC FUNDAMENTALISM AND THE SCOPE OF THE INQUIRY

1. See the case studies that grew out of the Fundamentalism Project, published in: Martin Marty and Scott Appleby, eds., *Fundamentalisms Observed* (Chicago: University of Chicago Press, 1991).

2. Clifford Geertz, *The Interpretation of Cultures* (New York: Basic Books, 1973), in particular chapter 4 on religion as a cultural system. This Geertzian concept has been further developed and applied to Islam in: Bassam Tibi, *Islam and the Cultural Accommodation of Social Change* (Boulder, Colo.: Westview Press, 1990).

3. On organized religions within the context of crisis, see Leslie Lipson, *The Ethical Crises of Civilization: Moral Meltdown or Advance?* (Newbury and London: Sage, 1993), pp. 294–95.

4. Following the Cold War, civilizations became a pivotal issue in world politics. The major work on the study of civilization continues to be: Will and Ariel Durant, *The Story of Civilization*, 11 volumes, new printing (New York: Simon & Schuster, 1981–85). For a useful recent overview, see Fernand Braudel, *A History of Civilizations* (London: Penguin Press, 1994).

5. The best outline of citizenship known to me is in Anthony Giddens, *The Nation-State and Violence* (Berkeley: University of California Press, 1987), chapter 8.

6. Oliver Roy, *Islam and Resistance in Afghanistan* (Cambridge: Cambridge University Press, 1986). See also the books by Arnold and Lohbeck cited in note 49 to chapter 1.

7. Lipson, *The Ethical Crises of Civilization*, p. 297.

8. On this idea, see Robert Nisbet, *The Idea of Progress* (New York: Basic Books, 1980).

9. See Theodor Nikolaou, Die Orthodoxie auf dem Balkan, in: *Litterae*, vol. 4, 1 (1994), pp. 27–35. See also note 51 to chapter 1.

10. See Bassam Tibi, Die Zerstörung des Religionsfriedens auf dem Balkan: Serbischer Ethno-Fundamentalismus, in: *Universitas*, vol. 49, 3 (March 1994) (German edition), pp. 205–15.

11. The basic work on cultural modernity is Jürgen Habermas, *The Philosophical Discourse of Modernity* (Cambridge, Mass.: MIT Press, 1987).

12. See the respective chapter in Sebastian de Grazia, *Machiavelli in Hell* (Princeton, N.J.: Princeton University Press, 1985), pp. 194ff.

13. See Anthony Giddens, *The Consequences of Modernity* (Stanford, Calif.: Stanford University Press, 1990), pp. 55ff.

14. See the contributions by Bull and Huntington cited in notes 2 and 3 to chapter 1.

15. Interview with Mahathir bin Mohammad in: *Der Spiegel*, issue 34, August 21, 1995, pp. 136–39, here p. 139.

16. John L. Esposito, *The Islamic Threat: Myth or Reality?* (New York: Oxford University Press, 1992), p. 186.

17. Yusuf al-Qaradawi, *Hatmiyyat al-hall al-Islami wa al-hulul al-mustawrada* (The Necessity of the Islamic Solution and the Imported Solutions), 3 volumes, here vol. 1: *Hatmiyyat al-hall al-Islami* (The Islamic Solution is Determined), new printing (Beirut: al-Risalah, 1980).

18. On this issue, with details and references, see Bassam Tibi, *Im Schatten Allahs: Der Islam und die Menschenrechte* (Munich: Piper Press, 1994), part 4, in particular chapter 12.

19. See Nicholas Pelham, Islamic Extremists Join Battle in Britain, in: *The Sunday Telegraph*, August 7, 1994, p. 7, and the commentary/editorial in the same paper: The Enemies Within, p. 27.

20. Reymer Kluever, Fundamentalisten auf dem Vormarsch: Radikale Türken in der Bundesrepublik, in: *Süddeutsche Zeitung*, April 28, 1995, p. 3. See also the contributions in Tomas Gerholm and Georg Lithman, eds., *The New Islamic Presence in Western Europe* (London: Mansell, 1988).

21. Abdulrahman A. Kurdi, *The Islamic State: A Study Based on the Islamic Holy Constitution* (London: Mansell, 1984).

22. Mark Juergensmeyer, *The New Cold War? Religious Nationalism Confronts the Secular State* (Berkeley: University of California Press, 1993).

23. See William McNeill, *The Rise of the West* (Chicago: University of Chicago Press, 1963); and, more recently, Wolfgang Reinhard, *Geschichte der europäischen Expansion*, 4 volumes (Stuttgart: Kohlhammer Press, 1983–90).

24. Jamaluldin al-Afghani, *al-A'mal al-kamilah* (Collected Writings), Muhammad 'Imara, ed. (Cairo: Dar al-Katib al-'Arabi, 1968), p. 328.

25. Bassam Tibi, The Worldview of Sunni Arab Fundamentalists (see note 43 to chapter 1).

26. Abu al-A'la al-Mawdudi, *al-Islam wa al-madaniyya al-haditha* (Islam and Modern Civilizations), as quoted by Muhammad Darif, *al-Islam al-siyasi fi al-watan al-'Arabi* (Political Islam in the Arab World) (Rabat, Morocco: Maktabat al-Umma, 1992), p. 99.

27. For more details on this concept of *hakimiyyat Allah,* see Muhammad Darif, *al-Islam al-siyasi* (see note 26), pp. 87–110.

28. Leslie Lipson, *The Ethical Crises of Civilization* (see note 3), p. 62.

29. Mourad Wahba, ed., The Paradoxon of Averroës, in: *Proceedings of the First International Islamic Philosophy Conference: Islam and Civilization*, November 19–22, 1979 (Cairo: Ain Shams University Press, 1982), pp. 81–84.

30. Bassam Tibi, *Krieg der Zivilisationen* (Hamburg: Hoffman & Campe, 1995).

31. Bassam Tibi, Fundamentalismus und Totalitarismus, in: Richard Saage, ed., *Das Scheitern diktatorischer Legitimationsmuster und die Zukunftsfähigkeit der Demokratie* (Berlin: Duncker & Humblot, 1995), pp. 305–18.

32. Eric Hobsbawm and Terence Ranger, eds., *The Invention of Tradition* (Cambridge: Cambridge University Press, 1983), introduction.

33. See the writings of Mawdudi (listed in Darif, see note 26) and Sayyid Qutb (see notes 42 to 45, chapter 3).

34. John L. Esposito, *The Islamic Threat* (see note 16), p. 186.

35. See Bassam Tibi, A Typology of Arab Political Systems (with Special Reference to Islam and Government as Exemplified in Arab Monarchies Legitimized by Islam: Morocco and Saudi Arabia), in: Samih Farsoun, ed., *Arab Society: Continuity and Change* (London: Croom Helm, 1985), pp. 48–64. On the introduction of the *shura* in Saudi Arabia, see Bassam Tibi, Das Königsdilemma, in: *Frankfurter Allgemeine Zeitung*, December 17, 1993, p. 14.

36. On this subject, see the interesting contributions by W. Montgomery Watt, *Islamic Fundamentalism and Modernity* (London: Routledge, 1988); and Youssef Choueiri, *Islamic Fundamentalism* (Boston: Twayne, 1990).

37. See Charles C. Adams, *Islam and Modernism in Egypt: A Study of the Modern Reform Movement Inaugurated by Muhammad 'Abduh*, new printing (New York: Russell & Russell, 1968; first printing 1933).

38. The major writing of Muhammad 'Abduh on this topic is: *al-Islam wa al-nasraniyya bain al-'ilm wa al-madaniyya* (Islam and Christianity between Science and Civilization), new printing (Beirut: Dar al-Hadatha, 1983).

39. The jurist Abdullahi A. An-Na'im, a disciple of Sheikh Taha, published: Mahmoud M. Taha, *The Second Message of Islam*, translated and edited and with an introduction by A. An-Na'im (Syracuse, N.Y.: Syracuse University Press, 1987).

40. See Tore Lindholm and Kari Vogt, eds., *Islamic Law Reform* (Oslo, Lund, and Copenhagen: Nordic Human Rights Publications, 1993). With contributions by Mohammed Arkoun, Abdullahi A. An-Na'im, Ann E. Mayer, and Bassam Tibi.

41. Among others, in the introduction to Bassam Tibi, *Arab Nationalism: Between Islam and the Nation-State*, third edition (London and New York: Macmillan and St. Martin's Press, 1996), in particular pp. 25–26.

42. I strongly disagree with Martin Riesebrodt, *Fundamentalismus als patriarchalische Protestbewegung* (Tübingen: Mohr Press, 1990).

43. John Kelsay, *Islam and War: The Gulf War and Beyond* (Louisville: John Knox Press, 1993), pp. 7–27.

44. See Bernard Lewis, *The Emergence of Modern Turkey*, second edition (Oxford: Oxford University Press, 1979), pp. 45–50; and Bernard Lewis, *The Muslim Discovery of Europe* (New York: W. W. Norton, 1982), chapter 9, Science and Technology, pp. 221–38.

45. David B. Ralston, *Importing the European Army: The Introduction of European Military Techniques and Institutions into the Extra-European World, 1600–1914* (Chicago: University of Chicago Press, 1990).

46. The industrialization of warfare that led to the superiority of the West and the decay of Islamic civilization is described by Anthony Giddens, *The Nation-State and Violence* (see note 5), chapter 9, pp. 222–54.

47. On world order in general, see Lynn H. Miller, *Global Order: Values and Power in International Politics*, second edition (Boulder, Colo.: Westview Press, 1990).

48. On both segments of this international morality, see Bassam Tibi, Islamic Law/Shari'a, Human Rights, Universal Morality and International Relations, in: *Human Rights Quarterly*, vol. 16, 2 (1994), pp. 277–99; and Tibi, Democracy and Democratization in Islam: The Quest for Islamic Enlightenment, in: *Universitas: Journal for Science and Humanities*, vol. 36, 4 (1994) (English edition), pp. 244–54.

3. WORLD ORDER AND THE LEGACY OF SADDAM HUSSEIN

1. See the published five volumes (Chicago University Press) of the Fundamentalism Project/American Academy of Arts and Sciences (see notes 1 and 8 to chapter 1).

2. On Islamic minorities in the world, see M. Ali Kettani, *Muslim Minorities in the World Today* (London: Mansell, 1986).

3. On the concept of "defensive culture," see Bassam Tibi, *The Crisis of Modern Islam: A Preindustrial Culture in the Scientific-Technological Age* (Salt Lake City: Utah University Press, 1988), introduction. See also W. Montgomery Watt, *Islamic Fundamentalism and Modernity* (London: Routledge, 1988).

4. The concept of world order employed in this book draws heavily on Hedley Bull, *The Anarchical Society: A Study of Order in World Politics* (New York: Columbia University Press, 1977). See also the book by Lynn H. Miller (see note 47 to chapter 2).

5. See Hedley Bull and Adam Watson, eds., *The Expansion of International Society* (Oxford: Oxford University Press, 1984).

6. The Gulf War as President Bush's war is noted by Stephen R. Graubard, *Mr. Bush's War: Adventures in the Politics of Illusion* (New York: Hill & Wang, 1992).

7. Mohammed Yacine Kassab, *Après l'Irak à qui le tour? L'Islam face au Nouvel Ordre Mondial* (Algiers: Edition Salama, 1991); see in particular the conspiracy chapter: Une vaste conspiration judeo-chrétienne, pp. 75–93.

8. See Abu al-'Abbas Ahmed Ibn Taimiyya (1263–1328), *al-Siyasa al-shar'iyya fi islah al-ra'i wa al-ra'iyya* (The *Shari'a*-Oriented Politics for the Guidance of the Ruler and His Subjects), new printing (Beirut: Dar al-Jil, 1988). On the topicality of Ibn Taimiyya, see Emmanuel Sivan, *Radical Islam* (New Haven, Conn.: Yale University Press, 1985).

9. The notion *hakimiyyat Allah* / God's rule was coined by Sayyid Qutb and Mawdudi. For more details, see Muhammad Darif, *al-Islam al-siyasi fi al-watan al-'Arabi* (Political Islam in the Arab World) (Rabat, Morocco: Maktabat al-umma, 1992), pp. 89–134.

10. See Raymond Aron, *Paix et guerre entre les nations* (Paris: Calmann Lévy, 1962). German translation *Frieden und Krieg* (Frankfurt am Main: S. Fischer, 1986),

pp. 468–69. On the ensuing disorder, see Zbigniew Brzezinski, *Out of Control: Global Turmoil on the Eve of the 21st Century* (New York: Charles Scribner, 1993), in particular part four, pp. 147ff.

11. See John Kelsay, *Islam and War: The Gulf War and Beyond* (Louisville: John Knox Press, 1993), chapter 5. I do not share the view of Trevor N. Dupuy, *Future Wars* (New York: Warner Books, 1993) that all coming major wars will be inter-state wars.

12. Fred Halliday, The Politics of Islamic Fundamentalism, in: Akbar S. Ahmed and Hastings Donnan, eds., *Islam, Globalization and Postmodernity* (London: Routledge, 1994), pp. 91–113.

13. Samuel P. Huntington, The Clash of Civilizations?, in: *Foreign Affairs*, vol. 72, 3 (1993), pp. 22–49. See also Bassam Tibi, *Krieg der Zivilisationen* (Hamburg: Hoffman & Campe, 1995).

14. Kelsay, *Islam and War*, pp. 26–27.

15. These documents, in Arabic, are included in the special issue of *al-Muntada* (Amman, Jordan), vol. 5, 60 (1990), pp. 19–22.

16. Ibid.

17. Kelsay, *Islam and War*, p. 8.

18. Rick Atkinson, *Crusade: The Untold Story of the Persian Gulf War* (Boston: H. Mifflin Co., 1993), pp. 500–501.

19. On the Middle East as a regional subsystem, see Bassam Tibi, *Conflict and War in the Middle East, 1967–1991: Regional Dynamic and the Superpowers* (London: Macmillan, 1993), chapter 2.

20. Charles Tilly in his edited volume *The Formation of National States in Western Europe* (Princeton, N.J.: Princeton University Press, 1975), p. 45.

21. Tibi, *The Crisis of Modern Islam* (see note 3). See also chapter 3 in Bassam Tibi, *Die fundamentalistische Herausforderung*, second edition (Munich: C. H. Beck, 1993), pp. 57ff.

22. See Bassam Tibi, The European Tradition of Human Rights and the Culture of Islam, in: Francis Deng and Abdullahi A. An-Na'im, eds., *Human Rights in Africa: Cross-Cultural Perspectives* (Washington, D.C.: The Brookings Institution, 1990), pp. 104–32; and Bassam Tibi, Universality of Human Rights and Authenticity of Non-Western Cultures, in: *Harvard Human Rights Journal*, vol. 5 (1994), pp. 221–26. See also note 48 to chapter 2.

23. The former Egyptian general Sa'duldin al-Shadhli, in his best-seller *al-Harb al-salibiyya al-thamina* (The Eighth Christian Crusade) (Casablanca, Morocco: Matba'at al-Najah al-Jadida, 1991), presents the Gulf War as a Western crusade against what he calls "the strongest Islamic army since the decline of Islam" (sub-title). On the meaning of the crusades in a historical perspective, see Karen Armstrong, *Holy War: The Crusades and Their Impact on Today's World* (New York: Anchor Books, 1991).

24. See the critical analysis by Wolfgang G. Lerch, Der serbische Kreuzzug: Die Bosnienkrise und das islamische Jahrhundert, in: *Frankfurter Allgemeine Zeitung*, July 22, 1995, issue 168/weekend supplement. The West was unable to contain the policy of greater Serbia leading to the "destruction of Bosnia." On this issue, see

Noel Malcolm, *Bosnia* (London: Macmillan, 1994), chapter 16; and Viktor Meier, *Wie Jugoslawien verspielt wurde* (Munich: C. H. Beck, 1995).

25. On this issue, see the interesting essay: Michiko Kakutani, Opinion versus Reality, in: *The New York Times*, January 28, 1994, p. B1, continued on p. B12.

26. On this debate, with many references, see Bassam Tibi, Culture and Knowledge: The Islamization of Knowledge as a Postmodern Project?, in: *Theory, Culture and Society*, vol. 12, 1 (1995), pp. 1–24.

27. Bassam Tibi, *Krieg der Zivilisationen* (see note 13).

28. Ernest Gellner, *Postmodernism, Reason and Religion* (London: Routledge, 1992). Against religious fundamentalism, Gellner ironically pleads for "rationalist fundamentalism," pp. 80–96.

29. See the article by Henry Siegman, Don't Ignore Bosnia's Parallels with the Holocaust, in: *International Herald Tribune*, July 16, 1993; and also Bassam Tibi, Die islamische Dimension des Balkan-Krieges, in: *Europa-Archiv*, vol. 48, 22 (1993), pp. 635–44.

30. For references, see Bassam Tibi, The Iranian Revolution and the Arabs: The Quest for Islamic Identity and the Search for an Islamic System of Government, in: *Arab Studies Quarterly*, vol. 8, 1 (1986), pp. 29–44.

31. On Indonesia, see Adam Schwarz, *A Nation in Waiting: Indonesia in the 1990s* (Boulder, Colo.: Westview Press, 1994); and for a historical survey, see M. C. Ricklefs, *A History of Modern Indonesia since ca. 1300*, second edition (Stanford, Calif.: Stanford University Press, 1993). See also the article on Indonesia by Fred van der Mehden, in: *The Oxford Encyclopedia of the Modern Islamic World* (New York: Oxford University Press, 1995), 4 volumes, here vol. 2, pp. 196–203.

32. More about the relations between these two regions of Islamic civilization is given in Fred van der Mehden, *Two Worlds of Islam: Interaction between Southeast Asia and the Middle East* (Miami and Jacksonville: The University of Florida Press, 1993); see in particular p. 97. In the view of Mehmet, the Islamic periphery (by which he means Malaysia and Turkey) could serve as a model for other Muslims: Ozay Mehmet, *Islamic Identity and Development: Studies of the Islamic Periphery* (London: Routledge, 1990), in particular pp. 218–33. See my essay on my observations in Indonesia published in the foremost German daily: *Frankfurter Allgemeine Zeitung*, October 27, 1995, pp. 10–11.

33. Tibi, *Conflict and War in the Middle East* (see note 19). See also the review by Fred Halliday, in: *International Affairs*, vol. 70, 1 (Winter 1994), p. 162.

34. See Bull, *The Anarchical Society* (see note 4), pp. 260–61.

35. In my book *Conflict and War in the Middle East* (see note 19), chapters 1 and 2, I suggest that we view world regions as units of world politics in terms of the subsystem approach.

36. See Fouad Ajami, *The Arab Predicament: Arab Political Thought and Practice since 1967* (Cambridge: Cambridge University Press, 1981), pp. 50ff, 177ff.

37. Mohammad 'Imara, *al-Sahwa al-Islamiyya wa al-tahaddi al-hadari* (The Islamic Awakening and the Civilizational Challenge) (Cairo: Dar al-Shuruq, 1991).

38. See Hassan al-Hanafi, *al-Usuliyya al-Islamiyya* (Islamic Fundamentalism) (Cairo: Maktabat Madbuli, 1988).

39. On the different meaning of *umma*, see Bassam Tibi, Islam and Arab Nationalism, in: Barbara Freyer Stowasser, ed., *The Islamic Impulse* (Washington, D.C.: Center for Contemporary Arab Studies, 1987), pp. 59–74.

40. See the Islamic view presented by Muhammad Shadid, *al-Jihad fi al-Islam* (Jihad in Islam), seventh printing (Cairo: Mu'assasat al-Risalah, 1985). On the primeval concept of *jihad* in Islam and its use in contemporary history, see Bassam Tibi, Jihad, in Roger S. Powers and William Vogele, eds., *Protest, Power, and Change: An Encyclopedia of Nonviolent Action from ACT-UP to Women's Suffrage* (New York and London: Garland Publishing, 1997), pp. 277–81; see also Bassam Tibi, War and Peace in Islam, in: Terry Nardin, ed., *The Ethics of War and Peace: Religious and Secular Perspectives* (Princeton, N.J.: Princeton University Press, 1996), pp. 128–45.

41. Dilip Hiro, *Holy Wars: The Rise of Islamic Fundamentalism* (London: Routledge, 1989); and Kurt Lohbeck, *Holy War, Unholy Victory: Eyewitness to the CIA's Secret War in Afghanistan* (Washington, D.C.: Regnery Gateway, 1993).

42. Sayyid Qutb, *al-Salam al-'alami wa al-Islam* (World Peace and Islam), tenth printing (Cairo: Dar al-Shuruq, 1992), pp. 172–73.

43. On Qutb in America, see Salah A. al-Khalidi, *Amerika min al-dakhil bi min-dar Sayyid Qutb* (America from Within Seen through the Lens of Sayyid Qutb) (Jeddah, Saudi Arabia: Dar al-Minarah, 1987).

44. Sayyid Qutb, *al-Islam wa mushkilat al-hadara* (Islam and the Predicament of Civilization), ninth "legal printing" (Cairo: Dar al-Shuruq, 1988).

45. Sayyid Qutb, *al-Mutaqbal li hadha al-din* (The Future Belongs to This Religion) (Cairo: Dar al-Shuruq, 1981); and Qutb, *Ma'alim fi al-tariq* (Signposts), thirteenth "legal printing" (Cairo: Dar al-Shuruq, 1989).

46. See the translated documents in Johannes J. G. Jansen, *The Neglected Duty: The Creed of Sadat's Assassins and Islamic Resurgence in the Middle East* (New York: Macmillan, 1986).

47. See the survey and documents included in Omar Massalha, *Towards the Long Promised Peace* (London: Saqi Books, 1994).

48. For more details, see Ziad Abu-Amr, *Islamic Fundamentalism in the West Bank and Gaza* (Bloomington: Indiana University Press, 1994).

49. Jadulhaq Ali Jadulhaq, for al-Azhar, *Bayan li al-nas* (Declaration to Humanity) (Cairo: al-Azhar Press, 1984, 1988), 2 volumes, here vol. 1, pp. 368ff, vol. 2, pp. 273ff.

50. On *jihad*, see the equally influential and impassioned treatise by the founder of the Muslim Brethren, Hassan al-Banna, in his collection *Majmu'at rasa'il al-imam al-shahid Hassan al-Banna* (Collected Essays of the Martyr Imam Hassan al-Banna) (Cairo: Dar al-Da'wah, 1990), pp. 271–91.

51. On Islamic "irregular war," see Kelsay, *Islam and War* (see note 11), pp. 77ff. See also the chapter by David Rapoport, Sacred Terror: A Contemporary Example from Islam, in: Walter Reich, ed., *Origins of Terrorism* (New York: Cambridge University Press, 1990), pp. 103–30; see also Edgar O'Ballance, *Islamic Fundamentalist Terrorism, 1979–1997* (New York: New York University Press, 1997).

52. Fundamentalists ridicule the sheikh of al-Azhar, Jadulhaq (in Arabic, *al-haq* means *righteous*, and *jad* means *the one who deals best*, so that Jadulhaq means "the

one who does right in the best manner"), in naming him Jadul Batil ("the one who does wrong best").

53. See the documents in *al-Muntada* (see note 15).

54. John Piscatori, ed., *Islamic Fundamentalisms and the Gulf Crisis* (Chicago: The American Academy of Arts and Sciences/The Fundamentalism Project, 1992).

55. These are the words of Qutb in his *Ma'alim fi al'tariq* (see note 45), p. 6.

56. Kanan Makiya, *Cruelty and Silence: War, Tyranny, Uprising, and the Arab World* (New York: W. W. Norton, 1993), pp. 260–62.

57. The constraints underpinning the political revival of Islam are dealt with in Bassam Tibi, *Islam and the Cultural Accommodation of Social Change* (Boulder, Colo.: Westview Press, 1990), chapter 8, pp. 122–34.

58. Here I follow Everett Mendelsohn, *A Compassionate Peace* (New York: Noonday Press, 1989).

59. Kelsay, *Islam and War* (see note 11), p. 117.

60. See Ann Elizabeth Mayer, *Islam and Human Rights: Tradition and Politics*, second edition (Boulder, Colo.: Westview Press, 1995); and Bassam Tibi, *Im Schatten Allahs: Der Islam und die Menschenrechte* (Munich: Piper Press, 1994).

4.   THE SOCIOCULTURAL BACKGROUND AND THE EXPOSURE TO CULTURAL MODERNITY

1. See Mary Kaldor, *The Imaginary War: Understanding the East-West Conflict* (Oxford: Basil Blackwell, 1990).

2. Anthony Giddens, *The Consequences of Modernity* (Stanford, Calif.: Stanford University Press, 1990), pp. 55ff.

3. Jürgen Habermas, *The Philosophical Discourse of Modernity* (Cambridge, Mass.: MIT Press, 1987).

4. Bassam Tibi, Strukturelle Globalisierung und kulturelle Fragmentierung: Dialog der Zivilisationen, in: *Internationale Politik*, vol. 51, 1 (January 1996), pp. 29–36.

5. David Apter, *The Politics of Modernization* (Chicago: University of Chicago Press, 1965); and recently and more revisionist, Apter, *Rethinking Development* (London: Sage, 1987).

6. Raymond Aron, *Paix et guerre entre les nations* (Paris: Calmann Lévy, 1962). German translation: *Frieden und Krieg* (Frankfurt am Main: S. Fischer, 1986), p. 468.

7. Bassam Tibi, Islamic Dream of Semi-Modernity, in: *India International Quarterly*, vol. 22, 1 (Spring 1995), pp. 79–87. This notion of "halbe Moderne / semi-modernity" for denoting the divorcing of instrumental modernity (techno-science) from the worldview related to it was first published in my article Der Traum von der halben Moderne, in: *Frankfurter Allgemeine Zeitung*, February 19, 1991, p. 35, and then developed further as an introduction to Bassam Tibi, *Islamischer Fundamentalismus, moderne Wissenschaft und Technologie* (Frankfurt am Main: Suhrkamp Press, 1992, second edition 1993).

8. Clifford Geertz, *The Interpretation of Cultures* (New York: Basic Books, 1973). My book *Islam and the Cultural Accommodation of Social Change* (Boulder, Colo.: Westview Press, 1990) is based on this Geertzian approach, but goes beyond cultural anthropology in considering the globalization processes.

9. For a conceptual proposition, see Bassam Tibi, The Interplay between Social and Cultural Change: The Case of Germany and the Arab Middle East, in: George Atiyeh and Ibrahim Oweiss, eds., *Arab Civilization: Challenges and Responses* (New York: SUNY Press, 1988), pp. 166–82. On the topicality of the study of civilizations, see also Bassam Tibi, *Krieg der Zivilisationen* (Hamburg: Hoffman & Campe, 1995).

10. Hedley Bull, The Revolt against the West, in: Hedley Bull and Adam Watson, eds., *The Expansion of International Society* (Oxford: Oxford University Press, 1984), pp. 217–28, here p. 223.

11. See Bassam Tibi, The Worldview of Sunni Arab Fundamentalists: Attitudes toward Modern Science and Technology, in: Martin Marty and Scott Appleby, eds., *Fundamentalisms and Society* (Chicago: University of Chicago Press, 1993), pp. 73–102.

12. Geoffrey Parker, *The Military Revolution: Military Innovation and the Rise of the West, 1500–1800* (Cambridge: Cambridge University Press, 1989).

13. David B. Ralston, *Importing the European Army: The Introduction of European Military Techniques and Institutions into the Extra-European World, 1600–1914* (Chicago: University of Chicago Press, 1990).

14. Fatma M. Goçek, *East-West Encounter* (New York: Oxford University Press, 1987); and Bernard Lewis, *The Muslim Discovery of Europe* (New York: W. W. Norton, 1982).

15. Franz Borkenau, *Der Übergang vom feudalen zum bürgerlichen Weltbild: Studien zur Geschichte der Philosophie der Manufakturperiode,* new printing (Darmstadt: Wissenschaftliche Buchgesellschaft, 1988). First published in Paris, 1934.

16. Edgar Zilsel, *Die sozialen Ursprünge der neuzeitlichen Wissenschaft* (Frankfurt am Main: Suhrkamp Press, 1976).

17. Martin van Creveld, *Technology and War* (New York: The Free Press, 1989), part two; and Anthony Giddens, *The Nation-State and Violence* (Berkeley: University of California Press, 1987), chapter 9.

18. On Tahtawi's venture into European civilization, see Bassam Tibi, *Arab Nationalism: Between Islam and the Nation-State,* third edition (London and New York: Macmillan and St. Martin's Press, 1996), pp. 84–88.

19. See Hichem Djaït, *Europe and Islam: Cultures and Modernity* (Berkeley: University of California Press, 1985); and W. Montgomery Watt, *Muslim-Christian Encounters* (London: Routledge, 1991).

20. Bassam Tibi, The Simultaneity of the Unsimultaneous: Old Tribes and Imposed Nation-States in the Modern Middle East, in: Philip Khoury and Joseph Kostiner, eds., *Tribes and State Formation in the Middle East* (Berkeley: University of California Press, 1990), pp. 127–52. See also chapter 6, this volume.

21. On the tensions between orthodox Islam and Islamic rationalism in Islamic civilization, see part 2 in: Bassam Tibi, *Der wahre Imam* (München: Piper Press, 1996), in particular chapter 4 on al-Farabi and chapter 5 on al-Mawardi and Ibn Taimiyya.

22. See Bassam Tibi, *Islam and the Cultural Accommodation* (see note 8).

23. Leslie Lipson, *The Ethical Crises of Civilization: Moral Meltdown or Advance?* (Newbury and London: Sage, 1993), pp. 62–63. On the Renaissance, see Peter Burke, *The Italian Renaissance* (Princeton, N.J.: Princeton University Press, 1986), in particular pp. 229–40 on social and cultural change.

24. Science can set down roots in a civilization only by becoming institutionalized. On this notion, see Robert Wuthnow, *Meaning and Moral Order: Explorations in Cultural Analysis* (Berkeley: University of California Press, 1987), chapter 8; and for the Islamic records, see George Makdisi, *The Rise of Colleges: Institutions of Learning in Islam and the West* (Edinburgh: Edinburgh University Press, 1981), in particular pp. 75–76.

25. Joseph Schacht, *An Introduction to Islamic Law* (Oxford: Oxford University Press, 1964, reprinted 1979), p. 1.

26. For more details on this issue, see Bassam Tibi, *The Crisis of Modern Islam: A Preindustrial Culture in the Scientific-Technological Age* (Salt Lake City: Utah University Press, 1988), chapters 2 and 3.

27. Daniel Pipes, *In the Path of God: Islam and Political Power* (New York: Basic Books, 1983).

28. 'Ali M. Jarisha and Muhammad Sh. Zaibaq, *Asalib al-ghazu al-fikri li al-'alam al-Islami* (Methods of the Intellectual Invasion of the Islamic World), second edition (Cairo: Dar al-I'tisam, 1978).

29. John Piscatori, ed., *Islamic Fundamentalisms and the Gulf Crisis* (Chicago: The Fundamentalism Project, 1992).

30. Bassam Tibi, The Worldview of Sunni Arab Fundamentalists: Attitudes toward Modern Science and Technology, in: Martin Marty and Scott Appleby, eds., *Fundamentalisms and Society* (Chicago: University of Chicago Press, 1993). On this project, see notes 1 and 8 to chapter 1.

31. Reinhard Bendix, *Nation-Building and Citizenship: Studies of Our Changing Social Order,* new edition (Berkeley: University of California Press, 1977), pp. 411 and 416.

32. See the illuminating remarks by Gerald Holton, *Science and Anti-Science* (Cambridge, Mass.: Harvard University Press, 1993), in particular pp. 145ff. An example of this anti-science is the publication of the Washington, D.C.-based International Institute of Islamic Thought, ed., *Toward Islamization of Disciplines* (Herndon, Va.: Institute of Islamic Thought, 1989).

33. Christian Meier, *Die Entstehung des Politischen bei den Griechen* (Frankfurt am Main: Suhrkamp Press, 1989), pp. 469–99.

34. Bruce Lawrence, *Defenders of God: The Fundamentalist Revolt Against the Modern Age* (San Francisco: Harper and Row, 1989).

35. On the Enlightenment component of the French Revolution and its anti-religious attitudes, see Roger Chartier, *The Cultural Origins of the French Revolution* (Durham: Duke University Press, 1991), chapter 5.

36. On the continued killings by Islamic fundamentalists, see Chris Hedges, Islamic Guerillas in Algeria Gain, in: *The New York Times,* January 24, 1994, p. 1, continued p. A4; and also Chris Hedges, Egypt Loses Ground to Muslim Militants and Fear, in: *The New York Times,* February 11, 1994, p. A3.

37. For more details, see chapter 11 on Morocco and Saudi Arabia in Tibi, *Islam and the Cultural Accommodation* (see note 8), pp. 160–77.

38. Ernst Bloch, *Thomas Müntzer als Theologe der Revolution* (Frankfurt am Main: Suhrkamp Press, 1972), p. 56.

39. For a reference, see note 17 to chapter 2.

40. Tibi, *Arab Nationalism* (see note 18). See also Tibi, Islam and Modern European Ideologies, in: *International Journal of Middle East Studies*, vol. 18, 1 (1986), pp. 15–29.

41. Abdulrahman A. Kurdi, *The Islamic State* (London: Mansell, 1984).

42. Bassam Tibi, Fundamentalismus und Totalitarismus, in: Richard Saage, ed., *Das Scheitern diktatorischer Legitimationsmuster* (Berlin: Duncker & Humblot, 1995), pp. 305–18.

43. Jean François Revel, *Democracy against Itself* (New York: The Free Press, 1993), in particular chapter 12, on Islamic fundamentalism. See also Bassam Tibi, Fundamentalism, in: Seymour M. Lipset, ed., *The Encyclopedia of Democracy*, 4 volumes, here vol. 2 (Washington, D.C.: Congressional Quarterly, 1995), pp. 507–10.

44. See the authoritative study by Richard P. Mitchell, *The Society of the Muslim Brothers* (Oxford and London: Oxford University Press, 1969).

45. Wolfgang G. Lerch, Der serbische Kreuzzug: Die Bosnienkrise und das islamische Jahrhundert, in: *Frankfurter Allgemeine Zeitung*, July 22, 1995, issue 168/weekend supplement. See also Bassam Tibi, Die islamische Dimension des Balkan-Krieges, in: *Europa-Archiv*, vol. 48, 22 (1993), pp. 635–44.

46. Bassam Tibi, Die Zerstörung des Religionsfriedens auf dem Balkan: Serbisher Ethno-Fundamentalismus, in: *Universitas*, vol. 49, 3 (March 1994) (German edition), pp. 205–15.

47. Habermas (see note 3).

5. CULTURAL FRAGMENTATION, THE DECLINE IN CONSENSUS, AND THE DIFFUSION OF POWER IN WORLD POLITICS

1. Hedley Bull, The Revolt against the West, in: Hedley Bull and Adam Watson, eds., *The Expansion of International Society* (Oxford: Oxford University Press, 1984), pp. 217–28.

2. Samuel P. Huntington, The Clash of Civilizations?, in: *Foreign Affairs*, vol. 72, 3 (1993), pp. 22–49. See also the response of Huntington to his critics: If Not Civilizations, What? Paradigms of the Post-Cold War World, in: *Foreign Affairs*, vol. 72, 5 (1993), pp. 2–10.

3. Bassam Tibi, *Krieg der Zivilisationen* (Hamburg: Hoffman & Campe, 1995), chapters 2 and 6.

4. See the editorial article by Charles Krauthammer, in: *International Herald Tribune*, August 18–19, 1990.

5. Interview with Hisham Djaït in: *North African News* (Washington, D.C.), vol. 1, 3 (September 1990), p. 5. Djaït is the author of the book: *Europe and Islam* (Berkeley: University of California Press, 1985).

6. See Joseph Nye, *Bound to Lead: The Changing Nature of American Power* (New York: Basic Books, 1990), parts 2 and 3.

7. Lionel Caplan, ed., *Studies in Religious Fundamentalism* (London: Macmillan, 1987), introduction, p. 1. See also the chapter on Islamic fundamentalism in the interesting book by Bruce B. Lawrence, *Defenders of God: The Fundamentalist Revolt against the Modern Age* (San Francisco: Harper and Row, 1989), pp. 189–226;

and Gilles Kepel, *La revanche de Dieu: Chrétiens, Juifs et Musulmans à la reconqueste du monde* (Paris: Edition du Seuil, 1991).

8. Joel S. Migdal, *Strong Societies and Weak States: State-Society Relations and State Capabilities in the Third World* (Princeton, N.J.: Princeton University Press, 1988). With respect to the Middle East, see some of the interesting chapters in: Milton J. Esman and Itamar Rabinovich, eds., *Ethnicity, Pluralism, and the State in the Middle East* (Ithaca, N.Y.: Cornell University Press, 1988), in particular the contribution of Gabriel Ben-Dor, pp. 71–92.

9. John Kelsay, *Islam and War: The Gulf War and Beyond* (Louisville: John Knox Press, 1993). See also Bassam Tibi, War and Peace in Islam, in: Terry Nardin, ed., *The Ethics of War and Peace* (Princeton, N.J.: Princeton University Press, 1996), pp. 128–45.

10. Nye, *Bound to Lead*, p. 187.

11. Theda Skocpol, *States and Social Revolutions* (Cambridge: Cambridge University Press, 1987), p. 23.

12. Hedley Bull, *The Anarchical Society: A Study of Order in World Politics* (New York: Columbia University Press, 1977), p. 68.

13. Ibid., pp. 13–14.

14. H. L. A. Hart, *The Concept of Law*, second edition (Oxford: Oxford University Press, 1970), p. 221.

15. See Robert Jackson, *Quasi-States: Sovereignty, International Relations and the Third World* (Cambridge: Cambridge University Press, 1990), pp. 21–26.

16. Bull, *The Anarchical Society*, p. 54.

17. Sayyid Qutb, *Ma'alim fi al-tariq* (Signposts), thirteenth "legal printing" (Cairo: Dar al-Shuruq, 1989), p. 6. See also Sayyid Qutb's call for a *"thaura 'alamiyya/*world revolution" in his *al-Salam al-'alami wa al-Islam* (World Peace and Islam), tenth printing (Cairo: Dar al-Shuruq, 1992), pp. 171–73.

18. Bull, *The Anarchical Society*, p. 257.

19. Ibid., p. 273.

20. Zbigniew Brzezinski, *Between Two Ages* (New York: Viking Press, 1970), p. 3.

21. Anthony Giddens, *The Consequences of Modernity* (Stanford, Calif.: Stanford University Press, 1990), in particular part 2, on the globalization of modernity.

22. On this issue, see Bassam Tibi, Politische Ideen in der Dritten Welt während der Dekolonisation, in: Iring Fetscher and Herfried Münkler, eds., *Pipers Handbuch der Politischen Ideen*, 5 volumes, here vol. 5 (Munich: Piper Press, 1987), pp. 361–402.

23. Bull, The Revolt against the West (see note 1), p. 223.

24. Ibid., p. 227. It is important to note here that this cultural revolt against Western values is paired with an interest conflict. On the latter, see Stephen Krasner, *Structural Conflict: The Third World against Global Liberalism* (Berkeley: University of California Press, 1985).

25. This is, for instance, the tenor of the book by Munir Muhammad Najib, *al-Harakat al-qawmiyya al-haditha fi mizan al-Islam* (Modern Nationalism Viewed from the Vantage-Point of Islam), second edition (al-Zarqa, Jordan: al-Manar Press, 1983). On the tensions between Islam and Arab nationalism, see Bassam Tibi, *Arab Nationalism: Between Islam and the Nation-State*, third edition (London and New

York: Macmillan and St. Martin's Press, 1996), chapter 8, in particular the new chapter to the second edition, pp. 1–26, and part 5 to the third edition.

26. On the international relationists' views of Islam, see Sabir Tu'ayma, *al-Shari'a al-Islamiyya fi 'asr al-'ilm* (Islamic *Shari'a* in the Age of Science) (Beirut: Dar al-Jil, 1979), pp. 208–29. On the perception of Western conspiracy, see Mohammed Yacine Kassab, *L'Islam face au nouvel ordre mondial* (Algiers: Edition Salama, 1991), in particular pp. 75–93.

27. Qutb (see note 17).

28. Abu al-A'la al-Mawdudi, *Bayn yadi al-shabab* (In the Hands of the Youth), Saudi edition (Jeddah, Saudi Arabia: al-Dar al-Saudiyya, 1987), pp. 59–61.

29. See Bassam Tibi, Islamic Law/Shari'a, Human Rights, Universal Morality and International Relations, in: *Human Rights Quarterly*, vol. 16, 2 (1994), pp. 277–99. See also chapter 10, this volume.

30. Jürgen Habermas, *The Philosophical Discourse of Modernity* (Cambridge, Mass.: MIT Press, 1987), p. 17.

31. See Bassam Tibi, *Im Schatten Allahs: Der Islam und die Menschenrechte* (Munich: Piper Press, 1994), chapter 3, pp. 99–116. See also note 29.

32. See the earlier book by R. J. Vincent, *Human Rights and International Relations* (Cambridge: Cambridge University Press, 1986), pp. 42–44; and also Bassam Tibi, The European Tradition of Human Rights and the Culture of Islam, in: Francis Deng and Abdullahi A. An-Na'im, eds., *Human Rights in Africa: Cross-Cultural Perspectives* (Washington, D.C.: The Brookings Institution, 1990), pp. 104–32.

33. René Descartes, *Von der Methode / Discours de la Méthode*, German edition (Hamburg: Felix Meiner, 1960), p. vi.

34. Tu'ayma, *al-Shari'a al-Islamiyya* (see note 26), p. 208.

35. Stephen D. Krasner, ed., *International Regimes* (Ithaca, N.Y., and London: Cornell University Press, 1988), p. 2.

36. See Qutb (see note 17); Mawdudi (see note 28); and, for the interpretation of this claim for an Islamic world order, Kelsay, *Islam and War* (see note 9), chapter 6, in particular p. 117.

37. Jamaluldin al-Afghani, *al-A'mal al-kamilah* (Collected Writings), Muhammad 'Imara, ed. (Cairo: Dar al-Katib al-'Arabi, 1968), p. 328.

38. Nikki R. Keddie, ed., *An Islamic Response to Imperialism: Political and Religious Writings of Sayyid Jamal ad-Din "al-Afghani,"* second edition (Berkeley: University of California Press, 1983), quoted from the introduction to the new edition: "From Afghani to Khomeini," p. xxi.

39. Hasan al-Sharqawi, *al-Muslimun 'ulama' wa-hukama'* (The Muslims as Scientists and as Wise Men) (Cairo: Mukhtar Press, 1987), p. 12.

40. See Bassam Tibi, The Worldview of Sunni Arab Fundamentalists: Attitudes Toward Modern Science and Technology, in: Martin Marty and Scott Appleby, eds., *Fundamentalisms and Society* (Chicago: University of Chicago Press, 1993), pp. 73–102.

41. See the historical survey by Adam Watson, *The Evolution of International Society* (London: Routledge, 1992).

42. Charles Tilly, ed., *The Formation of National States in Western Europe* (Princeton, N.J.: Princeton University Press, 1975), p. 45.

43. Tu'ayama, *al-Shari'a al-Islamiyya* (see note 26), pp. 211ff.

44. For more details, see Geoffrey Parker, *The Military Revolution: Military Innovation and the Rise of the West, 1500–1800* (Cambridge: Cambridge University Press, 1989).

45. See the chapter Aslamat al-teknologia (Islamization of Technology), in: 'Imaduldin Khalil, *al-'Aql al-Muslim wa al-ru'ya al-hadariyya* (Muslim Rationality and the Civilizational Outlook) (Cairo: Dar al-Haramayn, 1983), pp. 43–53.

46. Syed M. N. al-Attas, *Islam, Secularism and the Philosophy of the Future* (London: Mansell, 1985), pp. 127ff. For a critical view, see Bassam Tibi, Culture and Knowledge: The Politics of Islamization of Knowledge, in: *Theory, Culture and Society*, vol. 12, 1 (1995), pp. 1–24.

47. Ziauddin Sardar, *Islamic Futures: The Shape of Ideas to Come* (London: Mansell, 1985), pp. 85ff.

48. Al-Attas, *Islam, Secularism* (see note 46), p. 138.

49. See Bernard Lewis, *The Emergence of Modern Turkey*, second edition (Oxford: Oxford University Press, 1979).

50. See Bassam Tibi, Islam and Arab Nationalism, in: Barbara Freyer Stowasser, ed., *The Islamic Impulse* (Washington, D.C.: Center for Contemporary Arab Studies, 1987, reprinted 1989), pp. 59–74.

51. For a full account on Husri, see Bassam Tibi, *Arab Nationalism* (see note 25), parts 3 and 4.

52. Samir al-Khalil, *The Republic of Fear: The Politics of Modern Iraq* (Berkeley: University of California Press, 1989), pp. 152–60.

53. For more detail, see Bassam Tibi, *Conflict and War in the Middle East, 1967–1991: Regional Dynamic and the Superpowers* (London: Macmillan, 1993), part two.

54. The foremost analytical account of these processes is the book by Fouad Ajami, *The Arab Predicament: Arab Political Thought and Practice since 1967* (Cambridge: Cambridge University Press, 1981), in particular pp. 28–40, with a reference to my contribution.

55. See the translations and interpretations in John L. Esposito, ed., *Voices of Resurgent Islam* (New York: Oxford University Press, 1983).

56. Fouad Ajami, The End of Pan-Arabism, reprinted in: Tawific E. Farah, ed., *Pan-Arabism and Arab Nationalism: The Continuing Debate* (Boulder, Colo.: Westview Press, 1987), pp. 96–114.

57. See 'Ali M. Jarisha and Muhammad Sh. Zaibaq, *Asalib al-ghazu al-fikri li al-'alam al-Islami* (Methods of Intellectual Invasion of the Islamic World), second edition (Cairo: Dar al-I'tisam, 1978).

58. See, for instance, Anwar al-Jundi, *Ahdaf al-taghrib fi al'alam al-Islami* (The Targets of Westernization of the Islamic World) (Cairo: al-Azhar Books, 1987). See also the fundamentalist pamphlet quoted in note 57.

59. Yusuf al-Qaradawi, *Bayinat al-hall al-Islami wa shabahat al-'ilmaniyyin wa al-mustaghribin* (The Basic Elements of the Islamic Solution and the Suspicions of the Secularists and the Westernized), vol. 3 of Qaradawi's book series *Hatmiyyat al-hall al-Islami* (The Islamic Solution Is Determined) (Cairo: Wahba Press, 1988). Vols. 1 and 2 were first published in Beirut, in 1971 and 1974; they have been

reprinted frequently throughout the Middle East. The three volumes cover the basic formulae of current Islamic fundamentalism.

60. On this "repoliticization," see Bassam Tibi, *Islam and the Cultural Accommodation of Social Change* (Boulder, Colo.: Westview Press, 1990), part four, pp. 119–77.

61. Bassam Tibi, Islam and Modern European Ideologies, in: *International Journal of Middle East Studies,* vol. 18, 1 (1986), pp. 15–29.

62. Muhammad al-Mubarak, *al-Umma al-'Arabiyya fi ma'rakat tahqiq al-dhat* (The Arab Nation in the Struggle for Self-Identity) (Damascus: al-Matbu'at al-'Arabiyya, 1959), pp. 67ff. See also part 2, pp. 86ff.

63. On the basic distinctions between *tribe, umma* / community, and *nation* in the context of Arab-Islamic history up to the present, see Bassam Tibi, The Simultaneity of the Unsimultaneous: Old Tribes and Imposed Nation-States in the Modern Middle East, in: Philip Khoury and Joseph Kostiner, eds., *Tribes and State Formation in the Middle East* (Berkeley: University of California Press, 1990), pp. 127–52.

64. For a full elaboration of Islam as a cultural system, and of its politicization, see my book cited in note 60.

65. See Bassam Tibi, Islam and Secularization, in: Mourad Wahba, ed., *Proceedings of the First International Islamic Philosophy Conference (November 19–22, 1979): Islam and Civilization* (Cairo: Ain Shams University Press, 1982), pp. 65–79.

66. Jarisha and Zaibaq, *Asalib al-ghazu* (see note 57), pp. 15ff.

67. On the Islamic dimension and on its global implications, for the West in particular, see chapter 13 in Tibi, *Im Schatten Allahs* (see note 31), pp. 315–35.

68. For an enlightened Islamic debate on the caliphate, see Muhammad Said al-Ashmawi, *al-Kilafah al-Islamiyya* (The Islamic Caliphate) (Cairo: Dar Sina, 1990), in particular pp. 13–28.

69. Jarisha and Zaibaq (see note 57), pp. 38–39.

70. On this conspiracy-ridden thought, see Bassam Tibi, *Die Verschwörung: Das Trauma arabischer Politik* (Hamburg: Hoffmann & Campe, 1993).

71. Jarisha and Zaibaq (see note 57), pp. 75–84.

72. Ibid., p. 248.

73. Ibid., p. 244.

74. Mahmud 'Abdulmawla, *Anzimat al-mujtama' wa al-dawla fi al-Islam* (The Organization of Society and State in Islam) (Tunis: al-Sharika al-Tunisiyya, 1973), p. 44.

75. Muhammad Salim al-'Awwa, *Fi al-nizam al-siyasi li al-dawla al-Islamiyya* (On the Political System of the Islamic State), sixth edition (Cairo: al-Maktabat al-Misri, 1983), p. 22. A seventh edition of this major fundamentalist book was published in 1989 by Dar al-Shuruq, Cairo.

76. On this issue, see R. Stephen Humphreys, *Islamic History,* revised edition (Princeton, N.J.: Princeton University Press, 1991).

77. Al-'Awwa (see note 75), p. 11.

78. Ibid., p. 259.

79. Ibid., p. 280.

80. Bassam Tibi, Die Entwestlichung des Rechts: Die islamische Schari'a und der Krieg der Zivilisationen, in: *Frankfurter Allgemeine Zeitung*, June 23, 1995, pp. 13–14.

81. For more details on this point, see Bassam Tibi, *The Crisis of Modern Islam: A Preindustrial Culture in the Scientific-Technological Age* (Salt Lake City: Utah University Press, 1988). See also the review of this book by Fred Halliday, in: *The Times Literary Supplement*, issue for April 14–20, 1989.

82. R. K. Ramazani, *Revolutionary Iran: Challenge and Response in the Middle East* (Baltimore: Johns Hopkins University Press, 1986); and Bassam Tibi, The Iranian Revolution and the Arabs: The Quest for Islamic Identity and the Search for an Islamic System of Government, in: *Arab Studies Quarterly*, vol. 8, 1 (1986), pp. 29–44. See also Graham Fuller, *The Center of the Universe: The Geopolitics of Iran* (Boulder, Colo.: Westview Press, 1991).

83. Khalid Muhammad Khalid, *Min huna nabda'* (Here We Start), tenth edition (Cairo and Baghdad: al-Khanji Press and Maktabat Muthanna, 1963), p. 184.

84. Khalid Muhammad Khalid, *al-Dawla fi al-Islam* (The State in Islam), third edition (Cairo: Dar Thabit, 1989), p. 28.

85. Joseph Mughaizil, *al-'Uruba wa al-'ilmaniyya* (Arabism and Secularism) (Beirut: Dar al-Nahar, 1980).

86. Bassam Tibi, al-Islam wa al-almanah (Islam and Secularization), in: *Qadaya 'Arabiyya* (Beirut), vol. 7, 3 (1980), pp. 12–23; and Tibi, al-Islam wa al-taghyir al-itjtima'i fi al-sharq (Islam and Social Change in the Middle East), in: *al-Waqi'* (Beirut), vol. 1, 2 (1981), pp. 61–80.

87. 'Imaduldin Khalil, *Tahafut al-'ilmaniyya* (The Refutation of Secularism) (Beirut: Mu'assasat al-Risalah, 1979), pp. 108–11 and p. 136.

88. Ibid., p. 166.

89. These writings cannot be covered here, owing to lack of space. Exemplary, however, is the book by Yahya H. H. Farghal, *Haqiqat al-'ilmaniyya* (The Truth about Secularism) (Cairo: Dar al-Sabuni, 1989), in particular the chapter: Secularism Is Synonymous with Intellectual Invasion, pp. 250–71.

90. See Bassam Tibi, *Krieg der Zivilisationen* (Hamburg: Hoffman & Campe, 1995).

91. See Fred Halliday, *Islam and the Myth of Confrontation* (London: Tauris, 1996). It is unfortunate that Islam and fundamentalism are confused. Islam is no threat, but fundamentalism is.

92. Bassam Tibi, Strukturelle Globalisierung und kulturelle Fragmentierung, in: *Internationale Politik* (Bonn: German Council of Foreign Affairs/DGAP), vol. 51, 1 (January 1996), pp. 29–36.

93. Clifford Geertz, *The Interpretation of Cultures* (New York: Basic Books, 1973), pp. 87–125.

94. In the tradition of Islam, the *imam* is a religious and political leader, that is, an incumbent of power. The character of an underground *imam* has been a fundamentalist addition to Islam insofar as an underground *imam* leads illegal opposition and creates disorder in calling for overthrowing the existing order, unlike the traditional *imam*, who maintains the very existing order. For more details, see Bassam

Tibi, *Der wahre Imam: Der Islam von Mohammed bis zur Gegenwart* (München: Piper Press, 1996); on the underground *imam*, see the chapters of part four.

95. F. S. C. Northrop, *The Taming of the Nations: A Study of the Cultural Bases of International Policy*, new printing (Woodbridge, Conn.: Ox Bow Press, 1980), pp. 2–3.

96. Ibid., p. 172.

97. Richard Falk, Religion and Politics: Verging on the Postmodern, in: *Alternatives*, vol. 13, 3 (1988), pp. 379–84, here p. 391.

98. Ibid., p. 380.

99. On these underground Islamic fundamentalists, see the survey chapters included in the volume of the Beirut-based Markaz Dirasat al-Wihda al-'Arabiyya/Center for Arab Unity Studies/CAUS, ed., *al-Harakat al-Islamiyya al-mu'asira fi al-watan al-'Arabi* (Contemporary Islamist Movements in the Arab Homeland) (Beirut: CAUS-Press, 1987).

100. Robert D. Kaplan, The Coming Anarchy, in: *The Atlantic Monthly*, 2 (February 1994), pp. 44–76.

6.   THE CRISIS OF THE NATION-STATE: ISLAMIC,
     PAN-ARAB, ETHNIC, AND SECTARIAN IDENTITIES
     IN CONFLICT

1. See David Apter, *The Politics of Modernization* (Chicago: University of Chicago Press, 1965); and, two decades later, David Apter, *Rethinking Development* (London: Sage, 1987).

2. See Bohadan Nahaylo and Victor Swoboda, *Soviet Disunion: A History of the Nationalities Problem in the USSR* (New York: The Free Press, 1990).

3. See Christopher Chase-Dunn, *Global Formation* (Cambridge, Mass.: Basil Blackwell, 1989), in particular part 2.

4. See the five volumes of this project published by University of Chicago Press, referred to in notes 1 and 8 to chapter 1.

5. On the area studies of the Middle East, see Leonard Binder, ed., *The Study of the Middle East* (New York: John Wiley and Sons, 1976); and, more recently, Tareq Y. Ismael, ed., *Middle East Studies: International Perspectives on the State of the Art* (New York: Praeger, 1990). In the latter volume, see Bassam Tibi, The Modern Middle East in German Political Science, pp. 131–48.

6. Eric Hobsbawm, The Missing History, in: *The Times Literary Supplement*, June 23–29, 1989.

7. See Theda Skocpol, ed., *Vision and Method in Historical Sociology* (Cambridge: Cambridge University Press, 1984); and Charles Tilly, *Big Structures, Large Processes, Huge Comparisons* (New York: Russell Sage Foundation, 1984).

8. For more on this issue, see Bassam Tibi, *Krieg der Zivilisationen: Politik und Religion zwischen Vernunft und Fundamentalismus* (Hamburg: Hoffman & Campe, 1995).

9. See Marshall G. S. Hodgson, *The Venture of Islam*, 3 volumes (Chicago: University of Chicago Press, 1974).

10. See David Fromkin, *A Peace to End All Peace: The Fall of the Ottoman Empire and the Creation of the Modern Middle East* (New York: Avon Books, 1989).

11. For more details, see Bassam Tibi, The Simultaneity of the Unsimultaneous: Old Tribes and Imposed Nation-States in the Modern Middle East, in: Philip Khoury and Joseph Kostiner, eds., *Tribes and State Formation in the Middle East* (Berkeley: University of California Press, 1990), pp. 127–52.

12. This is a critique of the approach employed by James Piscatori, *Islam in a World of Nation-States* (Cambridge: Cambridge University Press, 1987).

13. The best and most authoritative overview of the nation-state is Anthony Giddens, *The Nation-State and Violence* (Berkeley: University of California Press, 1987).

14. See, for instance, Munir Muhammad Najib, *al-Harakat al-qawmiyya al-haditha fi mizan al-Islam* (Modern Nationalist Movements in the Balance of Islam), second edition (al-Zarqa, Jordan: Maktabat al-Manar, 1983), in particular pp. 259ff and 273ff.

15. Yusuf al-Qaradawi, *al-Hulul al-mustawrada wa qaif janat 'ala ummatina* (The Imported Solutions: How They Entrenched in Our Community) (Beirut: Mu'assasat al-Risalah, 1980), in particular pp. 49ff and 307ff.

16. Bassam Tibi, *Arab Nationalism: Between Islam and the Nation-State*, third edition (London and New York: Macmillan and St. Martin's Press, 1996).

17. On the Middle East as a subsystem, see Bassam Tibi, *Conflict and War in the Middle East, 1967–1991: Regional Dynamic and the Superpowers* (London: Macmillan, 1993), part 1. See also the review of this book by Fred Halliday, in: *International Affairs*, vol. 70, 1 (1994), p. 162. See also note 10.

18. See Bassam Tibi, *The Crisis of Modern Islam: A Preindustrial Culture in the Scientific-Technological Age* (Salt Lake City: Utah University Press, 1988).

19. See, for instance, Hassan Hanafi, *al-Usuliyya al-Islamiyya* (Islamic Fundamentalism) (Cairo: Maktabat Madbuli, 1989).

20. Benedict Anderson, *Imagined Communities*, revised edition (London: Verso, 1991).

21. For a historical review, see Jonathan Riley-Smith, *The Crusades* (New Haven, Conn.: Yale University Press, 1987). For a reference to contemporary history, see Karen Armstrong, *Holy War: The Crusades and Their Impact on Today's World* (New York: Anchor Books, 1991).

22. As an example of this perception, see 'Ali M. Jarisha and Muhammad Sh. Zaibaq, *Asalib al-ghazu al-fikri li al-'alam al-Islami* (Methods of Intellectual Invasion of the Islamic World) (Cairo: Dar al-I'tisam, 1978); on reviving the crusader memories, see pp. 16ff.

23. For more details, see Bassam Tibi, The Worldview of Sunni Arab Fundamentalists: Attitudes toward Modern Science and Technology, in: Martin Marty and Scott Appleby, eds., *Fundamentalisms and Society*, vol. 2 of the Fundamentalism Project (Chicago: University of Chicago Press, 1993), pp. 73–102.

24. Abdulrahman A. Kurdi, *The Islamic State: A Study Based on the Islamic Holy Constitution* (London: Mansell, 1984).

25. Jürgen Habermas, *The Philosophical Discourse of Modernity* (Cambridge, Mass.: MIT Press, 1987).

26. On the notion of *nizam Islami*, see Muhammad Salim al-'Awwa, *Fi al-nizam al-siyasi li al-dawla al-Islamiyya* (On the Political System of the Islamic State), sixth edition (Cairo: Maktabat al-Misri, 1983).

27. This is the vision of Sayyid Qutb, *al-Salam al-'alami wa al-Islam* (World Peace and Islam), tenth printing (Cairo: Dar al-Shuruq, 1992). On Qutb, see Ahmed S. Mousalli, *Radical Islamic Fundamentalism: The Ideological Discourse of S. Qutb* (Beirut: AUB, 1992).

28. Abussi Madani in *al-Munqith,* as quoted by Ahmidah 'Ayashi, *al-Islamiyyun al-jaza'iriyyun bain al-sulta wa al-rasas* (The Algerian Fundamentalists between State Authority and Bullets) (Algiers: Dar al-Hikma, 1991), p. 120.

29. On the history of this concept, see Francis H. Hinsley, *Sovereignty,* second edition (Cambridge: Cambridge University Press, 1986). On its basis for statehood, see Alan James, *Sovereign Statehood: The Basis of International Society* (London: Allen and Unwin, 1986). See also the chapter on sovereignty in Giddens, *The Nation-State and Violence* (see note 13), pp. 198–221.

30. For an example of the revival of this medieval notion in Algeria, see 'Ayashi, *al-Islamiyyun* (see note 28). The basic writing of Ibn Taimiyya spread most thoroughly among fundamentalist circles is: *al-Siyasa al-shar'iyya fi islah al-ra'i wa al-ra'iyya* (The *Shari'a*-Oriented Politics for the Guidance of the Ruler and His Subjects), new printing (Beirut: Dar al-Jil, 1988). See also Emmanuel Sivan, *Radical Islam: Medieval Theology and Modern Politics* (New Haven, Conn.: Yale University Press, 1985).

31. Hisham Sharabi, *Neopatriarchy: A Theory of Distorted Change in Arab Society* (New York: Oxford University Press, 1988).

32. Robert Jackson, *Quasi-States: Sovereignty, International Relations and the Third World* (Cambridge: Cambridge University Press, 1990).

33. On the legitimacy issue in Arab politics, see Michael Hudson, *Arab Politics: The Search for Legitimacy* (New Haven, Conn.: Yale University Press, 1977), pp. 1–30.

34. See Adam Seligman, *The Idea of Civil Society* (New York: The Free Press, 1992).

35. See the chapter on citizenship in Giddens, *The Nation-State* (see note 13), chapter 8, pp. 198ff.

36. Samir al-Khalil, *Republic of Fear: The Politics of Modern Iraq* (Berkeley: University of California Press, 1989). See also Bassam Tibi, Saddam Hussein und kein Ende, in: *MUT,* no. 348 (August 1996), pp. 38–53.

37. On this matter, see Bassam Tibi, Islam and Arab Nationalism, in: Barbara Freyer Stowasser, ed., *The Islamic Impulse* (Washington, D.C.: Center for Contemporary Arab Studies, 1987), pp. 59–74.

38. On the ideology of Iraqihood, see Amatzia Baram, *Culture, History and Ideology in the Formation of Ba'thist Iraq, 1968–1989* (New York: St. Martin's Press, 1991), in particular chapters 9–12.

39. See Sayyid Qutb, *Ma'alim fi al-tariq* (Signposts), thirteenth "legal printing" (Cairo: Dar al-Shuruq, 1989), p. 10.

40. For more details, see Haidar Ibrahim 'Ali, *Azmat al-Islam al-siyasi: al-Jabha al-Islamiyya al-qawmiyya fi al-Sudan namuzajan* (Crisis of Political Islam: The Case of the Islamic National Front in Sudan) (Casablanca, Morocco: Dar Qurtubah, 1991); and also the concise article by Carolyn Fluehr-Lobban, Protracted Civil War

in the Sudan: Its Future as a Multi-Religious, Multi-Ethnic State, in: *The Fletcher Forum of World Affairs*, vol. 16, 2 (Summer 1992), pp. 67–79. See also the chapter on Sudan in: Bassam Tibi, *Die Verschwörung: Das Trauma arabischer Politik* (Hamburg: Hoffman & Campe, 1993), pp. 191–208.

41. Leslie Lipson, *The Ethical Crises of Civilization: Moral Meltdown or Advance?* (Newbury and London: Sage, 1993), pp. 278–79.

42. See the reference to Fred Halliday in note 34 to chapter 1.

43. On the Shi'i opposition in Iraq, see A. Baram, From Radicalism to Radical Pragmatism, in: James Piscatori, ed., *Islamic Fundamentalisms and the Gulf Crisis* (Chicago: The Fundamentalism Project, 1991), pp. 28–51.

44. For a Sunni fundamentalist view on this issue, see Umar F. Abd-Allah, *The Islamic Struggle in Syria* (Berkeley, Calif.: Mizan Press, 1983).

45. The authoritative work on ethnicity is Donald L. Horowitz, *Ethnic Groups in Conflict* (Berkeley: University of California Press, 1985). For ethnosociological and anthropological studies, see John Rex and David Mason, eds., *Theories of Race and Ethnic Relations* (Cambridge: Cambridge University Press, 1988).

46. For an overview of the subsystem debate in international relations and its application to the Middle East, see Tibi, *Conflict and War* (see note 17), part 1, pp. 19–60.

47. On France and England, which provided this model, see Reinhard Bendix, *Kings or People* (Berkeley: University of California Press, 1978); on the globalization of this model, see Francis H. Hinsley, *Nationalism and the International System* (London: Hodder and Stoughton, 1973), pp. 35ff, 67ff; on its introduction to the World of Islam, see Tibi, The Simultaneity of the Unsimultaneous (see note 11).

48. Giddens, *The Nation-State* (see note 13), pp. 214–16.

49. Peter Weinrich, The Operationalization of Identity Theory in Racial and Ethnic Relations, in: Rex and Mason, eds., *Theories* (see note 45), pp. 229–320, here p. 301.

50. Michael Hudson, *Arab Politics* (see note 33), p. 38.

51. Ibid., p. 79.

52. Tibi, *Arab Nationalism* (see note 16). See also the debate documented in Tawfic E. Farrah, ed., *Pan-Arabism and Arab Nationalism* (Boulder, Colo.: Westview Press, 1987), in particular the contribution by Elia Chalala, pp. 18–50.

53. Hudson, *Arab Politics*, pp. 56–57.

54. Anthony D. Smith, *The Ethnic Origins of Nations* (Oxford: Basil Blackwell, 1986), p. 15.

55. Milton J. Esman and Itamar Rabinovich, eds., *Ethnicity, Pluralism, and the State in the Middle East* (Ithaca, N.Y.: Cornell University Press, 1988), p. 3.

56. Smith, *The Ethnic Origins of Nations*, pp. 7–13.

57. Ibid., p. 10. See also the contributions in: Charles Tilly, ed., *The Formation of National States in Western Europe* (Princeton, N.J.: Princeton University Press, 1975).

58. Ali Eddin Hilal-Dessouki and J. Matar, *al-Nizam al-iqlimi al-'Arabi* (The Arab Regional System) (Beirut: Center for Arab Unity Studies, 1983); and Saad Eddin Ibrahim, *The New Arab Social Order: A Study of the Social Impact of Oil Wealth* (Boulder, Colo.: Westview Press, 1982).

59. Ghassan Salamé, *al-Mujtama' wa al-dawlah fi al-mashraq al-'Arabi* (Society and State in the Arab East) (Beirut: Center for Arab Unity Studies, 1987), pp. 69–114.

60. Clifford Geertz, *The Interpretation of Cultures* (New York: Basic Books, 1973). With reference to this concept, see Bassam Tibi, *Islam and the Cultural Accommodation of Social Change* (Boulder, Colo.: Westview Press, 1990). See the review of the German edition by Barbara Freyer Stowasser in *International Journal of Middle Eastern Studies*, vol. 20, 4 (1988), pp. 564–68.

61. W. Montgomery Watt, *Islamic Political Thought* (Edinburgh: Edinburgh University Press, 1968), p. 14. See also W. Montgomery Watt, *Muhammad at Medina*, sixth printing (Oxford: Clarendon Press, 1977), pp. 144–49.

62. Smith, *The Ethnic Origins of Nations* (see note 54), pp. 35ff.

63. Marshall W. Murphree, Ethnicity and Third World Development, in: Rex and Mason, eds., *Theories* (see note 45), pp. 153–69, here p. 157.

64. John Waterbury, An Attempt to Put Patrons and Clients in Their Context, in: John Waterbury and Ernest Gellner, eds., *Patrons and Clients* (London: Duckworth, 1977), pp. 329–32.

65. Gabriel Ben-Dor, Ethnopolitics and the Middle Eastern State, in: Esman and Rabinovich, eds., *Ethnicity, Pluralism* (see note 55), pp. 71–94, here pp. 85–86.

66. Tilly, ed., *The Formation of National States* (see note 57), p. 45.

67. Bernard Lewis, *The Emergence of Modern Turkey*, second edition (Oxford: Oxford University Press, 1979), p. 45.

68. Kemal Karpat, The Ottoman Ethnic and Confessional Legacy in the Middle East, in: Esman and Rabinovich, eds., *Ethnicity, Pluralism* (see note 55), pp. 35–53, here pp. 43–45.

69. Philip Khoury, *Syria and the French Mandate: The Politics of Arab Nationalism, 1920–1945* (Princeton, N.J.: Princeton University Press, 1987), p. 13.

70. Hanna Batatu, Some Observations on the Social Role of Syria's Ruling Military Group and the Causes for Its Dominance, in: *Middle East Journal*, vol. 45, 3 (1981), pp. 331–34. See also Patrick Seale, *Asad: The Struggle for the Middle East* (Berkeley: University of California Press, 1989), pp. 8–11.

71. The *Muqaddimah*/Prolegomena of Ibn Khaldun has been translated into English by the prominent Yale scholar Franz Rosenthal, *The Muqaddimah of Ibn Khaldun: An Introduction to History*, 3 volumes (London: Routledge and Kegan Paul, 1967). On Ibn Khaldun, see chapter 6 in Bassam Tibi, *Der wahre Imam: Der Islam von Mohammed bis zur Gegenwart* (Munich: Piper Press, 1996), pp. 179–209.

72. Ghassan Salamé, *al-Mujtama' wa al-dawlah* (see note 59), p. 24.

73. Muhammad Y. Muslih, *The Origins of Palestinian Nationalism* (New York: Columbia University Press, 1988), pp. 214–15.

74. See the case study by John Waterbury, *The Egypt of Nasser and Sadat* (Princeton, N.J.: Princeton University Press, 1983), pp. 93–100.

75. Hedley Bull coined this term in his classical work about order in world politics in the context of the nation-state system: Hedley Bull, *The Anarchical Society: A Study of Order in World Politics* (New York: Columbia University Press, 1977).

76. Giddens, *The Nation-State* (see note 13), p. 214.

77. See Josef van Ess, *Theologie und Gesellschaft im 2. und 3. Jahrhundert Hidschra: Eine Geschichte des religiösen Denkens im frühen Islam,* 5 volumes, here vol. 1 (Berlin: de Gruyter, 1991).

7. THE FUNDAMENTALIST IDEOLOGY: CONTEXT AND THE TEXTUAL SOURCES

1. On this disputed issue, see Bassam Tibi, Fundamentalism, in: Seymour M. Lipset, ed., *The Encyclopedia of Democracy,* 4 volumes, here vol. 2 (Washington, D.C.: Congressional Quarterly, 1995), pp. 507–10. The opposite view is: John L. Esposito and John O. Voll, *Islam and Democracy* (New York: Oxford University Press, 1996).

2. See Bassam Tibi, The Iranian Revolution and the Arabs: The Quest for Islamic Identity and the Search for an Islamic System of Government, in: *Arab Studies Quarterly,* vol. 8, 1 (1986), pp. 29–44.

3. In this chapter I draw on Clifford Geertz's interpretation of "religion as cultural system." See Geertz, *The Interpretation of Cultures* (New York: Basic Books, 1973), pp. 87ff, which is one of the sources of the interpretive framework that I employ in my work for understanding Islam. See Bassam Tibi, *Islam and the Cultural Accommodation of Social Change* (Boulder, Colo.: Westview Press, 1990).

4. R. Hrair Dekmejian, *Islam in Revolution: Fundamentalism in the Arab World* (Syracuse, N.Y.: Syracuse University Press, 1985), in particular the chapter: Islamic Ideology and Practice, pp. 37–58.

5. See for instance Daniel Pipes, *In the Path of God: Islam and Political Power* (New York: Basic Books, 1983); and Edward Mortimer, *Faith and Power: The Politics of Islam* (London: Faber & Faber, 1982).

6. See for example the various contributions in James Piscatori, ed., *Islam in the Political Process* (Cambridge: Cambridge University Press, 1983); John Esposito, ed., *Islam and Development: Religion and Sociopolitical Change* (Syracuse, N.Y.: Syracuse University Press, 1980); and Shireen T. Hunter, ed., *The Politics of Islamic Revivalism* (Bloomington: Indiana University Press, 1988).

7. Very interesting is Olivier Roy, *Islam and Resistance in Afghanistan* (Cambridge: Cambridge University Press, 1985). Problematic, however, is Olivier Roy, *The Failure of Political Islam* (Cambridge, Mass.: Harvard University Press, 1994).

8. Emmanuel Sivan, *Radical Islam* (New Haven, Conn.: Yale University Press, 1985). See also Emmanuel Sivan, *Interpretations of Islam: Past and Present* (Princeton, N.J.: Darwin Press, 1985); Youssef M. Choueiri, *Islamic Fundamentalism* (Boston: Twayne, 1990); and Nazih Ayubi, *Political Islam* (London: Routledge, 1977).

9. The term *nizam* does not occur in the Qur'an or in the classical sources. See Wilfred C. Smith, *The Meaning and End of Religion,* second printing (New York: Mentor Books, 1978), p. 117.

10. See Bernard Lewis, *The Political Language of Islam* (Chicago: University of Chicago Press, 1988), pp. 3–6.

11. Anwar 'Abd al-Malek, *al-Fikr al-'Arabi fi ma'rakat al-nahda* (Arab Thought in the Battle of a Renaissance), second printing (Beirut: Dar al-Adab, 1978), p. 115.

12. Yusuf al-Qaradawi, *Hatmiyat al-hall al-Islami* (The Islamic Solution Is Determinable), 3 volumes: Vol. 1 *al-Hulul al-mustawrada* (The Imported Solutions)

(Beirut: al-Risalah, 1974); vol. 2 *al-Hall al-Islami faridah wa darurah* (The Islamic Solution Is an Obligation and a Necessity) (Beirut: al-Risalah, 1974). In 1988 al-Qaradawi published the third volume in this highly influential series as: *Bayinat al-hall al-Islami wa shabahat al-'ilmaniyyin wa al-mutagharibin* (The Distinctive Marks of the Islamic Solution and the Suspicions of the Secularists and the Westernized) (Cairo: Maktabat Wahba, 1988).

13. Ervand Abrahamian, *Khomeinism* (Berkeley: University of California Press, 1993).

14. Muhammad Salim al-'Awwa, *Fi al-nizam al-siyasi li al-dawla al-Islamiyya* (On the Political System of the Islamic State), sixth edition (Cairo: al-Maktab al-Misri al-Hadith, 1983).

15. Bernard Lewis, *The Emergence of Modern Turkey*, second edition (Oxford: Oxford University Press, 1979), pp. 21–39.

16. For more details on al-Husri and on pan-Arabism, see Bassam Tibi, *Arab Nationalism: Between Islam and the Nation-State*, third edition (London and New York: Macmillan and St. Martin's Press, 1996). See also the review of the first edition by Michael Hudson in: *International Journal of Middle East Studies*, vol. 17, 2 (1985), pp. 292–94.

17. Abdallah Laroui, *The Crisis of the Arab Intellectuals: Traditionalism or Historicism?* (Berkeley: University of California Press, 1986), pp. vii–xi. On the repercussions of the Six-Day War, see also the new part 5 in the third edition of Tibi, *Arab Nationalism* (see note 16).

18. Sadiq Jalal al-'Azm, *al-Naqd al-dhati ba'd al-hazimah* (Self-Criticism after the Defeat) (Beirut: Dar al-Tali'a, 1968, fourth printing 1970). The contributions alluded to (also by me) were published in the years 1967–70 in the Beirut-based journals *Dirasat 'Arabiyya, al-Adab, al-'Ulum*, and, in most cases, in *Mawaqif*. Fouad Ajami, in his book *The Arab Predicament: Arab Political Thought and Practice after 1967* (Cambridge: Cambridge University Press, 1981), covers only the debates published in *Mawaqif*, including the contributions by al-'Azm and me.

19. For a reference and a contextualization of this article of mine, see Fouad Ajami, *The Arab Predicament* (see note 18), pp. 28–29.

20. Bassam Tibi, The Renewed Role of Islam in the Political and Social Development of the Middle East, in: *The Middle East Journal*, vol. 37, 1 (1983), pp. 3–13. On the repercussions of the Six-Day War, see Bassam Tibi, *Conflict and War in the Middle East, 1967–1991: Regional Dynamic and the Superpowers* (London: Macmillan, 1993), pp. 80–104.

21. Concerning the political role of Islam in these cases, see the following studies: on the Muslim Brethren, see Richard P. Mitchell, *The Society of Muslim Brothers* (Oxford and London: Oxford University Press, 1969); on Wahhabi Saudi Arabia, see Helen Lackner, *A House Built on Sand* (London: Ithaca Press, 1978); and on Islam in colonial Algeria, see Ali Merad, *Le Réformisme Musulman en Algérie* (Paris: Press Universitaire, 1967).

22. See Bassam Tibi, Islam and Modern European Ideologies, in: *International Journal of Middle East Studies*, vol. 18, 1 (1986), pp. 15–29.

23. Anis Sayigh, *al-Hashimiyun wa al-thaurah al-'Arabiyya al-kubra* (The Hashimites and the Great Arab Revolt) (Beirut: Dar al-Tali'a, 1966), pp. 238–39.

24. Hassan al-Banna, *Majmu'at Rasi'il al-Imam al-shahid Hassan al-Banna* (Collected Letters of the Martyr-Imam Hassan al-Banna) (Beirut: Dar al-Andalus, 1965), p. 14.

25. Muhammad al-Mubarak, *al-Umma al-'Arabiyya fi ma'rakat tahqiq al-dhat* (The Arab Nation in the Battle of Self-Assertion) (Damascus: Mu'assasat al-Matbu'at al-'Arabiyya, 1959), pp. 43 and 108–9. See also Bassam Tibi, Islam and Arab Nationalism, in: Barbara Freyer Stowasser, ed., *The Islamic Impulse* (Washington, D.C.: Center for Contemporary Arab Studies, 1987), pp. 59–74.

26. See, for instance, 'Abdulrahman al-Bazzaz, *Hadhihi qawmiyatuna* (This Is Our Nationalism), second printing (Cairo: Dar al-Qalam, 1964), pp. 230ff. When it comes to modern times, al-Bazzaz speaks of "modern Arab Nationalism," ibid., pp. 369ff.

27. See Bassam Tibi, The Worldview of Sunni Arab Fundamentalists: Attitudes toward Modern Science and Technology, in: Martin Marty and Scott Appleby, eds., *Fundamentalisms and Society* (Chicago: University of Chicago Press, 1991). On secularization and social change, see Bassam Tibi, Islam and Secularization: Religion and the Functional Differentiation of the Social System, in: *Archives for Philosophy of Law and Social Philosophy*, vol. 66, 2 (1980), pp. 207–22.

28. Muhammad el-Bahy, *Muhammad Abduh: Eine Untersuchung seiner Erziehungsmethode zum Nationalbewusstsein und zur nationalen Erziehung in Ägypten* (doctoral dissertation, University of Hamburg, 1936). (Although the correct transliteration is *al-Bahi*, the dissertation was submitted with al-Bahi's name transliterated as cited.)

29. Muhammad al-Bahi, *al-Fikr al-Islami al-hadith wa silatuhu fi al-isti'mar al-gharbi* (Modern Islamic Thought and Its Connection with the Imperialism of the West), fourth printing (Cairo: Maktabat Wahbah, 1964), in particular pp. 15ff.

30. Ibid., p. 409.

31. Edward Said, *Orientalism* (New York: Random House, 1978), pp. 5–7.

32. Sadiq Jalal al-'Azm, *al-Istishraq wa al-istishraq ma'kusan* (Orientalism and Orientalism in Reverse) (Beirut: Dar al-Hadatha, 1981). This 1981 essay of al-'Azm is now also included in: Sadiq Jalal al-'Azm, *Dhihniyyat al-tahrim* (The Mentality of Taboo) (London: El-Rayyis Books, 1992), pp. 17–85. Regarding al-'Azm, see note 18.

33. The dualism of Orient and Occident is simply a modern version of a manichaeistic division of the world. Said's anti-orientalism clearly smacks of such romanticizing manichaeism. Maxime Rodinson, like this author, thinks that Said has an important point, but he warns, however, of "*jdanovisme,*" that is, of the worldview of dividing the cosmos into friends and enemies. See Maxime Rodinson, *La fascination de l'Islam* (Paris: Collection Maspero, 1980), pp. 14–15.

34. 'Abdulhalim Mahmud, *Urubba wa al-Islam* (Europe and Islam) (Cairo: Dar al-Ma'arif, 1979), pp. 39ff; and Ahmad M. Jamal, *Muhadarat fi al-thaqafa al-Islamiyya* (Lectures on Islamic Civilization), third printing (Cairo: Dar al-Sha'b, 1975), pp. 11–28.

35. See *The Islamization of Knowledge*, series published by The International Institute of Islamic Thought (Herndon, Virginia). For a critique of these views, see Bassam Tibi, Culture and Knowledge: The Politics of Islamization of Knowledge, in: *Theory, Culture & Society*, vol. 12, 1 (1995), pp. 1–24.

36. 'Ali 'Abd al-Raziq, *al-Islam wa usul al-hukm* (Islam and the Basis of Government), second printing (Beirut: Maktabat al-Hayat, 1966; first published 1925). This work was attacked by, among others, Mahmud 'Abdul-Aula, *Anzimat al-mujtama' wa al-dawla fi al-Islam* (Social Systems and the State in Islam) (Tunis: al-Sharika al-Tunisiyya li al-Tauzi', 1973), pp. 47ff; and by Mahmud Salim al-'Awwa (see note 14), pp. 131ff. Earlier attacks are included in the books referred to in note 41.

37. See Tareq and Jacqueline Ismael, *Government and Politics in Islam* (London: F. Pinter, 1985).

38. On scriptural Islam juxtaposed to historical Islam, see the assessment by Clifford Geertz, *Islam Observed*, second printing (Chicago: University of Chicago Press, 1971).

39. See Mohammed Arkoun, *Rethinking Islam* (Boulder, Colo.: Westview Press, 1994).

40. On Rida's views and for references, see the renowned study by Malcolm Kerr, *Islamic Reform: The Political and Legal Theories of Muhammad 'Abduh and Rashid Rida* (Berkeley: University of California Press, 1966).

41. The references are: Muhammad Yusef Musa, *Nizam al-hukum fi al-Islam* (The Political System of Islam) (Cairo, 1962); Muhammad Dia'uddin al Rayes, *al-Nazariyyat al-siyasiyya al-Islamiyya* (Political Theories of Islam) (Cairo, 1953); and 'Abdulhamid Mutawalli, *Mabadi' nizam al-hukm fi al-Islam* (Principles of the System of Government in Islam) (Alexandria, 1964).

42. Mahmud Shaltut, *al-Islam 'aqidah wa shari'a* (Islam, Doctrine and Law), tenth printing (Cairo: Dar al-Shuruq, 1980).

43. Ibid., p. 433.

44. Ibid., p. 440. See the *shura* chapter in Bassam Tibi, *Der wahre Imam: Der Islam von Mohammed bis zur Gegenwart* (Munich: Piper Press, 1996), chapter 10, pp. 315–32.

45. See Sheikh Jadulhaq Ali Jadulhaq, *Bayan li al-Nas* (Declaration to Humanity), 2 volumes (Cairo: al-Azhar, 1984, 1988). This Azhar sheikh died in March 1996. His successor is Sayyid Tantawi.

46. 'Ali M. Jarisha and Muhammad Sh. Zaibaq, *Asalib al-ghazu al-fikri li al-'Alam al-Islami* (Methods of Intellectual Invasion of the Islamic World), second printing (Cairo: Dar al-I'tisam, 1978), pp. 201–4.

47. On Tahtawi, see Albert Hourani, *Arabic Thought in the Liberal Age* (Oxford: Oxford University Press, 1992), pp. 67–82. See also the chapter on Tahtawi in Tibi, *Der wahre Imam* (see note 44), pp. 221–37, with references.

48. On conspiracy-driven thought in the contemporary Arab-Islamic Middle East, see Bassam Tibi, *Die Verschwörung: Das Trauma arabischer Politik*, second edition (Hamburg: Hoffman & Campe, 1994, first edition 1993).

49. Jarisha and Zaibaq (see note 46), p. 239.

50. Ibid., pp. 60–61. This antisemitic attitude can also be found in Faruq Abdel-Salam, *al-Ahzab al-siyasiyya wa al-fasl bain al-din wa al-siyasah* (Political Parties and the Separation of Religion and Politics) (Cairo: Maktab Qalyub, 1979), pp. 8–36 and 53–54.

51. See Abu al-Abbas Ahmed Ibn Taimiyya, *al-Siyasa al-shar'iyya* (The *Shari'a*-Bound Politics), new printing (Beirut: Dar al-Jil, 1988).

52. See Bassam Tibi, Authority and Legitimation, in: John L. Esposito, ed., *The Oxford Encyclopedia of the Modern Islamic World* (New York: Oxford University Press, 1995), 4 volumes, here vol. 1, pp. 155–60.

53. Jarisha and Zaibaq (see note 46), p. 239.

54. Ibid., pp. 248–49.

55. Mark Juergensmeyer, *The New Cold War? Religious Nationalism Confronts the Secular State* (Berkeley: University of California Press, 1993), p. 199.

56. See Muhammad al-Ghazali, *Huquq al-insan bain ta'alim al-Islam wa i'lan al-umam al-muttahida* (Human Rights between the Islamic Tenets and the UN Declaration), third revised edition (Cairo: Dar al-Kutub al-Islamiyya, 1984).

57. This *fetwa* is published in part in the London-based Arabic newspaper *al-Hayat*, June 23, 1993. On this *fetwa*, see Bassam Tibi, *Im Schatten Allahs: Der Islam und die Menschenrechte* (Munich: Piper Press, 1994), pp. 175–78.

58. See the *shari'a* chapter in Tibi, *Im Schatten Allahs* (referred to in note 57), pp. 194–216.

59. See Bassam Tibi, Islamic Law/Shari'a, Human Rights, Universal Morality and International Relations, in: *Human Rights Quarterly*, vol. 16, 2 (1994), pp. 277–99.

60. See Flora Lewis, In Algeria and Elsewhere: A War on Liberal Thought, in: *International Herald Tribune*, August 20, 1993.

61. 'Ali Husni al-Khartabuli, *al-Islam wa al-khilafah* (Islam and the Caliphate) (Beirut: Dar Beirut li al-Tiba'a wa al-Nashr, 1969), p. 39.

62. Muhammad Said al-Ashmawi, *al-Khilafah al-Islamiyya* (The Islamic Caliphate) (Cairo: Dar Sina, 1990), p. 21.

63. To these authors belongs Muhammad Said al-Ashmawi, *al-Islam al-siyasi* (Political Islam), second edition (Cairo: Dar Sina, 1989). Prominent among the Muslim exiles is Mohammed Arkoun, *Rethinking Islam* (see note 39).

64. Juergensmeyer, *The New Cold War?* (see note 55), p. 199.

8.   THE IDEA OF AN ISLAMIC STATE AND THE CALL FOR THE IMPLEMENTATION OF THE *SHARI'A*/DIVINE LAW

1. Political Islam is the term used and preferred by reformist Muslims for identifying religious fundamentalism. See the authoritative book by Muhammad Said al-Ashmawi, *al-Islam al-siyasi* (Political Islam), second edition (Cairo: Dar Sina, 1989). Herein the chapters *hakimiyyat Allah*/God's rule, pp. 11–70, and *al-usuliyya*/Fundamentalism, pp. 127–38. See also the informative survey by Hala Mustafa, *al-Islam al-siyasi fi Misr* (Political Islam in Egypt) (Cairo: Markaz al-Ahram, 1992).

2. On the caliphate, see the classic work of Sir Thomas Arnold, *The Caliphate*, second edition (London: Oxford University Press, 1965, originally published in 1924). For a reformist Islamic view, see Muhammad Said al-Ashmawi, *al-Khilafah al-Islamiyya* (The Islamic Caliphate) (Cairo: Dar Sina, 1990). On this notion of an Islamic state, see, among others, Abdulrahman A. Kurdi, *The Islamic State* (London: Mansell, 1984).

3. William C. Chittick, *The Sufi Path of Love* (Albany, N.Y.: SUNY Press, 1983).

4. On al-Farabi's perfect state (with references), see chapter 4 in Bassam Tibi, *Der wahre Imam: Der Islam von Mohammed bis zur Gegenwart* (Munich: Piper Press, 1996), pp. 133–50. In the same book, see also the chapter Democracy and Fundamentalism, pp. 333–48. These views are also included in my article Fundamentalism, in: Seymour M. Lipset, ed., *The Encyclopedia of Democracy*, 4 volumes, here vol. 2 (Washington, D.C.: Congressional Quarterly, 1995), pp. 507–10. I have problems with the interpretation given by John L. Esposito and John O. Voll, *Islam and Democracy* (New York: Oxford University Press, 1996). I miss in the Esposito and Voll book the distinction between Islam and political Islam/fundamentalism that is pivotal in this volume.

5. Mahmud 'Abdulmawla, *Anzimat al-mujtama' wa al-dawla fi al-Islam* (The Organization of Society and State in Islam) (Tunis: al-Sharika al-Tunisiyya, 1973). This work argues that Islam is a *din wa dawla* (unity of religion and state), whereas Hisham Qublan, *Ma'a al-Qur'an fi al-din wa al-dunya* (Along the Lines of the Qur'an in the Affairs of Religion and the World) (Beirut and Paris: Manshurat 'Uwaidat, 1986), pp. 125–33, emphasizes that Islam is a way of life, while not denying the political character of Islam. Thus, Islam is a *din wa dawla* (unity of religion and state) or a *din wa dunya* (religious way of life).

6. See 'Ali 'Abd al-Raziq, *al-Islam wa usul al-hukm* (Islam and the Basis of Government), second printing (Beirut: Maktabat al-Hayat, 1966, first published 1925). On this issue, see Bassam Tibi, *Arab Nationalism: Between Islam and the Nation-State*, third edition (London and New York: Macmillan and St. Martin's Press, 1996), pp. 107–77.

7. Muhammad Salim al-'Awwa, *Fi al-nizam al-siyasi li al-dawla al-Islamiyya* (The Political System of the Islamic State), sixth edition (Cairo: al-Maktab al-Misri al-Hadith, 1983), p. 22.

8. 'Ali M. Jarisha and Muhammad Sh. Zaibaq (see note 46 to chapter 7).

9. Al-'Awwa, *Fi al-nizam*, pp. 22–23.

10. See Max Weber, Die drei reinen Typen der legitimen Herrschaft, in: Max Weber, *Soziologie, Weltgeschichtliche Analysen, Politik* (Stuttgart: A. Kroener Verlag, 1964), pp. 151–66.

11. Marshall G. S. Hodgson, *The Venture of Islam: Conscience and History in a World Civilization*, 3 volumes, here vol. 1 (Chicago: University of Chicago Press, 1974), pp. 280–96.

12. On this Ibn Khaldunian observation of Islamic history, see Bassam Tibi, *Der wahre Imam* (see note 4), chapter 6, pp. 179–209.

13. Al-'Awwa, pp. 10–11.

14. On the Islamic liberalism of 'Abd al-Raziq, see Leonard Binder, *Islamic Liberalism* (Chicago: University of Chicago Press, 1988), pp. 128–69.

15. Al-'Awwa, pp. 11 and 130.

16. On this conspiracy-driven approach in Middle Eastern politics, see Bassam Tibi, *Die Verschwörung: Das Trauma arabischer Politik*, second edition (Hamburg: Hoffman & Campe, 1994, first edition 1993). Spanish edition: Bassam Tibi, *La Conspiración: El Trauma de la política árabe* (Barcelona: Editorial Herder, 1996).

17. Al-'Awwa, p. 127.

18. Joseph Schacht, *An Introduction to Islamic Law* (Oxford: Clarendon Press, 1964), p. 54.

19. Al-'Awwa, *Fi al-nizam*, pp. 75–82.

20. Ibid., p. 129.

21. See Bassam Tibi, The Worldview of Sunni Arab Fundamentalists, in: Martin Marty and Scott Appleby, eds., *Fundamentalisms and Society* (Chicago: University of Chicago Press, 1993), pp. 73–102. On this project, see chapter 1, this volume.

22. al-'Awwa (see note 7), pp. 146–47.

23. Ibid., pp. 191–252.

24. Ibid., pp. 255–60.

25. Ibid., p. 259.

26. Ibid., p. 280.

27. See Bassam Tibi, The Iranian Revolution and the Arabs: The Quest for Islamic Identity and the Search for an Islamic System of Government, in: *Arab Studies Quarterly*, vol. 8, 1 (1986), pp. 29–44.

28. Eric Hobsbawm and T. Ranger, eds., *The Invention of Tradition* (Cambridge: Cambridge University Press, 1983).

29. Husain Fawzi al-Najjar, *al-Islam wa al-siyasa: Bahth fi usul al-nazariyya al-siyasiyya wa nizam al-hukm fi al-Islam* (Islam and Politics: An Inquiry into the Origins of Political Theory and the Political System of Islam) (Cairo: Dar al-Sha'b, 1977), p. 64.

30. Ibid., p. 66.

31. Ibid., p. 172.

32. Ibid., pp. 202 and 205. On this issue, see the authoritative work by Sir Hamilton Gibb, *Studies on the Civilization of Islam* (Princeton, N.J.: Princeton University Press, 1982), in particular part two, pp. 141–65.

33. Al-Najjar (see note 29), p. 74.

34. Al-'Awwa (see note 7), pp. 153–54.

35. See Hisham Sharabi, *Neopatriarchy: A Theory of Distorted Change in Arab Society* (New York: Oxford University Press, 1988), in particular chapter 8, pp. 104–24.

36. See the references to Schacht and Coulson in notes 18 and 38; and the chapter on *shari'a* in Bassam Tibi, *Islam and the Cultural Accommodation of Social Change* (Boulder, Colo.: Westview Press, 1990), pp. 122–34.

37. See the chapter on Sudan in Tibi, *Die Verschwörung* (see note 16 above), pp. 191–208.

38. See the standard works of Schacht, *An Introduction to Islamic Law* (see note 18); and Noel J. Coulson, *A History of Islamic Law*, third printing (Edinburgh: Edinburgh University Press, 1978).

39. See Ann E. Mayer, The Shari'a, in: Nicholas Heer, ed., *Islamic Law and Jurisprudence* (Seattle and London: University of Washington Press, 1990), pp. 177–98.

40. Published in the London-based newspaper *al-Hayat*, June 23, 1993. For more on this *fetwa*, see Bassam Tibi, *Im Schatten Allahs: Der Islam und die Menschenrechte* (Munich: Piper Press, 1994), pp. 175–78.

41. Johannes J. G. Jansen, *The Neglected Duty: The Creed of Sadat's Assassins and Islamic Resurgence in the Middle East* (New York and London: Macmillan, 1986).

42. See Nabil 'Abdul al-Fattah, *al-Mishaf wa al-saif* (The Holy Book and the Sword) (Cairo: Maktabat Madbuli, 1984). 'Abdul al-Fattah, of the al-Ahram Center in Cairo, deals in this book with the ideology and action of the Islamic fundamentalist underground groups *al-Jama'at al-Islamiyya* in Egypt.

43. This and the following translations of Qur'anic verses are taken from the translation of the Qur'an by N. J. Dawood, *The Koran*, fourth revised edition (Harmondsworth, U.K.: Penguin Books, 1974).

44. Muhammad Said al-Ashmawi, *Usul al-shari'a* (The Origins of the *Shari'a*) (Cairo: Maktabat Madbuli, 1983), pp. 53 and 93. See also his *al-Shari'a al-Islamiyya wa alyanun al-Misri* (Islamic *Shari'a* and Egyptian Law) (Cairo: Maktabat Madbuli, 1996).

45. Al-Ashmawi, *Usul al-shari'a* (see note 44), p. 31. See also the critical study by al-Ashmawi, *al-Khilafah al-Islamiyya* (see note 2).

46. Nasr Hamid Abu-Zaid, *Naqd al-khitab al-dini* (Critique of Religious Discourse), new edition with all documents of the Abu-Zaid affair (Cairo: Maktabat Madbuli, 1995).

47. Hussain Ahmad Amin, *Dalil al-Muslim al-hazin / Haul al-da'wa ila tatbiq al-shari'a al-Islamiyya* (Guide of the Sad Muslim/Reflections on the Call for the Implementation of the Islamic *Shari'a*), third printing of the *"Dalil . . . "* and second printing of the *"Haul . . . "* in one volume (Cairo: Maktabat Madbuli, 1987), here p. 198.

48. Ibid., p. 290.

49. See Mahmoud M. Taha, *The Second Message of Islam*, ed. and trans. by Abdullahi A. An-Na'im (Syracuse, N.Y.: Syracuse University Press, 1987).

50. See the *shura* chapter in Bassam Tibi, *Der wahre Imam* (see note 4), pp. 315–32.

51. Mustafa Abu-Zaid-Fahmi, *Fan al-hukm fi al-Islam* (The Art of Governing in Islam) (Cairo: al-Maktab al-Masri al-Hadith, 1981), pp. 195–255.

52. Michael Hudson, Islam and Political Development, in: John L. Esposito, ed., *Islam and Political Development* (Syracuse: Syracuse University Press, 1980), pp. 1–24, here p. 12.

53. See Bassam Tibi, Democratie et Démocratisation en Islam: La quête d'un Islam éclaré et les contre-forces de l'autoritarisme et du fundamentalisme religiou, in: *Revue Internationale de Politique Comparée*, vol. 2, 2 (September 1995), pp. 285–99.

54. For more details on Mawdudi's views, see Muhammad Darif, *al-Islam al-siyasi fi al-watan al-'Arabi* (Political Islam in the Arab World) (Rabat: Maktabat al-Umma, 1992), pp. 98ff, in particular pp. 98–99.

55. Shakib Arslan, *Limatha ta'akhara al-Muslimun wa limatha taqadama ghairuhum* (Why Are Muslims Backward While Others Have Developed?), second printing (Beirut: Maktabat al-Hayat, 1965). In the recent Islamic political writings, even a professor of al-Azhar revived Arslan's concept of a synthesis of Islam and Arabism: Ahmed al-Sharbasi, *Shakib Arslan: Da'iyat al-'uruba wa al-Islam* (Shakib Arslan and His Call for Arabism and Islam), second printing (Beirut: Dar al-Habil, 1987).

56. Mohammed Arkoun, *Rethinking Islam: Common Questions, Uncommon Answers* (Boulder, Colo.: Westview Press, 1994).

57. Abdullahi A. An-Na'im, *Toward an Islamic Reformation* (Syracuse, N.Y.: Syracuse University Press, 1990).

58. For a discussion of the ideas of An-Na'im, see the contributions by Mohammed Arkoun, Bassam Tibi, Ann E. Mayer, Roy Mottahedeh, and others in: Tore Lindholm and Kari Vogt, eds., *Islamic Law Reform and Human Rights: Challenges and Rejoinders* (Copenhagen and Oslo: Nordic Human Rights Publications, 1993).

59. Abdallah Laroui, *The Crisis of the Arab Intellectuals: Traditionalism or Historicism?* (Berkeley: University of California Press, 1976), part 2.

9. DEMOCRACY AND DEMOCRATIZATION IN ISLAM:
AN ALTERNATIVE TO FUNDAMENTALISM

1. See the recent work by Anthony H. Birch, *Concepts and Theories of Modern Democracy* (London: Routledge, 1993); and the 1993 reprint of Carol C. Gould, *Rethinking Democracy* (Cambridge: Cambridge University Press, 1988).

2. David E. Apter, *The Politics of Modernization* (Chicago: University of Chicago Press, 1965), p. 457. See also the new contribution by David Apter, *Rethinking Development* (London: Sage, 1987).

3. Samuel P. Huntington, *The Third Wave: Democratization in the Late Twentieth Century* (Norman: University of Oklahoma Press, 1991).

4. A German version of this Harvard paper was published in the festschrift for my academic mentor Iring Fetscher: Herfried Münkler, ed., *Die Chancen der Freiheit: Grundprobleme der Demokratie* (Munich: Piper Press, 1992), pp. 199–223.

5. See Bassam Tibi, Fundamentalism, in: Seymour M. Lipset, ed., *The Encyclopedia of Democracy*, 4 volumes, here vol. 2 (Washington, D.C.: Congressional Quarterly, 1995), pp. 507–10.

6. Bassam Tibi, *Der wahre Imam: Der Islam von Mohammed bis zur Gegenwart* (Munich: Piper Press, 1996), part 2, in particular chapter 4.

7. The authoritative history of Islamic civilization is Marshall G. S. Hodgson, *The Venture of Islam: Conscience and History in a World Civilization*, 3 volumes (Chicago: University of Chicago Press, 1974).

8. John Kelsay, *Islam and War: The Gulf War and Beyond* (Louisville: John Knox Press, 1993), p. 117.

9. For further details on this concept, see Bassam Tibi, Islamic Law/Shari'a, Human Rights, Universal Morality and International Relations, in: *Human Rights Quarterly*, vol. 16, 2 (1994), pp. 277–99.

10. Robert Kaplan, The Coming Anarchy, in: *The Atlantic Monthly*, 2 (February 1994), pp. 44–76.

11. See Bassam Tibi, Nationalisten gefährden Indiens Vielvölkerstaat, in: *Berliner Morgenpost*, May 30, 1996, p. 4. See also chapter 7 on India in Bassam Tibi, *Der religiöse Fundamentalismus im Übergang zum 21. Jahrhundert* (Mannheim: BI & Brockhaus, 1995), pp. 97–106.

12. Fred van der Mehden, *Two Worlds of Islam: Interaction between Southeast Asia and the Middle East* (Miami and Jacksonville: University of Florida Press, 1993), p. 97.

13. See the German translation of Tahtawi's Paris diary (Arabic: *Takhlis al-ibriz fi takhlis Paris*): Karl Stowasser, ed., *Ein Muslim entdeckt Europa* (Munich: C. H. Beck, 1989), p. 223.

14. Leonard Binder, *Islamic Liberalism* (Chicago: University of Chicago Press, 1988).

15. 'Abbas Mahmud al-'Aqqad, *al-Demoqratiyya fi al-Islam* (Democracy in Islam) (Cairo, 1952). Many printings.

16. See W. Montgomery Watt, *Islamic Philosophy and Theology* (Edinburgh: Edinburgh University Press, 1962); and the contributions in the festschrift for Muhsin Mahdi: Charles Butterworth, ed., *The Political Aspects of Islamic Philosophy* (Cambridge, Mass.: Harvard University Press, 1992). See also the reference in note 19, and my book cited in note 6.

17. Leslie Lipson, *The Ethical Crises of Civilization: Moral Meltdown or Advance?* (Newbury and London: Sage, 1993), p. 63.

18. Ernst Bloch, *Avicenna und die aristotelische Linke* (Frankfurt am Main: Suhrkamp Press, 1963), p. 30.

19. For an elaboration of the two rival traditions in Islamic intellectual history, with full-scale source references, see Bassam Tibi, Politisches Denken im klassischen und mittelalterlichen Islam zwischen *Fiqh* und *Falsafa*, in: Iring Fetscher and Herfried Münkler, eds., *Pipers Handbuch der politischen Ideen*, 5 volumes, here vol. 2 (Munich: Piper Press, 1993), pp. 87–140. See also note 6.

20. Hamid Enayat, *Modern Islamic Political Thought* (Austin: Texas University Press, 1982), pp. 138–39.

21. Richard J. Payne, *The Clash with Distant Cultures: Values, Interest and Force in American Foreign Policy* (New York: SUNY Press, 1995).

22. See Bassam Tibi, *Arab Nationalism: Between Islam and the Nation-State*, third edition (London and New York: Macmillan and St. Martin's Press, 1996).

23. See the chapter by Roger Owen in: Ellis Goldberg et al., eds., *Rules and Rights in the Middle East: Democracy, Law, and Society* (Seattle and London: University of Washington Press, 1993), pp. 17–40.

24. On this war and its repercussions, see the two chapters of part 2 in Bassam Tibi, *Conflict and War in the Middle East, 1967–1991: Regional Dynamic and the Superpowers* (London: Macmillan, 1993).

25. This contention can be found in John L. Esposito, *The Islamic Threat* (New York: Oxford University Press, 1992), pp. 184–89. I agree with Esposito that Islam is compatible with democracy. The incompatibility is between Islamic fundamentalism/political Islam and democracy. Esposito fails to see the distinction between the two. See John L. Esposito and John O. Voll, *Islam and Democracy* (New York: Oxford University Press, 1996).

26. Goldberg et al. (see note 23), p. 8.

27. See the chapters based on observation in Algeria in: Bassam Tibi, *Die Verschwörung: Das Trauma arabischer Politik* (Hamburg: Hoffman & Campe, 1993), pp. 161ff, 228ff (also published in Spanish).

28. Abu al-A'la al-Mawdudi, *al-Islam wa al-madaniyya al-haditha* (Islam and Modern Civilization), reprint Cairo, no date, pp. 41–42. On these views of Mawdudi,

see also Muhammad Dharif, *al-Islam al-siyasi fi al-watan al-'Arabi* (Political Islam in the Arab World) (Casablanca, Morocco: Maktabat al-Umma, 1992), pp. 98–99.

29. Sayyid Qutb, *Ma'alim fi al-tariq* (Signposts), thirteenth "legal printing" (Cairo: Dar al-Shuruq, 1989), pp. 5–6.

30. Yusuf al-Qaradawi, *al-Hall al-Islami wa al-hulul al-mustawrada* (The Islamic Solution and the Imported Solutions), new printing (Beirut: Mu'assat al-Risalah, 1980), pp. 51 and 53.

31. See my interpretation of *"hakimiyyat Allah* / God's rule" as a new variety of totalitarianism in the festschrift for Professor Walter Euchner: Richard Saage, ed., *Das Scheitern diktatorischer Legitimationsmuster* (Berlin: Duncker & Humblot, 1995), pp. 305–18. See also the chapter on *hakimiyyat Allah* in Tibi, *Der wahre Imam* (see note 6), pp. 349–62.

32. As Muhammad Said al-Ashmawi, *Usul al-shari'a* (The Origins of the *Shari'a*) (Cairo: Maktabat Madbuli, 1983), pp. 52 ff., argues, *shari'a*, as Qur'anic ethics, is divine being the *din* / religion, whereas religious thought by humans (like the *fiqh* / jurisprudence) is simply an interpretation by humans and cannot be divine.

33. Enayat, *Modern Islamic* (see note 20), p. 131.

34. Authoritative is Joseph Schacht, *An Introduction to Islamic Law* (Oxford: Clarendon Press, 1964). See also chapter 7 in Bassam Tibi, *Im Schatten Allahs: Der Islam und die Menschenrechte* (Munich: Piper Press, 1994), pp. 194–216.

35. Enayat, *Modern Islamic* (see note 20), p. 131.

36. Ibid., p. 126.

37. Mohammed Arkoun, *Rethinking Islam* (Boulder, Colo.: Westview Press, 1994).

38. Bassam Tibi, *Islam and the Cultural Accommodation of Social Change*, second printing (Boulder, Colo.: Westview Press, 1991).

39. Enayat, *Modern Islamic* (see note 20), p. 135.

40. Ibid.

41. I refer here to Huntington's concept of a low degree of institutionalization: Samuel P. Huntington, *Political Order in Changing Societies* (New Haven, Conn.: Yale University Press, 1968). On this concept, with respect to the Middle East, see: Bassam Tibi, Schwache Institutionalisierung als politische Dimension der Unterentwicklung, in: *Verfassung und Recht in Übersee*, vol. 13, 1 (1980), pp. 3–26.

42. Centre for Arab Unity Studies, ed., *Azmat al-demoqratiyya fi al-watan al-'Arabi* (Crisis of Democracy in the Arab World) (Beirut: Centre Press, 1984). My paper (in Arabic) presented there, on the structural requirements for democratization, is included in this volume, pp. 73–87.

43. On the nominal states in the Middle East, see Bassam Tibi, The Simultaneity of the Unsimultaneous, in: Philip Khoury and Joseph Kostiner, eds., *Tribes and State Formation in the Middle East* (Berkeley: University of California Press, 1990), pp. 127–52.

44. See Hisham Sharabi, *Neopatriarchy: A Theory of Distorted Change in Arab Society* (New York: Oxford University Press, 1988).

45. On the role of Kuwaiti merchants, see Jill Crystal, *Oil and Politics in the Gulf: Rulers and Merchants in Kuwait and Qatar* (Cambridge: Cambridge University

Press, 1990). On Kuwait, see also the book by Jacqueline S. Ismael, *Kuwait: Social Change and Historical Perspective* (Syracuse, N.Y.: Syracuse University Press, 1982).

46. For more details, see the chapter on Kuwait in: Liesl Graz, *The Turbulent Gulf* (London: Macmillan, 1990), pp. 84–108, here p. 99.

47. See the chapter Demokratie spaltet die arabische Familie, in: Bassam Tibi, *Die Verschwörung* (see note 27), pp. 216–27.

48. On this matter, see the article by Bassam Tibi, Das Königs-Dilemma: Mit der Gründung einer Schura hat in Riad nicht die Demokratie begonnen, in: *Frankfurter Allgemeine Zeitung,* December 17, 1993, p. 14. See also the chapter on *shura* in Tibi, *Der wahre Imam* (see note 6), pp. 315–22.

49. For more on this, see Bassam Tibi, The Worldview of Sunni Arab Fundamentalists: Attitudes toward Modern Science and Technology, in: Martin Marty and Scott Appleby, eds., *Fundamentalisms and Society* (Chicago: University of Chicago Press, 1993), pp. 73–102.

50. See Bassam Tibi, Démocratie et Démocratisation en Islam: La quête d'un Islam éclaré et les contre-forces de l'autoritarisme et du fundamentalisme religiou, in: *Revue Internationale de Politique Comparée*, vol. 2, 2 (September 1995), pp. 285–99.

10.   HUMAN RIGHTS IN ISLAM AND THE WEST: CROSS-CULTURAL FOUNDATIONS OF SHARED VALUES

1. See the comparative study by Bassam Tibi, *Der religiöse Fundamentalismus im Übergang zum 21. Jahrhundert* (Mannheim: BI & Brockhaus, 1995).

2. On the charged Islamic-Western relations, see the pivotal contributions by W. Montgomery Watt, *Muslim Christian Encounters* (London: Routledge, 1991); Hichem Djaït, *Europe and Islam: Cultures and Modernity* (Berkeley: University of California Press, 1985); and the new edition of Norman Daniel, *Islam and the West: The Making of an Image* (Oxford: Oneworld, 1993).

3. See the comparative study by Leslie Lipson, *The Ethical Crises of Civilization: Moral Meltdown or Advance?* (Newbury and London: Sage, 1993).

4. Benjamin R. Barber, Jihad vs. MacWorld, in: *The Atlantic Monthly* 3 (March 1992), pp. 53–65.

5. See Bassam Tibi, Islam and Secularization: Religion and the Functional Differentiation of the Social System, in: *Archives for Philosophy of Law and Social Philosophy*, vol. 66, 2 (1980), pp. 207–22.

6. On the two waves of Hellenism in Islam, followed by a period of darkness, see W. Montgomery Watt, *Islamic Philosophy and Theology* (Edinburgh: Edinburgh University Press, 1962), parts 2, 3, and 4.

7. See Lipson, *The Ethical Crises*, pp. 62–63.

8. See note 5 and Bassam Tibi, *The Crisis of Modern Islam: A Preindustrial Culture in the Scientific-Technological Age* (Salt Lake City: Utah University Press, 1988), pp. 127–48.

9. See Bassam Tibi, Islamic Law/Shari'a, Human Rights, Universal Morality and International Relations, in: *Human Rights Quarterly*, vol. 16, 2 (1994), pp. 277–99.

10. Abdullahi A. An-Na'im, *Toward an Islamic Reformation* (Syracuse, N.Y.: Syracuse University Press, 1990). For a discussion of An-Na'im's approach, see the

contributions by Mohammed Arkoun, Ann E. Mayer, Roy Mottahedeh, and Bassam Tibi, in: Tore Lindholm and Kari Vogt, eds., *Islamic Law Reform and Human Rights* (Oslo: Nordic Human Rights Publications, 1993).

11. See, for instance, the publication by the fundamentalist Mohammed 'Imara, *al-Islam wa huquq al-insan* (Islam and Human Rights) (Cairo: Dar al-Shuruq, 1989).

12. Jack Donnelly, *Universal Human Rights in Theory and Practice* (Ithaca, N.Y.: Cornell University Press, 1989).

13. For more details, see Ann E. Mayer, *Islam and Human Rights: Tradition and Politics* (Boulder, Colo.: Westview Press, 1991, second edition 1995); and Bassam Tibi, *Im Schatten Allahs: Der Islam und die Menschenrechte* (Munich: Piper Press, 1994).

14. Ann E. Mayer, *Islam and Human Rights* (see note 13), p. 53 (first 1991 edition quoted, as in note 13).

15. Ibid., p. 66.

16. See Wolfgang Günther Lerch, Der offene Islam und seine Feinde, *Frankfurter Allgemeine Zeitung*, May 4, 1995, review article of: Anke von Kügelgen, *Averroës und die arabische Moderne: Ansätze zu einer Neugründung des Rationalismus im Islam* (Leiden: E. J. Brill, 1994).

17. Mohammed Arkoun, *Rethinking Islam: Common Questions, Uncommon Answers* (Boulder, Colo.: Westview Press, 1994).

18. Theda Skocpol, *States and Social Revolutions* (Cambridge: Cambridge University Press, 1979), p. 23.

19. The seminal work on cultural modernity is that by Jürgen Habermas, *The Philosophical Discourse of Modernity* (Cambridge, Mass.: MIT Press, 1987).

20. See, for instance, Muhammad al-Ghazali, *Huquq al-insan* (Human Rights), third edition (Cairo: Dar al-Kutub al-Islamiyya, 1984).

21. Adam Watson, *The Evolution of International Society: A Comparative Historical Analysis* (London: Routledge, 1992), chapter 11: The Islamic System, pp. 112–19.

22. See Hedley Bull, *The Anarchical Society: A Study of Order in World Politics* (New York: Columbia University Press, 1977), p. 273.

23. See the contributions in: The Erasmus Foundation, ed., *The Limits of Pluralism: Neo-Absolutisms and Relativism* (Amsterdam: Praemium Erasmianum Foundation, 1994).

24. Hamid Enayat, *Modern Islamic Political Thought* (Austin: Texas University Press, 1982), p. 131.

25. See the thoughtful editorial article by Flora Lewis, In Algeria and Elsewhere: A War on Liberal Thought, in: *International Herald Tribune*, August 20, 1993.

Names Index

Subject Index

Compositor:	BookMasters, Inc.
Text:	10/13.5 Aldus
Display:	Sabon
Printer:	Data Reproductions Corp.
Binder:	John H. Dekker & Sons